Livelihood Insecurity and Social Conflict in Nepal

Edited by

Bishnu Raj Upreti
Ulrike Müller-Böker

ADROIT

Citation:
Upreti BR and Müller-Böker U, editors (2016). Livelihood Insecurity and Social Conflict in Nepal. New Delhi: Adroit Publishers.

Published by:
ADROIT PUBLISHERS
4675/21, Ganpati Bhawan, Ansari Road,
Daryaganj, New Delhi-110 002
Phones : 011-23266030
E-mail : adroitpublishers@gmail.com

ISBN: : 978-81-87393-18-4

Cover design/layout: Bhanu Design Unit

Printed in India on behalf of M/s Adroit Publishers by
Akhil Sharma E-mail : akhil21@gmail.com

This book was first published as research based monograph by the South Asia Regional Coordination Office of the NCCR North-South programme (an international research programme co-funded by the Swiss National Science Foundation [SNSF], the Swiss Agency for Development and Cooperation [SDC], and the participating institutions in Switzerland) and the Department of Development Studies, Kathmandu University.

Original citation: Upreti BR, Müller-Böker U, editors. 2010. *Livelihood Insecurity and Social Conflict in Nepal.* Kathmandu: South Asia Regional Coordination Office of the Swiss National Centre of Competence in Research (NCCR North-South) and Department of Development Studies, Kathmandu University.

Printed at Thompson Press (India) Limited, New Delhi.

Dedicated to:

The people contributing to promote co-existence, mutual trust and social harmony in Nepal

Preface and acknowledgements

Livelihood insecurity and social conflict are manifest in contemporary Nepal. The country is in the process of an enormous transformation. Nepalese society, historically organised as hierarchical and feudal, has experienced 10 years of armed conflict (February 1996 to November 2006), a conflict stimulating the quest for access to development, questioning traditional power relations and practices of social exclusion. To this date, the 19-day Jana Andolan II uprising of April 2006 and the subsequent change process has brought fundamental transformation and opened new avenues. There have been many positive steps forward in this change process: the signing of the Comprehensive Peace Agreement between the Government of Nepal and the Communist Party of Nepal (Maoist) [CPN (M)][1] on 21 November 2006, the successful completion of the Constituent Assembly election on 10 April 2008 and the declaration of Nepal as Democratic Federal Republic on 29 May 2008 ending the more than 245 years of the institution of monarchy. The accelerated change process of the last 18 years (1990 to 2008) clearly demonstrates that Nepal is moving towards an open, inclusive and liberal democracy and being integrated into the globalisation and liberalisation process. However, institutionalisation of these achievements requires sound livelihood security for the Nepalese people. As more than 30.9 per cent[2] of total population falls below poverty line, it is a tremendous challenge to initiate an inclusive development process. Hence, a proper analysis of the livelihood complexity of the poor and of the structural and proximate causes of livelihood insecurity is a precondition for addressing these challenges, and

1 In January 2009, the CPN (M) changed its name into the United CPN (M) once the Janamorcha Nepal and CPN (M) united. So, the terms UCPN (M) and CPN (M) throughout this book imparts interchangeable meanings.

2 See http://indexmundi.com/g/g.aspx?c=np&v=69 (accessed on 4 June 2009).

necessary to strengthen achievements made so far and guide the change process in a positive and sustainable direction.

The old established institutions (like the caste system and the monarchy), with their social norms and values legitimatising exclusion and discrimination and enforcing unbalanced power relations, have been challenged by new political actors, which has created enormous social conflict and unrest. Although such social conflicts are common during times of transition, analysis of their causes and exploration of options to address them is vitally important.

In this book, the basic causes of livelihood insecurity and social tension and conflict in Nepal are documented and analysed and possible ways of addressing these challenges envisioned. We do not claim that this book gives a comprehensive framework for addressing all the challenge this country is facing, but we firmly believe that its will contribute to a deeper understanding of the livelihood complexity of poor people and elucidate potential ways to enhance their livelihood security and contribute to solving social conflict in Nepal.

This book is the outcome of the collective efforts of several researchers, scholars and professionals engaged in the fields of livelihood, globalisation and food security. We would like to acknowledge their efforts and thank them. Our thanks go to Swiss National Centre of Competence in Research North-South for creating a conducive environment for preparing this book. We are also thankful to the staff of the South Asia Regional Coordination Office for their support in bringing this book into its present shape. Dr Abid Suleri, Director of the Sustainable Development Policy Institute, Islamabad is thanked for his time in reviewing parts of the chapters, and for constant input and support we would like to thank Professor Ruedi Baumgartner of ETH, Zurich. We would like to thank Susan Sellars-Shrestha for her efforts in English language editing and Safal Ghimire for general editorial support and proofreading. Constructive suggestions and comments from the readers are always welcome.

The editors

2015

Acronyms and abbreviations

AAN	ActionAid Nepal
ACAP	Annapurna Conservation Area Project
ADBN	Agriculture Development Bank of Nepal
AGDP	Agricultural gross domestic product
AI	Amnesty International
AoA	Agreement on Agriculture
APP	Agricultural Perspective Plan
APP-SP	Agricultural Perspective Plan-Support Program
BS	Bikram Sambat (Government calendar in Nepal)
CBD	Convention on Biological Diversity
CBS	Central Bureau of Statistics
CF	Community Forestry
CFUG	Community Forest User Group
CPA	Comprehensive Peace Agreement
CPN (M)	Communist Party of Nepal (Maoist)
CPN (UML)	Communist Party of Nepal (United Marxist-Leninist)
DAO	District Administration Office
DFID	Department for International Development (UK)
DFO	District Forest Officer
DoA	Department of Agriculture
ETH	Swiss Federal Institute of Technology Zurich
EU	European Union
FAD	Food Availability Decline
FAO	Food and Agriculture Organisation
FECOFUN	Federation of Community Forest Users-Nepal

FINIDA	Finish International Development Agency
FUG	Forest User Group
GATT	General Agreement on Tariffs and Trade
GCAP	Global Call to Action against Poverty
GDP	Gross Domestic Product
GM	Genetically Modified
GMO	Genetically Modified Organism
GoN	Government of Nepal
GOVNET	Network on Governance
GPID	Guiding Principles on Internal Displacement
HDI	Human Development Index
HRBA	Human Rights Based Approach
ICG	International Crisis Group
IDD	Internal Displacement Division
IDMC	International Displacement Monitoring Centre
IDP	Internally Displaced Person
IDS	Institute of Development Studies
IFI	International Financial Institution
INGO	International Non-governmental Organisation
INSEC	Informal Sector Service Centre
IRDA	Integrated Rural Development Approaches
JM	Jana Morcha
LDC	Least Developed Country
LIRP	Low Input Resource Poor
LLDC	Land Locked Developing Country
MDD	Marketing Development Directorate
MDG	Millennium Development Goal
MNC	Multinational Corporation
MoA	Ministry of Agriculture
MoF	Ministry of Finance
MoFSC	Ministry of Forest and Soil Conservation

MoHP	Ministry of Health and Population
MoPR	Ministry of Peace and Reconstruction
MPFS	Master Plan for the Forestry Sector
MT	Metric Tons
NC	Nepali Congress
NCCR	Swiss National Centre of Competence in Research North-South
NFC	Nepal Food Cooperation
NGO	Non-governmental Organisation
NPC	National Planning Commission
NRM	Natural Resource Management
NRs.	Nepali Rupees
NSCFP	Nepal Swiss Community Forestry Project
NSP	Nepal Sadbhawana Party
NTFP	Non-timber Forest Product
NWPP	Nepal Workers and Peasant Party
OECD	Organization for Economic Cooperation and Development
OFMP	Operational Forest Management Plan
PF	Panchayat Forest
PLA	Peoples Liberation Army
PPF	Panchayat Protected Forest
RCIW	Rural Community Infrastructural Works
RECOFTC	Regional Community Forestry Training Centre
RLS	Rural Livelihood System
RPP	Rashtriya Prajatantra Party
RRN	Rural Reconstruction Nepal
S&DT	Special and Differential Treatment
SAARC	South Asian Association for Regional Cooperation
SAFTA	South Asia Free Trade Agreement
SCF-US	Save the Children-United States

SDC	Swiss Agency for Development and Cooperation
SL	Sustainable Livelihoods
SLA	Sustainable Livelihoods Approach
SLF	Sustainable Livelihoods Framework
SLLP	Sustainable Livelihoods Learning Platform Email Conference
SNV	Netherlands Development Organisation
SPA	Seven Party Alliance
SPS	Sanitary and Phytosanitary
TNC	Transnational Corporation
TRIPS	Trade-Related Aspects of Intellectual Property Rights
UK	United Kingdom
UML	Unified Marxist-Leninist
UN	United Nations
UNCTAD	United Nations Conference for Trade and Development
UNDP	United Nations Development Programme
UNMIN	United Nations Mission in Nepal
UPF	United Peoples Front
USA	United States of America
USAID	United States Agency for International Development
VDC	Village Development Committee
WFP	World Food Programme
WTO	World Trade Organization

Conversion rate: USD 1 =NRs101(approximately)

List of contents

List of tables

List of figures

List of boxes

CHAPTER 1

Introduction

Bishnu Raj Upreti,
Ulrike Müller-Böker

Nepalese society, historically organised as hierarchical, discriminatory and feudal, has encountered 10 years of armed conflict – a conflict that stimulated the quest for access to development and questioned traditional power relations and practices of social exclusion. After more than 240 years of rule by the monarchy and the Rana regime, Nepal is now a federal democratic republic and is in the process of transforming into an inclusive, decentralised, modern state.

However, livelihood insecurity and social conflict are still manifest in contemporary Nepal. The country is undergoing enormous societal change and is in the process of negotiating the future form of the country through the drafting of a new constitution. There is widespread discrimination based on sex, caste, ethnicity and religion; discriminated groups are raising their voices and some segments of the Nepalese elite are expressing concern. To resolve these issues and achieve peace and stability requires visionary leadership, democratic practices, and the protection of human rights and social justice, as well as economic development and political stability, which are major challenges for the coming years. These factors will determine people's livelihood options in the 'New Nepal'.

As more than 30.9 per cent of the total population of Nepal lives below the poverty line[1], it is a tremendous challenge to initiate inclusive development for poor and disadvantaged groups. Hence, a proper analysis of the livelihood complexity of poor people and the structural and proximate causes of livelihood insecurity is necessary to address these challenges in order to strengthen achievements made so far and guide the change process in a positive and sustainable direction.

This book looks at livelihood insecurity and social tension in Nepalese society. Conceptual links between livelihood insecurity, social tension and conflict in Nepal have seldom been made. Therefore, we examine this relationship from different perspectives. Nepalese experts, campaigners, academic and non-academic scholars engaged in the fields of public policy analysis, food rights and globalisation, livelihoods, conflict transformation and social change were invited to contribute their views and analysis. Their contributions provide the reader with a wide range of perspectives on livelihood insecurity and social conflict. Another aim of the book is to test the explanatory power of the livelihood approaches and to enrich the livelihood perspective by constructive and evidence-based criticism.

It is hoped that the book will initiate a debate on the importance of livelihood security in minimising social tension and conflict and to provide a conceptual basis and empirical evidence for politicians, policymakers, researchers and people engaged in the field of social transformation and agrarian change. Each chapter has a specific topic and theoretical entry point, but all chapters tackle the meaning, concepts and the framework of various livelihood approaches and their linkages with social tension, conflict and peace building.

Chapter 2 looks at the decade of armed conflict and livelihood insecurity in Nepal, focusing on the structural and proximate causes of conflict in Nepal. Bishnu Raj Upreti argues that the armed conflict in Nepal is the cumulative effect of

---

1 See http://indexmundi.com/g/g.aspx?c=np&v=69 (accessed on 4 June 2009) for details on poverty trends (42 per cent of the population lived below the poverty line in 2000 decreasing to 30.9 percent in 2008).

structural causes, proximate causes, changing international security dimensions, psychological aspects, the failure of leadership and geo-political specificity, not the sole product of the failure of multiparty democracy. It is the reflection of more than 240 years of a top-down, exclusionary, centralist, autocratic and feudal political and social system that nurtured social exclusion, marginalisation, poverty, discrimination and subordination in Nepalese society.

The structural causes of the conflict are identified as poverty, discrimination and exclusion, skewed distribution of production resources, as well as geographic marginalisation. The proximate causes include governance failure, the absence of a vibrant civil society and of non-violent mechanisms to manage public differences, the strategies and tactics used by the Government and the CPN (M), a culture of denial and resistance, and the ineptitude and lack of vision of political leaders. This chapter also highlights the ideological dimensions of Nepal's conflict, the monopolisation of Nepalese politics, and the international dynamics of ongoing conflict and its relationship to development. Further, a link is established between development, conflict and the livelihood insecurity of the people, and the increase in insecurity during the 10-year Maoist insurgency is pointed out. Finally, Chapter 2 sheds some light on the people's movement of April 2006 and subsequent political changes such as the completion of the CA elections and the declaration of a federal democratic republic.

In Chapter 3, Netra Prasad Timsina examines natural resource governance practices and the livelihood dimensions in Nepal from the perspectives of the political economy and the political ecology. He discusses the power structure of society, which is determined by the political and economic processes, and their role in shaping livelihood security/insecurity, and highlights the production, distribution, exchange and consumption systems of a society as important components of the political economy determining the institutions and policies that frame the allocation of, access to, and control over natural resources.

The notion of the political ecology is considered an extension of the political economy in order to accommodate ecological considerations, i.e., society and nature. As this chapter deals with natural resources and people, the combination of the two theoretical perspectives provides a conceptual and pragmatic basis for analysing the livelihood security/insecurity dichotomy. The author broadly examines the political and economic history of natural resources in Nepal, focusing on forest resources, and analyses resource ownership, use and management patterns over time, depicting how the government's bureaucratic interests maintains control over valuable forest resources. Chapter 3 offers interesting insights into how the conservation and elitist discourse sidelines the needs and priorities of people in the name of participatory resource management, and how the political and economic interests of the ruling class controls natural resources through top-down policy processes and rigid institutional arrangements. Based on the examples of various forestry programmes, Timsina argues that poverty and livelihoods are political issues and cannot be fixed with technical instruments that ignore resource management politics.

He also discusses new thinking and debate on development, which includes the natural resource management sector. The author's core message is that freedom of agency is important if individuals are to capture the social, political and economic opportunities. Freedom can only be achieved with an organised and conscious people's movement that exerts pressure for a complete transformation of the institutions and policies in favour of the poor and marginalised sections of society. The author concludes that the policies and governance of natural resources need a complete transformation, as existing institutions are not able to ensure the rights of people over resources.

Chapter 4 presents the overall situation of food security and livelihood threats in Nepal. Jagannath Adhikari investigates the food security situation and its relationship with livelihood insecurity in the context of the armed conflict in Nepal. He discusses different approaches used to analyse food security and argues that food security has been defined in different ways because it is affected by many factors, including the changing domestic and international contexts. The author feels that it is becoming increasingly difficult to develop and apply specific methodological approaches to investigate food security, especially during times of crisis. He emphasises that the political crisis in Nepal made people vulnerable in different ways, and the factors that determine vulnerability change frequently, making it difficult to focus only on currently food insecure people. The conflict deteriorated the food security situation in Nepal after both internal and external policies and practices had made this situation precarious.

The author concludes that food security is a complex phenomenon and, therefore, solutions must incorporate different dimensions, ranging from policy and institutional responses to access and equitable distribution. In discussing pathways to solving the problem of food insecurity, the author advocates reinforcing local food systems that use diverse technical, social and economic resources to improve the availability and accessibility of food produced on a sustainable basis and distributed to all as part of the 'right to life' principle. Last, but not least, he emphasises citizens' participation in shaping the food system.

In Chapter 5, Yamuna Ghale presents the relationship between corporate globalisation, hunger and livelihood insecurity in Nepal. She discusses hunger and livelihood insecurity from the perspective of the economic reform process and control over the means of production and distribution systems. She looks at different forms of hunger and analyses them from a wide range of perspectives, including physical access to the systematic denial of access to resources. The conventional school of thought on hunger, which focuses on short-term measures to alleviate hunger and livelihood insecurity, is challenged. Emphasis is placed on service delivery for the symptomatic treatment of the phenomenon of hunger, which is criticised for being unable to address the present food crisis. The author contends that livelihood insecurity in Nepal and other developing countries is due to conventional thinking, which has dominated policies and practices in developing countries. She emphasises the need for new thinking and a new perspective in addressing livelihood insecurity and hunger, which is gradually emerging. The newly-emerging perspective considers hunger as a political issue caused by the continuous and structural denial of access to and control over means of production. Such structural denial paralyses production and purchasing capacity. The philosophy behind the 'right to food' and the 'right to livelihood security' is to change this structural denial and to ensure that people have the freedom to organise and mobilise resources for sustained food sovereignty and a dignified life, especially for socially and economically disadvantaged people.

The author assesses hunger, food insecurity, exclusion and the denial of an individual's right to secure a dignified life as the main components of livelihood security. She argues that, as millions of Nepalese people are engaged in agriculture for their livelihood, priority should be given to eliminating agricultural resource- based discrimination and denial. If not properly handled, economic globalisation could present serious problems for poor and marginalised farmers in Nepal. She concludes in that hunger is a central element of food and livelihood security and, therefore, addressing poverty and resource-based discrimination and ensuring Nepalese people's access to production resources is one of the most essential elements of a broader social safety net.

Chapter 6 presents a critical reflection on sustainable livelihood approaches and their application to Nepal's community forestry sector. Bharat Pokharel introduces four livelihood approaches promoted by development agencies such as OXFAM, UNDP, CARE, DFID and RLS, and compares the DFID and RLS approaches. Based on Nepal's experience, the author critically analyses livelihood approaches in terms of their contribution and argues that livelihood approaches are useful tools for understanding various elements of livelihoods. However, these approaches are unable to provide an analytical framework for political and structural transformation processes, power relations and wider social change. The livelihood approaches do acknowledge the importance of the transformation of policy, institutions and social processes and capital formation, but do not offer any clues on how the transformation actually takes place or how people can increase their capital and reduce vulnerability. The author further highlights that livelihood approaches are silent on the means of structural and policy change, such as a people's movement. Rather, as with other development approaches, the livelihood approaches tend to promote 'reformist' ways and means of social and policy change. Although the approaches provide development practitioners with a coherent and flexible framework for programming, their core principles, such as people-centred, holistic, dynamic, building on strengths, macro-micro links and sustainability, are yet to be proven in ensuring livelihood security for poor and marginalised people. However, the livelihood approaches 'add value' to various existing development approaches, as they capture the experience and learning of most of the leading concepts of the past.

Despite these limitations, Chapter 6 demonstrates the usefulness of the livelihood approaches as tools for analysing development programmes such as community forestry. This is exemplified by outlining a community forestry case in Nepal where the DFID and RLS frameworks are used to examine the contributions of the project to the livelihoods of people in the project areas. Although the chapter portrays livelihood approaches as widely practised in development organisations, the author contends that the approach must be broaden conceptually and methodologically to accommodate a human rights based approach to development. A human rights based approach would enhance the focus on political and civil rights together with livelihood.

Chapter 7 deals with the livelihoods of internally displaced persons (IDPs) in Nepal. Based on an in-depth case study of an IDP camp situated in Rajhena, Banke district in Western Nepal and in the Kathmandu Valley, Anita Ghimire, Bishnu Raj Upreti and Subash Pokharel discuss the different dimensions of the livelihoods of people internally displaced by the armed conflict. The livelihood realities of IDPs are examined using and further developing DFID's Sustainable Livelihoods Framework (SLF) (DFID 2002) and the Rural Livelihood System (RLS) (Baumgartner 2006) as analytical tools. In order to understand the specific psychological and emotional situation of refugees and to integrate the humanitarian and human rights aspects, the classical frameworks are broadened by the Human Security Framework (Deng 1998).

The authors present the overall situation of conflict-induced IDPs and are concerned with the political-administrative concept of 'IDP' on the national and international agenda, as well as the Government's response to the IDP problem. The case study informs not only about livelihood insecurities and coping strategies, but also about the emotional stress and trauma experienced by IDPs. Issues such as returning back to their village of origin, rehabilitation, reconciliation and reintegration into society, as well as the uncertainties and risks faced by IDPs are taken up. Furthermore, different types IDPs and their knowledge, networks and power relations, and how these factors shape their course of action, are examined. Finally, the authors suggest some practical steps, mechanisms and procedures to address the problems of IDPs in Nepal.

Chapter 8 presents the need for thorough research into and analysis of livelihood options to formulate conducive policy, institutional frameworks, and regulatory and procedural provisions to secure the livelihoods of the poor and marginalised people in Nepal. Chapter 8 proposes restructuring the fundamental pillars of the state, such as security, the judiciary and the bureaucracy, to enable them to address the new challenges and opportunities presented by the political changes in Nepal.

References

Bhattarai BR. 2003. *The Nature of Underdevelopment and Regional Structure of Nepal: A Marxist Analysis.* New Delhi: Adroit Publishers.

Bhattarai BR. 2005. *Monarchy vs Democracy: The Epic Fight in Nepal.* New Delhi: Samakalin Teesari Dunya.

Baumgartner R. 2006. *Poverty and Livelihoods in Development Cooperation* (First draft). Zurich: NADEL-ETH [Postgraduate Course on Developing Countries Swiss Federal Institute of Technology Zurich].

de Haan L, Zoomers A. 2005. Exploring the frontier of livelihood research. *Development and Change*. 36(1):27-47.

Deng FM. 1998. *Guiding Principles on Internal Displacement.* Washington: United Nation Office for the Co-ordination of Humanitarian Affairs.

DFID [Department for International Development]. 2002. *Sustainable Livelihoods Guidance Sheets*. London: DFID.

Onesto L. 2005. *Dispatches from the People's War in Nepal.* London: Pluto Press and Chicago: Insight Press.

Upreti BR. 2004a. *The Price of Neglect: From Resource Conflict to the Maoist Insurgency in the Himalayan Kingdom.* Kathmandu: Bhrikuti Academic Publications.

Upreti BR. 2004b. Resource conflicts and their resolution practices in Nepal. *Mountain Research and Development Journal* 24(1):60-66.

Upreti BR. 2004c. Land conflict in Nepal: Peasants' struggle to change unequal agrarian social relations. *Journal of Community, Work and Family* 7(3):371-394.

Upreti BR. 2004d. Neglected reality: Resource governance and conflict in Nepal. *In:* Mukti Rijal, editor. *Readings on Governance and Development Vol. 3.* Kathmandu: Institute of Governance and Development, pp 95-111.

Upreti BR. 2006. *Armed Conflict and Peace Process in Nepal: The Maoist Insurgency, Past Negotiation and Opportunities for Conflict Transformation.* New Delhi: Adroit Publishers.

* * * * *

CHAPTER 2

A decade of armed conflict and livelihood insecurity in Nepal

Bishnu Raj Upreti

Abstract

This chapter looks at the different sources of the decade-long armed conflict in Nepal and their interrelationship with livelihood insecurity. The complexity and interwovenness of the different causes is highlighted and their collective impact on the livelihoods of the poor and marginalised people examined. Poverty, discrimination, exclusion, skewed distribution of production resources, malgovernance, failure of development, weak civil society and geographical isolation are some of the main sources of livelihood insecurity and conflict in Nepal. The strategies of the Government and the Communist Party of Nepal (Maoist) during the armed conflict, were another source of conflict and livelihood insecurity, as well as the culture of denial, political ineptitude, ideological conflict, and external forces. The Nepalese people have faced severe livelihood insecurity over the last decade, mainly because of the negative impact of the armed conflict on important sectors such as health, education, agriculture and transportation, which previously provided a livelihood for millions of people. The shift of resource from social/development sectors to military to fight the insurgency severely affected livelihoods. However, after the end of the armed conflict in November 2006 with the signing of the Comprehensive Peace Agreement (CPA) between the government and the CPN (M), the peaceful exit by the King, the successful completion of the Constituent Assembly election in April 2008, and the declaration of Nepal as a republic, a broader framework for stable political change is in place. It is hoped that the changes that are afoot within this new framework will provide livelihood security for the Nepalese people.

2.1 Context

From 1996 to 2006, Nepal was in the midst of a violent conflict, which claimed more than 13,000 lives and caused billions of rupees worth of damage to property and infrastructure. On 4 October 2002 King Gyanendra took over legislative power, claiming that the Government had failed to deal with the insurgency; on 1 February 2005, he declared direct rule, ending multiparty democracy. In reaction to this, in April 2006, there was a 19-day popular uprising referred to as Jana Andolan II, in which the people, political parties and CPN (M) rose up to overthrow the monarch and restore multiparty democracy. This precipitated the signing of the signing of the Comprehensive Peace Agreement (CPA) in November 2006 and the ended of the armed conflict between the CPN (M) and the State. Nepal is now in a state of transition towards a federal democratic republic, with a Constituent Assembly elected to write a new constitution.

Although the means were questionable, and the pain and suffering inflicted upon the Nepal people considerable, the conflict challenged the centuries-old feudal socio-cultural and political systems of Nepal. The country now has a tremendous opportunity to restructure the previously centrally controlled, feudalistic, unitary state. Hence, it is highly relevant at this point in Nepal's development to analyse the root causes of conflict and livelihood insecurity to ensure that the new state structure provides an opportunity for all Nepali people to prosper.

The notion of livelihood is complex in its scope, nature and understanding. Generally, the term livelihood comprises the capabilities, assets (both material and social resources) and activities required for a means of living. An livelihood is sustainable when it can cope with, and recover from, stresses and shocks and maintain or enhance its capabilities and assets both now and in the future, while not undermining the natural resource base (Chambers & Conway 1992). According to the UK Department for International Development (DFID), the livelihoods of Nepalese people will improve if they have:

1. Access to basic rights established through international conventions and access to high-quality education, information, technologies and training, and better nutrition and health

2. A supportive and cohesive social environment
3. Secure access to, and better management of, natural resources
4. Better access to basic and facilitating infrastructure, and financial resources
5. A policy and institutional environment that supports multiple livelihood strategies and promotes equitable access to competitive markets for all (DFID 1999)

Based on these criteria, the livelihoods of the poor and marginalised were severely threatened during the armed conflict, and are still at great risk.

Poverty; gender, caste and ethnic-based discrimination; social and political exclusion; skewed distribution of production resources; malgovernance (weak, ineffective and corrupt governance); failure of development; weak civil society; and geographical isolation are the root causes of the armed conflict and sources of the persistent livelihood insecurity of the poor people of Nepal (Thapa & Sijapati 2003; Upreti 2006). The strategies of the Government and the CPN (M) during the armed conflict, a culture of denial, political ineptitude, ideological conflict, and external forces are some of the other sources of conflict and livelihood insecurity. This chapter aims to develop an understanding of these causes and the complexity of their interrelationship with livelihood insecurity.

2.2 Sources of conflict and livelihood insecurity

The armed conflict in Nepal was the cumulative effect of structural causes, proximate causes, changing international security dimensions, psychological factors, failure of leadership and geo-political specificity. The Maoist insurgency was not the sole product of the 'failure' of multiparty democracy, as claimed by some sources. Rather, it was the manifestation of the centuries-old, exclusionary, centralist, autocratic and feudal political and social system in Nepal, which had nurtured social and political exclusion, discrimination, poverty and subordination in Nepalese society.

Table 2.1 presents a broad overview of the various sources of insecurity and conflict in Nepal.

Table 2.1 Overview of sources of insecurity and conflict

Structural sources	External sources	Triggers and catalysts
• Political sources • Socio-economic sources (e.g., caste, class and religion based discrimination and inequality; poverty and unemployment; social exclusion, etc.) • Geographical isolation • Constitutional and legal sources • Ideological sources	• Changes in the international security paradigm • Interests of powerful nations (political, economic, e.g., in natural resources such as gas, oil, water and forests; historical legacy • of autocracy; religious; strategic and military) • Information technology, global advancement	• Vested interests • Unforeseen events (e.g., the Royal massacre in Nepal on 1 June 2001) • Failure of political leadership • Failure of development • Psychological factors (e.g., revenge and retaliation) • Irresponsibility factor and a culture of denial

Source: Modified from Upreti (2007)

In summary, poverty and inequality, social and political exclusion, gender disparity, caste and ethnic-based discrimination, corruption and malgovernance can be identified as root causes of the conflict. The following sections discuss the different sources/ causes of the armed conflict and livelihood insecurity in Nepal.

2.2.1 Poverty

It is well known that poverty and livelihood insecurity are closely interrelated and that they are both a cause and consequence of conflict. Poverty in Nepal is one of the major determining factors of livelihood insecurity, as the vast majority of the population live below the absolute poverty line and face immense livelihood insecurity. They are excluded from access to food and other resources necessary for their bare subsistence including shelter, safe drinking water, health care and education. This causes malnutrition and high infant mortality, among other things (Seddon & Hussein 2002). In 2008, it was estimated that 30.9 per cent of the population in Nepal were living below the poverty line (dropping from 42 per cent in 2000).[1] Hence,

1 http://indexmundi.com/g/g.aspx?c=np&v=69 (accessed on 4 June 2009)

we can assume that poverty and livelihood insecurity were the primary root causes of the armed conflict, and are potential sources of new/ongoing conflict in Nepal.

Poverty in Nepal is a function of many things including discrimination and exclusion, skewed distribution of production resources, malgovernance and geographic isolation, among others. These will be discussed in more detail in the sections below.

2.2.2 Discrimination

State-nurtured discrimination (based on caste, ethnicity, gender and religion), and interrelated political and social exclusion, are also main causes of the armed conflict and of livelihood insecurity in Nepal. The state structures in Nepal are discriminatory and exclusionary in structure and operation. For example, the state constitutionally declared Nepal a 'Hindu state' in the Constitution of 1990, implicitly excluding other religious groups; Madheshi and Newari people are not properly represented in the military; citizenship certificates have been denied to those applying under the name of their mother, and to some Madheshi cultural and ethnic groups; and landless people have not only been denied access to land, but to other livelihood resources including traditional sources such as fish and forests. As well as struc-tural discrimination, the state has applied policies and laws in a discriminatory way, and remained passive in relation to 'untouchability' and discrimination, despite the abolition of the caste system in the Civil Code of 1963 (Muluki Ain 1963).

It is widely perceived by many ethnic groups, marginalised sections of society, and social and political analysts that the 1990 Constitution, which was regarded as one of the best constitutions in the world, is sexist and racist (Lawoti 2005). The 1990 Constitution promoted one language, one culture and one religion, thereby discriminating on the basis of race, and it did not treat men and women equally in fundamental issues like citizenship, thereby discriminating on the basis of gender. The Constitution of 1990 also protected authoritarian institutions, which discriminate against minority religious groups, women and so-called 'lower' caste people. Another common criticism of the 1990 Constitution is that, although it enshrined freedom of expression, it failed to ensure equity (Upreti & Dhungana 2006). In addition to the Constitution, many legal provisions are also exclusionary and discriminatory, and are unable to ensure justice to poor, marginalised and socially excluded sections of society.

Deep-rooted social cleavages along the lines of caste, ethnicity, gender, region, culture, language and religion are characteristics of Nepalese society and are a structural source of conflict. People had great expectations that these divisions would be overcome with the political change and reintroduction of democracy in 1990. However, with the poor performance of successive governments, the Nepalese people became disillusioned with political parties and the government. The highly unsatisfactory democratic transition of the 1990s, in terms of the transformation of the state, politics and society, contributed to the emergence of the armed conflict in 1996. The dominance of certain groups such as Brahmins, Chhetris and high-caste Newars in all social, political and economic sectors, and the exclusion of ethnic groups and so-called 'low' caste people created strong feelings of injustice and a need for revenge. It is also widely documented that the livelihood insecurity of a vast majority of Nepalese people is the outcome of such exclusion and marginalisation (Seddon & Hussein 2002; Upreti 2006).

2.2.3 Social and political exclusion

Intentional social and political exclusion is common and serious in Nepal. Intentional social exclusion is the deliberate action of certain powerful elites to protect their vested interests and to maintain the prevailing economic and social structures upon which their existence is largely based (Karki & Seddon 2003; Upreti 2004a). These elite groups overtly and covertly developed filtering mechanisms (such as higher fees for health and other basic services, the need for literacy and numeric skills to access certain facilities, and rigid regulations) to limit poor people from accessing resources and services, and from obtaining power (Kumar 2006; Upreti 2004c). Overt social exclusion includes the inheritance of traditional exclusionary social practices, myths, belief systems (e.g., caste-based hierarchy, untouchability, and restrictions in relation to marriage, religion and occupation). The structural basis of Hindu society is principally shaped by a notion of exclusion that goes beyond the general social division of society (Lawoti 2005; Upreti 2004d). The Hindu system has promoted centralised exclusionary practices in the lives of individuals including in their food habits, marriage, religious beliefs, education and day-to-day activities. The Hindu system has maintained a rigid social hierarchy in Nepal. This blatantly exploitative social structure has not been eradicated by any political system in Nepal and still has tremendous influence in Nepalese society (Baral 2006; Aditya et al. 2006). Discrimination against women in the form of polygamy; discrimination against girls and women on the basis of gender, which affects the distribution of resources, decision making power and division of labour; untouchability of women; sexual harassment and exploitation; and the inhumane treatment of women who are deemed witches is still common in Nepal.

As well as social exclusion, the vast majority of the Nepali people have been politically excluded. Nepal's national politics has been historically monopolised by a few oligarchic families (e.g., Shah, Rana and Koirala). Like fixed property, politics (leadership and control of power) is inherited in these elite families. This feudal transfer of power within elite families is backed and supported by traditional culture, values and religious systems nurtured by the exclusionary and feudal state.

The current conflict is the cumulative outcome of the monopolisation of national politics and the failure of political systems, which goes back 240 years. The Shah and Rana regimes (including the partyless Panchayat regime) systematically denied inclusive political processes and focused on capturing power and resources. The Nepalese people have protested against this by participating in various democratic movements in 1950, 1979, 1990 and 2006. The general public has had great expectations of each political change. However, after every movement, the Nepalese people have been (ab)used as a ladder for oligarchic families and their coteries to capture state power and resources. The ruling elites have consistently failed to govern the country based on democratic ideals and norms (Thapa 2002; Upreti

2006; Kumar 2006). The resulting frustration provided fertile ground for social unrest and conflict. It is widely recognised that the post-1990 politics in Nepal failed to democratically govern the country or to alleviate the most urgent economic, social and political needs (Baral 2006; Upreti 2006; Aditya et al. 2006). Hence, the CPN (M)'s proposal of agragami chhalang (progressive political change) and a total restructuring of the state were able to attract a large proportion of the Nepalese people.

The political parties created and nurtured a narrowly politicised civil administration and security apparatus. The bureaucracy, the stable government, has been increasingly engaging in fulfilling vested personal and political (party) interests. This helped develop a widespread distrust in the democratic process and spurred civil unrest and conflict. Even democratic parties and governments enacted and used draconian legislation (such as the Terrorist Control Act), committed severe human rights violations (including killing innocent civilians and non-combatants, unlawful detention, disappearances, torture), which led to the development of negative feelings in ordinary people toward the political parties, the government and the security forces.

Certain caste and ethnic groups dominate all of the political structures and processes in Nepal. This is reflected in the representation of certain castes and ethnic groups in parliament and in the central committees of political parties, a vivid example of exclusionary politics (see Table 2.2).

Table 2.2 Political representation of different groups (% total)

Caste/ ethnicity	House of representatives			Parties' central committees					
	1991	1994	1999	NC	UML	RPP	JM	NSP	NWPP
Total seats	205	205	205	29	46	41	38	29	9
Brahmin	37.6	42	37.6	62.06	65.21	19.51	44.73	-	22.22
Chhetri	19.1	19.5	20.5	10.34	10.86	31.70	7.84	-	11.11
Newar	6.8	6.3	6.8	3.44	13.04	4.87	10.52	-	66.66
Hill ethnic groups	15.2	12.2	14.7	13.79	6.52	26.82	21.05	-	-
Terai communities	21.0	20.0	19.5	10.34	4.34	17.07	5.26	100	-
Others	2.9	2.0	2.5	-	-	-	10.52	-	-
Total	100	100	100	100	100	100	100	100	100

Source: Adapted from Hachhethu (2003, p 16, Table 3)

2.2.4 Skewed distribution of resources

Centralised policies, regional imbalances in the allocation of state resources, and highly skewed ownership, distribution, access and control of land and other productive resources have also contributed to the armed conflict in Nepal. Among the production resources, land is the main means of livelihood for the Nepalese people. Owning land is also a form of social status, which provides the basis for securing other rights such as citizenship, eligibility for loans from banks, birth certificates and so forth. If people are landless they not only lose their means of livelihood, they are also deprived of many other rights and entitlements.

Table 2.3 Land distribution in Nepal

S. N.	Category of people	% of Total population
1	Landless	24.44
2	Semi-landless (owning less than 0.20 acres or 0.08 hectares)	6.98
3	Marginal cultivators (owning 0.21 to 1 acres or 0.084 to 0.4046 hectares)	27.59
4	Small cultivators (1.01 to 2 acres or 0.4087 to 0.809 hectares)	20.15
5	Semi-medium (2.01 to 4 acres or 0.809 to 1.618 hectares)	13.42
6	Medium cultivators (4 to 10 acres or 1.659 to 4.05 hectares)	6.25
7	Large cultivators (more than 10.01 acre or 4.06 hectares)	1.17

Source: Adapted from UNDP (2004, p 176,)

Table 2.3 shows the general landholding pattern prevalent in Nepal. More than 24 per cent of the population is landless and another 6.98 per cent of the population is semi-landless. If more than 30 per cent of the population of an agricultural country is landless or semi-landless, they face livelihood insecurity, and, if the state fails to provide a means for their survival, they will become frustrated and may take up arms (Hutt 2004).

The series of rallies and mass protests (in Siraha, Saptari, Dang, Kailali and Chitwan) organised by tenants, Dalits, landless, squatters and ex-Kamaiyas (bonded labourers) is evidence of the frustration of these groups. When people feel ignored, neglected or victimised by the state, they become organised and protest from time to time to demand their rights. This is one of the perennial sources of conflict and instability in Nepal. Similar inequalities can be observed in relation to access to and control over forest resources (e.g., threats to forest-based livelihoods, lack of decision-making power of poor and women over forest resources) and water resources (e.g., privatisation of water and high user fees). This situation is discussed further in chapter three.

The work of Seddon and Hussein (2002) shows that in rural areas 20 per cent of the population are wealthy landowners and peasants, and the remaining 80 per cent experience livelihood insecurity. The lives and livelihoods of women, girls and children were especially threatened by the armed conflict because many remained in the village where resources for their basic needs were scarce, whereas men were often out of the village. The poor, marginalised and socially excluded were engaged in a constant struggle for their survival because of lack of control over and access to productive resources, weak social capital and networks, and the lack of a stable or regular source of income, among other things (Upreti 2006; Seddon & Hussein 2002).

When there is a huge accumulation of land and other natural resources in the hands of a small section of society and other large sections have to depend on limited resources, there is always competition. When some people have more and others have to suffer, feelings of injustice develop. The unequal distribution of land in Nepal (see Table 2.3) not only threatens the livelihoods of people with little or no land, but has also implanted feelings of injustice. The Maoist insurgents capitalised on this, gaining the sympathy of the exploited and marginalised. The state was simply not able, or unwilling, to address the concerns of poor and marginalised people (Lawoti 2005; Kumar 2006; Upreti 2004c).

Examining the local dynamics of resource use patterns from the perspective of power relations, the 'winner-takes-all' model appears to be common; local elites hold almost all production resources and exploit poor and marginalised sections of society. The inequitable use of natural resources by powerful elites in villages is depriving poor people. Previous studies conducted by this author (Upreti 2001 and 2002a) show, for example, that it is almost impossible for poor Dalits to get access to water for irrigation in dry summers before it is used by the local elites. Furthermore, exploitation is not limited to physical resources. Elites have not only captured productive resources, but are also controlling the negotiation and peace process. None of the three negotiations (2001, 2003, and 2006) between the Government of Nepal and the CPN (M) involved representatives from civil society, women or socially excluded/marginalised groups. The need for broader participation (i.e., representation of the interests of a broad cross-section of society) was ignored, and the peace process was neither transparent nor accountable. The main reason for this was to protect the vested interests of the elites in the negotiations (Upreti 2006; Baral 2006).

2.2.5 Malgovernance

Lack of democratic legitimacy and effective governance was one of the proximate causes of the conflict (Kumar 2006). Successive governments not only failed to address social exclusion, inequality, poverty and lack of access to resources, but also blatantly engaged in corruption (Thapa 2002), nepotism and favouritism (Shrestha 1997; Pandey 1999).

Table 2.4 World Bank institute governance index for Nepal (1996–2006)

Year	Dimensions of governance (in %)					
	Voice and accountability	Political stability	Government effectiveness	Regulatory quality	Rule of law	Control of corruption
1996	50.2	25.0	48.3	23.4	51.4	44.7
1998	44.2	23.6	37.4	24.4	52.4	43.2
2000	44.7	14.4	39.3	27.3	45.2	40.3
2002	22.6	6.7	36.5	30.7	41.0	46.1
2003	23.6	5.3	32.2	32.7	36.7	51.0
2004	17.8	2.9	22.3	24.4	33.9	34.5
2005	13.9	1.4	15.6	26.3	24.8	28.6
2006	13.0	1.9	19	28.8	29.0	25.2
South Asia Average (2006)	25.5	26.8	37.7	37.0	39.3	33.9

Source: Manandhar (2007)

Table 2.4 shows that the governing situation in Nepal has deteriorated since the armed conflict started in 1996. All of the six governance indices used to measure the various dimensions of governance indicate a worsening trend.

The Nepalese state has consistently failed to reduce poverty, provide a decent means of livelihood, control exploitation and generate employment opportunities (Upreti 2002a and 2002b). Consequently, semi-educated, left-out, unemployed and frustrated youths have become a source of civil unrest. Corruption and irregularity are blatant characteristics of the governing system and political process in Nepal, which have diverted state resources that should have been invested in the livelihood security of poor and marginalised people (Pokharel 2004).

Another factor leading to the armed conflict was the Government's repressive behaviour towards the supporters of the United Peoples' Front (UPF) in the early 1990s. In the parliamentary election of 1991, one of the factions of the UPF won nine seats in parliament, becoming the third largest party. However, the ruling party (the Nepali Congress) tried to wipe out the UPF in its stronghold areas in the Mid- Western Development Region using state power and resources. Under Operation Romeo, the state used local administration and police to brutally suppress the members of UPF and their supporters. As a result, ordinary people did not feel secure, even though democracy had been reinstated in the widely acknowledged political change of 1990. The excessive and unlawful acts of the police under Operation Romeo terrorised the local people. The Parliamentary Investigation Committee made the following statement (summarised by Pahari 2003, p 7):

> *Between 1990 and 1996 successive regimes in Kathmandu, starting with that of strongly anti-communist Girija Koirala, pursued a conscious policy of trying to undermine and ultimately dismantle the considerable electoral clout of the Maoists in Rukum, Rolpa, Salyan and Jajarkot – a region with strong left support since 1950s. [...] mobilising not only party cadre, but local and regional civil administration and the police force as available and necessary, the Girija government started a trend of committing and compromising state resources to undermine opposition parties to win local and national elections. ...If free and fair elections are to be regarded as forming the most inviolable aspects of democracy, then the trend*

initiated by the Nepali Congress government under Koirala in the Maoist hinterland and beyond can be taken as the beginning of a series of egregious and systematic violence of democracy from within the state in post 1990 period.

A major boost to the Maoist cause was the local governance structure. The CPN (M) wanted to make local bodies dysfunctional to create a political vacuum, which they could then fill with their local janasarkar (People's government). The then Deuba Government greatly assisted the Maoists in meeting this objective by neither conducting local elections nor extending the tenure of existing elected bodies. Instead, he assigned the responsibilities of the elected local representatives to central government officials, which virtually eradicated local government. The CPN (M) emerged even stronger in the absence of local government, maintaining their high degree of their control. Most of the office bearers in the local government offices (except teachers and health workers) withdrew from the villages.

2.2.6 Development failure

In the history of Nepal's planned development, policies, strategies and practices have consistently discriminated against and excluded poor people and ethnic minorities (Pandey 1999; Shrestha 1997; Upreti 2004a). The exploitative nature of development in Nepal has created tension, fear, mistrust, feelings of injustice and resentment. It is widening the gap between the rich and the poor, promoting the accumulation of wealth by certain elite groups at the cost of grave livelihood insecurity for the vast majority of the Nepalese population (Pandey 1999). This created a group of oppressed people looking for an opportunity to oppose the ruling elite. The Maoists presented them with such an opportunity; hence, development failure is one of the main reasons for the expansion of the Maoist conflict in Nepal. It is naive to believe that all development interventions have a positive impact on the wellbeing of socially excluded and marginalised people. The experiences of the five decades of planned development in Nepal have proved that development is not able to secure the livelihoods of poor and marginalised people. Development interventions often overlook or exclude the poorest members of society (Upreti 2004a; Shrestha 1997; Pandey 1999). Despite the rhetoric on decentralisation, Nepal's development practices are still strongly centralised, elite-biased and exclusionary, and ultimately create livelihood insecurity and social tension.

More than 60 per cent of Nepal's development budget comes from the international community. Hence, the role and influence of donors through development assistance is substantial. Donors have a significant influence over development policy, strategy, structure, process and practice in Nepal. However, the role and influence of development assistance has so far been sectoral, producing competition on particular development issues and resulting in contradictory advice to the Government. Development assistance is also rigid and conditional (e.g., on relinquishing incentive systems or on price rises in basic goods and services like electricity and water, which often leads to severe conflict), and priorities change frequently, ultimately leading to development failure (Pandey 1999; Shrestha 1997).

It is worth stating one of the findings of research on the impact of donor assistance in Nepal (Seddon & Hussein 2002):

> *Despite a heavy donor presence and sustained high levels of aid to Nepal (with foreign agencies contributing some 60 per cent of Nepal's development budget) and the existence of a wide variety of development programmes, the number of people falling below the poverty line has not decreased over the last twenty years. There can be little doubt that, even after half a century of development interventions, Nepal is still in crisis. (Seddon & Hussein 2002, p 2)*

There is an extensive corpus of material that evaluates the impact of donor interventions in Nepal (Acharya 1998; Panday 1999; Shrestha 1997; Upreti 2004b; Mainali 2003; Sharma & Rana 2006), but the following remains symptomatic of the negative repercussions of the contribution and effectiveness of donor funded development interventions in addressing the root causes of the conflict and livelihoods security of poor and marginalised people in Nepal. For example, USAID invested 50 million US dollars in a 15 year project (from 1980-1995) called the Rapti Zone Rural Area Development Project (later called the Rapti Development Project) to fulfil the basic needs of the poor people in the project area by improving household food production and consumption, and improving income generating opportunities for poor farmers, landless labourers, occupational castes and women. However, this project failed to improve the wellbeing of poor people in the project area specifically because of failure of the project to reach the poor. Instead, the CPN (M) began their armed movement with the support of poor and marginalised people in the project area (Mainali 2003).

2.2.7 Weak civil society

As in many developing countries, there has been an absence of civil society sector to closely watch the political, economic and social processes in Nepal and to hold the government and political actors accountable if they do wrong. Only after the political change of 1990 did the non-governmental organisation (NGO) sector emerge strongly and, claiming to be an important civil society actor, has started to raise its voice in some crucial areas such as human rights, women's rights, children's rights, access to resources for poor and marginalised groups, and the right to education, food and shelter, and so forth. However, this sector has also lost its credibility due to its non-transparent dealings in relation to external funding and the use of resources (often charged as *dollorko kheti garne haru*[2]), its adoption of the agendas of donors and its fragmentation in terms of political ideology. However, after the grand failure of the Government to respect human rights and civil liberties, the civil society movement emerged strongly, starting in the Kathmandu Valley and quickly moving to district headquarters. If a vibrant civil society existed, it could perform the role of a watchdog in relation to malgovernance, human rights abuses, and so on, minimising the potential for conflict to erupt.

One of the proximate causes of the conflict was a lack of effective non-violent mechanisms to address problems and overcome differences. The legal system was ineffective, exclusionary, expensive and ultimately unable to deal with the social cleavages reflected in terms of caste, ethnicity, gender

---

[2] Meaning 'the harvesters of money'.

and discrimination (Upreti 2001). When people have no other way of resolving their differences they opt for coercive or violent means. Some of the traditional non-violent mechanisms such as guthis (a special endowment arrangement), *dharma bhakaris* (a fund created for a special purpose) existed, but these were also religiously biased, elitist and hierarchical in nature, and they excluded people who did not believe in them (Upreti 2002a). If there had been a common platform available to the poorest, marginalised groups, development agencies, government offices and political parties promoting a non-violent approach to negotiation it would have helped to mitigate conflict. For example, local government bodies (village development committees) could have been one such platform, but the Government did not enable them to function.

2.2.8 Geographical isolation

Remoteness, especially in the Mid-Western and Far West Development Regions and other remote areas, is associated with widespread poverty and spatial disparities. The unwillingness of the state to invest in infrastructure, such as roads, schools, hospitals, electricity, drinking water and irrigation, has exacerbated social exclusion and increased livelihood insecurity. Spatial disparities have caused feelings of injustice. One reason for the start and rapid expansion of the Maoist insurgency in the Mid-Western Development Region (Rolpa, Rukum, Salyan and Jajarkot) is its geographical isolation and the state's neglect of the area (Hutt 2004; Mackinlay & Upreti 2003).

Lack of good networks for transport and communication in these remote regions favoured the launching of the rebellion, partly because these uncontrolled areas (forests) served as hideouts and training centres for the rebels. Hence, geographical isolation became one of the main causes of conflict and livelihood insecurity.

2.2.9 The Maoist's war strategy

The CPN (M) learnt from the strategies and tactics of the Peruvian communist party, the Shining Path; Mao's strategy of protracted people's war (developing in rural areas and expanding to urban centres to capture state power); and the Russian strategy of armed insurrection. The CPN (M) dealt with very sensitive issues and aligned themselves with the agenda of the poor, attracting large portions of Nepal's population. In addition to poor people, peasants and workers, they also tactfully used media, intelligentsia and politicians in their favour. The power struggle between, and within, the political parties over the past 10 years greatly contributed to the expansion and strengthening of the Maoist movement.

The CPN (M) adopted Mao Zedong's strategy of three weapons for the people's revolution: (i) party (to develop and maintain ideology, and formulate policies and strategies related to people's war), (ii) people's army (responsible for attacking enemies and defending areas under control) and (iii) united front (to consolidate friendly forces). One of the main strategies of the CPN (M) was to mobilise the frustrations and aspirations of ethnic minorities (Upreti 2006; Thapa & Sijapati 2003). The Maoists created a strong united front, bringing several ethnic and regional forces together like the Kirat National Liberation Front, Magrat National Liberation Front, Tharuwan National Liberation Front, Tamang National Liberation Front, Thami National Liberation Front, Majhi National Liberation Front, Madheshi National Liberation Front, and the Karnali Regional Liberation Front. These fronts are coordinated by the CPN (M) Ethnic and Regional Coordination Committee. Ethnic support was one of the foundational strengths of the Maoist insurgency (Sharma 2003).

The CPN (M) became successful by dichotomising identities such as 'oppressor- oppressed', 'ruler-ruled', 'rich-poor', 'landlord-landless' and 'patriot-non patriot' to establish political, social, cultural and economic cleavages. These dichotomies fuelled the already developed feelings of injustice and frustration of the Nepalese people. Hence, the Maoist gained wider sympathy for their cause (Seddon & Hussein 2002). The differences between ethnic groups and caste groups are based on language (Nepali language versus ethnic languages), cultural practices and religious practices (Hindu versus non-Hindu). The different groups have been discriminated against in various ways, including legally and judicially, through the denial of their indigenous identity, political exclusion and by denial of citizenship by the state. These injustices were used by the CPN (M) to gather support.

2.2.10 The Government's war strategy

The Government's strategy for dealing with the Maoist insurgency had a negative impact on the conflict, leading to further insecurity and livelihood stress. Instead of trying to resolve the conflict through dialogue and negotiation, the Government opted for a coercive approach. It launched a police operation called 'Operation Kilo Sierra II' against the CPN (M) in 18 districts between May 1998 and 1999. This operation was counterproductive because of the high number of casualties. Many people, especially the victims' families and relatives joined the insurgency to take revenge (Sharma 2003). In 1999, the Government provided an extra allowance for members of the police force working in Maoist influence areas. This also helped to expand the Maoist movement, because the police acted unlawfully to prove the presence of the CPN (M) in their working area so that they would be eligible for the allowance. Police operations such as Operation Romeo, Kilo Sierra II, Operation Jungle Search (1998-99), Operation Silent Kilo Sierra III, and Operations Delta and Chakrabyuha (2000-May 2001) were unsuccessful in controlling the rebellion and contributed to the development of anti-government feelings in ordinary people. This strategy helped to escalate conflict in certain geographical areas. The Integrated Development Programme (November 2000 to March 2001), in Rolpa, Rukum, Salyan, Kalikot and Jajarkot, and the Integrated Security and Development Programme (ISDP) implemented by the Government in Maoist stronghold districts (since May 2001) were ineffective (Thapa & Sijapati 2003; Upreti 2006). Until 1999, the confrontations, actions and counter-actions were limited to between the police and CPN (M). Although the Army was deployed in the Maoist affected areas (Rolpa, Rukum, Salyan, Jajarkot and Pyuthan) under the Integrated Security and Development Programme (ISDP), there were no confrontations between the Army and the CPN (M) at that time. Later, after an attack by the CPN (M) on a military barrack in Dang district in 2001, the Government mobilised the Nepalese Army to control the CPN (M). However, the Nepalese Army was not able to control the insurgency. Instead, the Army bore heavy losses and lost the trust of the Nepalese people because of its grave human rights violations (AI 2005a and 2005b; ICG 2003; INSEC 2005). The serious mistrust by the people of the military caused permanent damage to the Nepalese Army. The Government's strategy of issuing red corner notices to CPN (M) through Interpol, fixing bounties on the heads of Maoist leaders, repeatedly imposing a state of emergency, issuing Terrorist and Destructive Activities Control Ordinances, creating a special Armed Police Force, and forming a unified command by bringing police, armed police, intelligence and military under the command of the Nepal Army were all ineffective and unsuccessful in controlling the insurgency. Instead, the CPN (M) gained tremendously from the Government's failed counter-insurgency tactics and strategy.

2.2.11 Culture of denial

People's reaction to the political situation in Nepal, especially to the armed conflict, was largely either denial, coercion or revenge. Politicians and bureaucrats often preferred to ignore or deny the existence of exclusion, discrimination, hunger, and civil and human rights violations, rather than accept the reality and acknowledge the need to reform the state and society (Upreti 2004c). All major actors in society used denial as a powerful mechanism. Those in power denied the seriousness of the country's situation, afraid to admit that their weaknesses were reflected in the attitudes, behaviour and practices responsible for the country's problems. They were even more defensive when confronted with evidence of their bad governance and corruption. In Nepal, denial is rooted in the psychological makeup of the individual and, at the institutional level, in political parties, government departments, and other power centres. The magnitude of denial is reflected in the ideas, values, greed, and orthodoxy of the major political and social actors in Nepal.

The self-interest of many of the key political and social actors in Nepal was the main factor influencing the dynamics of the conflict. For example, the urban elites feared that their privileges and comfortable lifestyles would be lost. Their needs and interests were, therefore, to protect this lifestyle by pacifying and neutralising those trying to restructure the state or advocating for social change. The urban elite used all available means at their disposal, such as the media, information, networks and strategic alliances, including a large segment of the international community, and national power centres. It is in their access to such diverse and powerful means that the elites display their potential to influence and direct the course of the conflict in Nepal. In sharp contrast, the poorest and most marginalised groups have few ways of influence the power/decision-making centres, and are, therefore, pushed to violence as a last resort. Although there is no established causal relationship between poverty and the use of violence, in Nepal it seems that the Maoists gained most of their early support from the poorest regions and the poorest and most marginalised groups.

2.2.12 Political ineptitude

It is very hard to find statesmanship in any of the current political leaders in Nepal (Baral 2006). Senior leaders are surrounded by coteries of people with vested interests. Nepal has received tremendous financial and technical support from the international community over the last five decades; however, misery caused by poverty, discrimination and exclusion is still rampant. India, South Korea, China and Nepal all started to develop economically at the same time (in the 1950s). All these countries, except for Nepal, have made huge economic progress. The single most important reason for the lack of development of Nepal is the ineptitude and lack of vision of the country's political leaders. Nepalese politicians have failed to prove themselves as leaders of the Nepalese people and have reduced themselves to leaders of their political faction (not even accepted by all members of their own political party). Hence, failure of the leadership and the absence of visionary leaders is one of main reasons for the lack of economic development, which in turn is a source of insecurity and livelihood stress.

2.2.13 Ideological conflict

The revolutionary politics of the CPN (M) are based on a clear ideology (Bhattarai 2005; Onesto 2005), that of Mao Zedong. The CPN (M) perceive Nepal's problems to be caused by deep-rooted oppression and feudalistic production relations, unequal power structures and the capitalist system (Upreti 2006; Bhattarai 2005; Sharma 2003). In contrast, the Government and the parliamentary parties advocated for a capitalist political system and constitutional monarchy. This resulted in an ideological conflict. The CPN (M) refined their theoretical orientation, calling it Prachandapath (after leader Pushpa Kamal Dahal whose alias during the insurgency was Prachanda), claiming that it was the way to address the challenges of the 21st Century. For their proletariat revolution, the Maoist combined the Chinese strategy of protracted people's war and the Russian strategy of armed insurrection with the discontentment of the Nepalese people with the state (Upreti 2006; Sharma 2003). Parliamentary parties and their successive governments were confused or unwilling to realise the strong ideological dimensions of the Maoist insurgency (Nickson 2003; Karki & Seddon 2003). Further, the state systematically underestimated and trivialised the United People's Front – the political wing of the CPN (Mashal) led by Baburam Bhattarai. This is reflected in the statement of the then Home Minister, "we will be able to bring the present activities under control within four five days" (Sharma 2003, p 371).

In the early years, Nepal's armed conflict was ideologically influenced by the Revolutionary Internationalist Movement (RIM) and the Coordination Committee of Maoist Parties and Organisations in South Asia (CCOMPOSA), as the CPN (M) was a member of both organisations (Upreti 2006). It even had some connection to, and official relations with, the communist party of the USA. However, none of these organisations influenced the armed conflict as much as the Peruvian communist party – the Shining Path – which was the real ideological, strategic and tactical source of Nepal's Maoist insurgency (Nickson 2003).

2.2.14 International dimensions

The armed conflict in Nepal has very strong international dimensions. The roles of India and the USA, and, to lesser extent, the UK were crucial during the entire duration of the conflict. India's role was particularly crucial in both the escalation and resolution of the armed conflict.

After 11 September 2001, the international security situation changed, greatly influencing the dynamics of the armed conflict in Nepal. Indian and American security interests in Nepal expanded. Although, the influence of the UK was not at the level of the other two countries, it had a significant influence on Nepal's armed conflict. The longstanding ties between Nepal and the UK (the role of the Gurkha soldiers in the British Army and the royal linkage between the two countries) enhanced the UK's interest in the armed conflict. Hence, it provided military aid to the Government of Nepal, despite the vehement opposition of human rights organisations such as Amnesty International. After 9/11, the USA took a very aggressive stance on terrorism, and Nepal was in its top six countries for military assistance. The USA also provided security intelligence, training and millions of US dollars in financial support to strengthen the Nepal Army. Even the Belgian Government provided 5000 weapons to Nepal. Selling arms was one of the major international interests in the Nepalese conflict (Upreti 2004a).

The open border (1808 km) between India and Nepal gave the CPN (M) easy access to India. The Maoists had easy access to India and strong ties with Indian ultra- leftists. They obtained training and weapons from India, and used Indian territory for meetings, to organise themselves, for publications, the collection of donations, to expand networks, and to access media. India has always been concerned with 'anti-Indian' activities in Nepal, particularly on the part of the Pakistani intelligence agency (ISI) and the support of the CPN (M) to Indian Maoists groups active in more than 12 states of India. After 9/11, India declared the CPN (M) as 'terrorists', started to extensively search for Maoist cadre and arms caches in India, reinforced border security by deploying troops, sealed borders, and provided military equipment and helicopters to crack down on the rebels. However, the CPN (M) continued its activities inside India. After the King's takeover on 1 February 2005, India changed its position. India not only supported the Seven Party Alliance (SPA) in its fight against the royal takeover, it also facilitated the meeting of the CPN (M) and the SPA and the 12-point understanding between these two political forces.

Although, China was close to the Palace in the past, it remained indifferent about the armed conflict saying that it was an 'internal problem' and that China does not want to engage in the internal politics of Nepal. However, it was watching developments very closely and used silent diplomacy. Contrary to the speculations of many people, China did not support the CPN (M) insurgency. Instead, it had frequently expressed dissatisfaction with the use of Mao's name in the conflict. After the 2006 people's movement, China changed its position on the monarchy, distancing itself and expressing support for the people's choice.

2.3 Effect of the armed conflict on livelihoods

Livelihoods are secure when they can cope with and recover from stresses and shocks and maintain or enhance capabilities and resources without undermining the resource base (Chambers & Conway 1992). Once capabilities and resources or assets are disturbed, people face livelihood insecurity. The armed conflict in Nepal disturbed these dynamics and consequently led to enormous livelihood insecurity. It also created some opportunities for alternative means of livelihood through the redistribution of land to landless, by forcing the Government to channel resources to pro-poor activities, and by prompting donors to focus on social exclusion and livelihood insecurity.

To achieve livelihood security for the Nepalese people, their basic rights must be guaranteed (according to international human rights conventions) in the constitution and legislated into national law. Furthermore, the Government must ensure the access of Nepali people to quality education, health services, markets, information and technology. Other important factors in livelihood security are secure access to and better management of natural resources; better access to basic and facilitating infrastructure and financial resources; and a policy and institutional environment that supports multiple livelihood strategies and promotes equitable access to basic services for all (DFID 1999). None of these conditions have been met to date and all were seriously disturbed by the armed conflict. Hence, the livelihoods of the vast majority of Nepalese people are insecure and vulnerable.

2.3.1 Diversion of state funds

One of the serious impacts of the armed conflict on the livelihoods of poor people was the resource shift from basic service sectors to unproductive military expenditure. The proportion of the budget dedicated to security invariably increases overtime. This increase in military expenditure and the disproportionate increase in the amount of 'administrative costs' compared to the development budget led to a decrease in the proportion of resources allocated to basic social service sectors (e.g., health, education, and drinking water).

Table 2.5 Comparative expenditure in different sectors in Nepal (million rupees/year) 1996-2004

Fiscal year	Total budget	Royal Nepal Army	Police	Royal Palace	General (administrative costs)	Development
1996/97	57566 (100%)	2425 (4.21%)	2235 (3.88%)	70 (0.12%)	24984 (43.40%)	32581 (56.60%)
1997/98	62022 (100%)	2629 (4.24%)	2521 (4.06%)	73 (0.12%)	27983 (45.12%)	34039 (54.88%)
1998/99	69693 (100%)	3028 (4.34%)	2922 (4.19%)	83 (0.12%)	31952 (45.85%)	37741 (54.15%)
1999/00	77238 (100%)	3511 (4.55%)	3324 (4.30%)	88 (0.11%)	35686 (45.81%)	41852 (54.19%)
2000/01	91621 (100%)	3897 (4.25%)	5271 (5.75%)	93 (0.10%)	43513 (47.50%)	48108 (52.50%)
2001/02	99792 (100%)	4521 (4.53%)	5795 (5.81%)	116 (0.12%)	49322 (49.42%)	50470 (50.58%)
2002/03	96125 (100%)	7228 (7.52%)	6304 (6.56%)	388 (0.40%)	57445 (59.76%)	38680 (40.24%)
2003/04	102400 (100%)	7179 (7.02%)	6279 (6.13%)	329 (0.32%)	60555 (59.14%)	41845 (40.86%)

Source: Pokharel (2004) Note: Numbers in parenthesis are percentage of total budget.

Table 2.5 demonstrates that administrative costs have increased from 43.40 per cent in 1997/98 to 59.14 per cent in 2003/04. The trend continues to increase further.

2.3.2 Damage to infrastructure

Table 2.6 shows the estimate of the value of damage to property and infrastructure during the armed conflict and the amount needed for reconstruction. The total destruction was estimated at about 5 billion rupees, out of which 3.8 billion rupees is required to reconstruct, and damage worth 1.2 billion rupees has already been reconstructed.

Table 2.6 Damage to physical infrastructure during the armed conflict in Nepal

S.N.	Ministries and constitutional commissions	Damage (NRs.)	Cost of Reconstruction (NRs.)
1	Ministry of Local Development	596446000	161722000
2	Ministry of Water Resources	342703000	297243000
3	Ministry of Health and Population	417000	130130000
4	Ministry of Forest and Soil Conservation	354461000	377123000
5	Ministry of Education and Sports	20960000	44984000
6	Ministry of Agriculture and Cooperatives	260755000	00
7	Ministry of Industry, Commerce and Supplies	18123000	15064000
8	Ministry of Environment, Science and Technology	3209000	00
9	Ministry of Information and Communication	741555000	145166000
10	Ministry of Culture, Tourism and Civil Aviation	134747000	26550000
11	Ministry of Physical Planning and Works	25174000	19746000
12	Ministry of Land Reform and Management	12187000	00
13	Ministry of Defence	24799000	00
14	Ministry of Finance	4666000	2270000
15	Home Ministry	2428646000	2428203000

16	Ministry of Women, Children and Social Welfare	230000	00
17	Supreme Court	27489000	165555000
18	Election Commission	2946000	00
19	Office of Attorney General	201000	00
20	Public Service Commission	4780000	00
21	Total	5004494000	3813756000

Source: Ministry of Peace and Reconstruction (2007)

2.3.3 Health

Access to health facilities is an important component of livelihood security, because physical and psychological readiness and ability to work and tap opportunities is higher if individuals are healthy. During the armed conflict ambulances, health posts and other health related infrastructure were damaged and the supply of medicines restricted in Maoist influenced areas to prevent them from falling into Maoist hands. Medical professionals were unwilling to go to remote areas for work, which led to a deficiency in health services. State investment in the health sector decreased leading to a rapid 'brain drain' as qualified doctors and nurses left Nepal for better opportunities. Frequent disruption of water supply and blockades of water sources by insurgents created serious problems in the health sector. Blockades and restrictions on visiting district headquarters by the insurgents has seriously disrupted or obstructed people's access to health facilities.

2.3.4 Education

Access to quality education is another important element of livelihood security. The armed conflict created anarchy in the education sector and warring parties held schools to ransom. Between 1996 and 2005 the CPN (M) killed 60 teachers and 66 students, caused the disappearance of 151 teachers and abducted 516 students and 62 teachers (not including mass abductions for indoctrination purposes). Similarly, the Army killed 44 teachers, 172 students, detained 158 teachers and 115 students, and caused the disappearance of 14 teachers (The Himalayan

Times 10 July 2005). Further, the mass abduction of students and teachers by CPN (M) and suspicion on the part of the security forces caused great insecurity. As a result, teachers and students left schools and colleges in rural remote areas. Strikes, bandhs (forced temporary closure of businesses and schools and the restriction of movement by vehicle) and the closure of schools have seriously obstructed the school and university calendars, and the teaching/learning environment. Schools were used as battlegrounds by the warring parties and as camps by security forces. Students and teachers felt confused and afraid when the CPN (M) forced them to follow their curriculum in schools. Regular extortion and payment of levies added an extra financial burden on parents, teachers and students.

The performance of community schools in villages and remote areas was very poor because the teachers, students and parents were obliged to participate in the programmes of the CPN (M). The School Leaving Certificate (SLC) examination results from conflict-affected areas were poor and a high percentage of students failed, creating frustration among the under-educated youth. School leavers who were unable to obtain (suitable) employment consequently became restless, angry and disconnected from society, and some of them joined the rebellion.

2.3.5 Transportation

The regular restriction or obstruction of the movement of people and goods during the insurgency (and since) has severely affected livelihood security, particularly of people in remote areas. Transportation was regularly obstructed, and for long periods of time, during the insurgency by the placement of landmines on major roads and due to physical damage to roads, transport infrastructure (civil aviation towers, roads, suspension bridges, etc.) and vehicles (burning or blasting of buses, loaded trucks, ambulances, cars, motorbikes, etc.). Blockades prevented truckloads of food and other goods from reaching markets and from reaching district headquarters, which severely disrupted market systems (leading to price rises; shortages of basic foods; increases in black marketing, smugglings, and cartels, etc.), all of which have caused severe livelihood insecurity.

The disruption of transport slowed down economic activities. Big construction projects (e.g., Melamchi Drinking Water Project, Kali Gandaki 'A' Hydro Power Project, various road construction projects, etc.), which required a huge amount of construction materials, were not able to continue work smoothly. This had a direct impact on daily wage labourers. Many ongoing infrastructure construction projects (e.g., the Chhinchu Jajarkot Road Construction Project) were stopped due to security risks and many other projects slowed down. All these transport and travel related problems created severe livelihood insecurity.

2.3.6 Market disruption

The Maoist strategy of sabotaging the infrastructure of large companies such as Uniliver Nepal, Surya Tobacco Company, Coca-Cola Bottlers Nepal, and various distilleries has had a negative effect on the employment of labour and created livelihood insecurity. It has also had a substantial negative impact on the economy, which affects the livelihoods of many people.

During the insurgency market opportunities were severely constrained and trade imbalances observed. The local hat-bazaar (a local market where people gather to buy and sell goods) system was disrupted and there were shortages of goods and services due to physical damage to goods and food stuff (hundreds of truckloads of goods were destroyed by the Maoists). As a result, the black market flourished. The diversion of scarce resources to unproductive uses and the destruction of capital severely weakened essential service delivery mechanism. Farmers were forced to throw away the milk, vegetables and other agricultural products on the road because of the frequent transport bandhs, which forced people towards bankruptcy. Employment opportunities were also severely constrained due to the scaling down of existing industries. All of these factors created an unfavourable environment for investing or establishing new enterprises. People engaged in self-employment, agriculture and small-scale cottage industries left their villages/occupations due to insecurity. Because of market disruption, uncertainty and insecurity (looting, robbery, etc.) the banking sector was also significantly affected. This has had a major impact on productive investment and employment generation in Nepal.

Tourism, an important livelihood sector in Nepal, was also severely affected during the conflict. Some big hotels closed due to onerous labour strikes. Demands by the Maoists for huge donations from big business were frequent and created a negative image internationally about the situation in Nepal. Forced donations and levies imposed on tourists and restrictions on the movement of tourists due strikes, bandhs (forced temporary closure of businesses, schools and transport) and blockades led to a reduction in the number of tourists visiting Nepal.

2.3.7 Food security and livelihoods

An examination of the food availability situation in Nepal, which is one of the most important elements of livelihood security, reveals that 60.2 per cent of households experience food insufficiency. Table 2.7 demonstrates the harsh reality.

Table 2.7 Food sufficiency of Nepali households

Household characteristics (food sufficiency situation)	Total no of households	Total number of households with land holdings
Total	3364139 (100%)	26700 (100%)
Sufficient to feed household	1337965 (39.8%)	1728 (6.5%)
Not sufficient to feed household	2026174 (60.2%)	24972 (93.5%)
1. 1-3 months insufficient	439592 (21.7%)	755 (3%)
2. 4-6 months insufficient	877362 (43.3%)	2250 (9%)
3. 7-9 months insufficient	342039 (16.9%)	2275 (9.1%)
4. 10-12 months insufficient	357544 (16.6%)	19633 (78.6%)

Source: Adapted from CBS (2004 pp 104-107, Table 2.32)

If the state fails to secure food for more than 60 per cent of households and more than 16 per cent households in Nepal have food insecurity all round the year, the legitimacy of the state is in serious question.

A study conducted by Seddon and Hussein (2002) reveals that during the insurgency security forces restricted local people from holding more than one-day's food supply at a time to deny the CPN (M) access to food, as against the general practice of people to hold a few months supply. This imposed great hardship on the people as in rural areas people have to walk up to three or four days to reach the nearest market.

The traditional livelihood opportunities of local poor were jeopardised by the conflict, as they were prohibited by the security forces from entering forests to collect forest based means of livelihood (e.g., mushrooms, young sprouts of plants, medicinal herbs, non-timber forest products, firewood, etc.). Anyone found in the forest by security forces was suspected to be Maoist. As a result, there were frequent famines in the Karnali region (Ibid, p 29) and other high-conflict areas.

2.3.8 Land, agriculture and water resources

Land is symbol of power, prestige and social status. It is also a means of production. Land is one of the natural resources that has been most affected by the armed conflict. During the conflict, power brokers and local elites captured valuable land resources using their networks and connections with state power centres and traditional power structures. Hence, land remained one of the major means of exploitation. As a result, the CPN (M) targeted landowners, evicting local landlords and village elites from Maoist controlled villages and capturing their lands. In some areas, especially in the Maoist controlled areas, they redistributed the land to the poor. However, because of intimidation by the security forces, the poor could not make use of the land. Local landlords were not able to cultivate their land and, consequently, scarce land resources were underutilised. The Government at that time started a Land Bank concept to buy land back from the landlords and sell it to the landless. However, critics say that it is a game plan of the feudal government to serve the interests of the feudal elites by buying their lands.

The Maoist slogan 'land to the tillers' gained the sympathy of the tenants, poor farmers and marginalised groups, but the conflict disrupted traditional production relations in rural areas. In a recent study (Upreti et al. 2008) key informants explained that most of the large landholdings were either directly controlled by the CPN (M) or the CPN (M) exerted pressure on tenants to stop paying contractual payments to landlords. The CPN (M) asked tenants to pay the landlords' share to them. This had a negative impact on the productivity of land, as lands were either uncultivated or under cultivated or cultivated with no/low investment. Some of the commercial farming (e.g., tea gardens in Ilam and Panchtahr, which are usually owned by middle class to rich farmers or local elites with strong links with power centres) was controlled or disturbed by the CPN (M). Such control ultimately forced the commercial farmers to leave the area. Rich and medium class commercial farmers faced continuous pressure to pay the Maoists huge sums of money. Such extortion greatly affected commercial farming including tea gardens, fruit farms, livestock farming, and cardamom, broom grass and ginger growing. In turn, this negatively affected agriculture processing and distribution systems.

Investment in the agriculture sector by the Agriculture Development Bank (ADB) and other financial institutions decreased. It became extremely difficult for ADBN staff to visit the field, as the insurgents were very negative towards ADBN loans and had damaged several branches of the ADBN destroying documents. Many farmers were unable to invest money loaned due to loss of their business. Big farmers and entrepreneurs were not ready to take the risk of investing in agriculture due to insecurity. In some cases farmers did not even draw down after the approval of the loan from the bank (Upreti 2005c).

The CPN (M) recognised the importance of agricultural development in their 75 point Common Minimum Policy and Programme. The 31st point states, "...Special attention shall be paid on the development of agricultural industries and proper arrangement shall be made for agricultural market". However, what they say (or write) and what they do are often different. The office buildings for agriculture and forestry (e.g., the Regional Agriculture Directorate in Biratnagar, Agriculture Development Office in Dhankuta, Forestry and Agriculture offices in Khotang, etc) were bombed by the insurgents. Several restrictive rules imposed by the Government directly hit farmers. For example, farmers needed a recommendation from the VDC Secretary to sell their rice, but there were no VDC secretaries available due to the conflict; the CPN (M) stopped the selling of timber by community forestry user groups; and communities/local people had to pay tax twice (to the Government and the CPN (M)) on the sale of non-timber forest products.

Similarly, investment in water resource was severely disturbed due to the armed conflict. Investment in water resources for hydropower, irrigation, drinking water, recreation and industrial uses was limited because the political environment was not conducive. Water sources were also polluted by the war and normal water supply systems disturbed.

2.3.9 Violation of human rights

Human rights abuses by the warring parties severely threatened the livelihood security of the Nepalese people as they were not able to freely engage in livelihood earning activities. The UN High Commissioner for Human Rights, Louise Arbor issued the following press statement highlighting the severe human right crisis during her visit to Nepal (23-26 January 2005): "I would warn the leaders of the insurgency not to misread development in the wider world or to believe that they can operate outside of the law." A series of reports by Amnesty International (Nepal: Killing with Impunity 20 January 2005; Nepal: State of Emergency Deepening Human Rights Crisis, 1 February 2005 and Nepal: A Long Ignored Human Rights Crisis Now on the Brink of Catastrophe, 18 February 2005) highlighted the worsening human rights situation in Nepal. Similarly, Amnesty International in its statement of 19 December 2004 stated:

> *The heightened threats occur as the international community reacts to the human rights situation with growing alarm. The UN Working Group on Enforced or Involuntary Disappearances (WGEID) concluded a visit to Nepal on Tuesday having received more reports of disappearance cases than from any other country in the world. (Upreti 2005a, p 7)*

The then Secretary General of the UN, Kofi Annan also repeatedly expressed his concern about the crisis in Nepal. His statement of 23 December 2004 issued by his office demonstrates his worries about the deteriorating situation in Nepal:

> *The Secretary-General is deeply troubled by reports of an escalation of fighting in Nepal and of continued grave human rights violations. The conflict is undermining democracy and human rights and seriously hindering development activities. Reports that human rights defenders in Nepal face grave threats to their safety and security are very disturbing. The safety and ability of the National Human Rights Commission and all human rights activists to carry out their essential work should be guaranteed. In that regard, the recent signing of a Memorandum of Understanding between His Majesty's Government of Nepal and the Office of the High Commissioner for Human Rights is a welcome step. The Secretary-General once again calls for an urgent cessation of fighting and the initiation of dialogue between the Government and the Communist Party of Nepal (Maoist) with the participation of all political and civil forces. He stands ready to assist such a national effort. (Upreti 2005a, p 7)*

The Secretary-General of the International Commission of Jurists (ICJ) while visiting Nepal said on 30 November 2004:

> *We are deeply concerned about the escalating and gross human rights abuses being committed by both sides of the conflict in Nepal. Addressing the breakdown of the rule of law cannot wait for a peace settlement. On the contrary, urgent steps can and must be taken to protect non-combatants, halt the spiralling descent into lawlessness and build the confidence for a political process. (Upreti 2005a, p 7)*

According to the reports of globally reputed organisations such as International Crisis Group and Amnesty International, the situation further worsened after the royal takeover of February 2005 (AI 2005a and 2005b; ICG 2005).

2.3.10 Displacement

Migration from rural areas to urban areas and from the hills to the Terai has been a general demographic phenomenon in Nepal for the last 40 years, particularly after the eradication of malaria in the Terai. Therefore, it is difficult to distinguish between conflict-induced Internally Displaced People (IDP) and voluntary migration (in search of a better life). The prevalence of both types of migration in Nepal is high. In the past decade the rate of migration continuously increased. Economic migration often positively contributes to secure livelihoods (Thieme 2006); conflict induced internal displacement, on the other hand, has devastating effects on the livelihoods of displaced people.

Conflict-induced internal displacement is one of the main forms of migration in Nepal (Pyakuryal et al. 2008). India is the destination for the largest number of migrants from Nepal, due to ease of accessibility (open border, similar religion, culture and language, relatives working there, and so forth). More information about conflict-induced displacement is discussed in Chapter 7.

2.3.11 Gender relations

Gender roles and gender relations in the villages have drastically changed in the areas most affected by the armed conflict (Upreti 2005). Because of displacement of men from the villages, the conventional roles of men and women have changed. For example, women have started to plough the fields in the absence of male family members, which was previously culturally forbidden. Women have also been starting to take on other functions performed by men such as participating in meetings and discussions, attending funerals and dealing with outsiders (e.g., security forces and insurgents). As well as changing the role of women, the conflict has increased the work burden of women as they now have to perform the tasks of their absent men folk, as well as their traditional roles.

Several cultural restrictions have been forcefully changed by the CPN (M) in Maoist influenced areas. Women have been empowered and opportunities opened up for them. For example, during the conflict, women took decisions and other responsibilities in the absence of their husbands and other male family members. Women participating in the armed conflict as combatants in the People's Liberation Army (PLA) discovered a new environment.

Gender violence is another dimension of the armed conflict. During the conflict, there were increased incidences of rape by perpetrators from both the armed forces and the Maoists. Both sides used rape as a deliberate tactic to intimidate the opposing side (AI 2005a and 2005a). The Nepalese press has frequently reported that incidents of rape were increasing. Reports of Amnesty International and various national human rights organisations stated that rape and intimidation were common characteristics of the armed conflict in Nepal. Rape survivors experience serious psychological effects and feelings of insecurity, anger and revenge. They are also often blamed by their family and the society and treated as social outcasts by the community. There were also some reported cases in the Nepalese media of a connection between the spread of HIV/AIDS and the armed conflict as some female IDPs were directly or indirectly forced into the commercial sex industry (Upreti 2006). Men forced to migrate for work or due to the conflict brought the disease back to their villages, infecting their wives and other partners. There has been a high increase in the commercial sex sector in IDP influx areas such as Nepalgunj, Surkhet and Kathmandu.

The number of single women and widows increased during the armed conflict. These women have difficulty in securing access to government compensation, basic rights and resources such as land and public services, etc. The subordination and exploitation of women is common during civil war. However, the situation in Nepal is exacerbated by cultural practices. If a women's husband is killed by either warring party, she and her children can end up displaced because of insecurity and fear.

In Nepal, women were not just victims of the conflict, they also actively participated as combatants. In the Maoist PLA, approximately 30 to 35 per cent of the fighting forces were women. This showed both men and women in Nepal that women are equally capable of fighting and serving in the armed forces. As a consequence, the Nepal Army has started to recruit female soldier.

In agriculture and resource management sectors in the conflict affected areas farming systems were very much dependent upon women as their men left the villages to avoid the warring parties. Field research (Upreti 2005a) revealed that women were taking responsibility for both the household and agriculture including crop production, livestock and the marketing of agricultural products.

2.3.12 Trigger for reforms

In a strategic sense, the armed conflict exposed the fundamental causes of livelihood insecurity prevalent in Nepal for centuries, making these issues a topic of national debate. The armed conflict has forced the promotion of transparency and the minimisation of corruption in development activities at the local level. The armed conflict has also increased the direct entitlement to land and assets of certain households and poor people in the Maoist stronghold areas (Onesto 2005). As discussed, gender roles in rural areas have also shifted, particularly since the CPN(M) vehemently opposed discrimination against, and the exploitation of, women. Thus, the conflict has helped to empower women, Dalits, ethnic groups and marginalised people in Nepal. Gambling and alcohol abuse has also decreased in Maoist controlled villages (Upreti 2006). Similarly, the exploitation of the poor and small farmers by village moneylenders has decreased in rural areas. All of these changes have contributed to addressing livelihood insecurity. The armed conflict has forced the Government to start some reform programmes on such as issues as the maximum landholding ceiling, women's property rights, the regulation of the sale and consumption of liquor, and the formulation of anti-corruption legislation. Further, the CPN (M) introduced various community decision-making mechanisms to deal with land issues, domestic violence, alcoholism, polygamy, and so forth, which have given a voice to socially excluded people, the poor and rural women. The CPN (M) raised legitimate questions regarding the performance and benefit of development projects in terms of the volume of budget spent and the types of people who have benefited. These concerns have contributed at a strategic level to improving the livelihoods of poor and marginalised sections of society.

2.4 Newly emerging sources of insecurity

In its transition towards an inclusive, federal democratic republic, Nepal is facing new challenges and threats to security and livelihoods. Even with a fully functional elected government, Nepal is still struggling with a weak law and order situation and increasing violence causing insecurity and livelihood stress. General strikes (bandhs), closures (even indefinite closures) and blockades are still routine, and even turn violent (burning vehicles, smashing or destroying public and private property, harassing travellers, etc.). Killing, bombing, kidnapping, looting and extortion continue. In addition, Nepal has experienced shortages of fuel (gasoline, kerosene, petrol) and power cuts of up to 16 hours a day. All of this has placed a burden on businesses (leading to the permanent closure of some businesses and factories), increased unemployment, and put pressure on daily wage earners who find it harder and harder to work. At the same time, rising commodity and food prices have increase the cost of living.

2.4.1 Ethnic movement

On the political front, the Terai region has become increasingly insecure and violent since the promulgation of the Interim Constitution. Some of the Madheshi[3] groups and political parties claim that their demands for ethnic autonomy (reflected in the slogan 'One Madhesh One Pradesh') are not being met. The movement is both powerful and aggressive. The Madhesh uprising in January/February 2007 (during which 27 people lost their lives) resulted in the amendment of the Interim Constitution 2007 to incorporate federalism and proportional representation, two of the main issues in the ethnic movement. It also succeeded in increasing the number of seats in Constituent Assembly allocated to the Terai from 43 per cent to 49 per cent. The regional parties have emerged as new political force in Nepal. The Madheshi movement regrettably turned out to be anti-Pahadi[4] (although the Pahadi's are not the only ones being targeted). Madheshi armed groups have been involved in kidnapping, extortion and killings (Hachhethu 2009). This lack of law and order in the Terai has brought about a new source of livelihood insecurity. Market disruption due to strikes and demonstrations, blockades preventing the transportation of goods from India and the Terai to urban centres in Nepal, and the closure of businesses and factories, some temporarily and others

---

3 'Madheshi' is a term used to describe the people from the Terai (or 'Madhesh'), the plain region of Nepal.

4 'Pahadi' is a term used to describe the people from the hills, as opposed to the people from the Terai.

permanently, are common place as the different political actors promote their causes. All these factors have created livelihoods insecurity.

2.4.2 Emergence of armed groups in the Terai

The security situation in the Terai is also severely affected by several small, armed groups that have emerged in the wake of the ethnic movement and are taking advantage of the extremely poor transitional security situation in the Terai. These groups include Janatantrik Terai Mukti Morcha (led by Jwala Singh), Janatantrik Madesh Mukti Morcha (led by Goit), Janatantrik Terai Mukti Morcha (led by Bisphot Singh), Madeshi Mukti Tiger, Terai Cobra; Python, Terai Baggi, Terai Army, Madeshi Virus Killers Party, Royal Defence Army, Gorkha Line Mukti Morcha, Liberation Tigers of Terai Ilem (LTTE) and the Kirat Workers Party (mainly in Udayapur and Khotang), and many more. There are more than `100 armed groups active in Nepal. Most of them have no political aim, but are encouraged by being reported in the media and perhaps by the Maoist access to power by use of violence to extort resources and to be popular leaders. There are only five or six armed groups with political aims and an organisational structure. Their formal demands are mostly related to the recognition of their community's/ ethnic group's interests and representation in state structures; however, some of these groups want autonomy or a separate state. The open border with India has greatly contributed to the organisation and expansion of several militant and fringe groups, most of whom have no political base, popular support, or clear organisational structure.

2.4.3 Criminal groups

There are also many criminal groups active in the Terai, based both in India and Nepal. Chhotelal Sahani, Sanju Baba, Raju Singh Rathor and the Munna Singh Groups are a few of the many groups mainly operating from India. This is creating severe insecurity and obstructing the normal livelihood activities of people. The open border between India and Nepal is becoming a haven for illegal arms traders and smugglers. The phenomena of criminal-led insecurity, such as the kidnapping of children, murder and attempted murder, robbery, the illegal trafficking of arms and ammunitions, human trafficking, drug trafficking, massacres, and forced displacement are continuing (Upreti 2009).

2.4.4 Militant arms of political parties

A new security dilemma is emerging as the main political parties are organising their youth as fighting forces against each other. Violent clashes between workers of different political parties are frequent. All the major political parties have created coercive sister youth organisations such as the Young Communist League (YCL) by CPN (M) (the largest party), Youth Force (YF) by the CPN (UML) (third largest party), Madesh Rakshya Bahini by Nepal the Sadbhavana Party, Madeshi Youth Force by Madheshi Janadhikar Forum. These organisations are operating without any legal mandate, reinforcing the 'might is right' culture that was prevalent during the worst of the Maoist insurgency, and are consequently creating enormous insecurity and fear all over Nepal. The Police Force is stretched, politicised and demoralised and consequently not able to act against the unlawful actions of these groups.

2.5 Changing political context

Nepal is now undergoing an historic transition from a feudal, centralist, autocratic and exclusionary state, to an inclusive, federal democratic republic. The popular uprising of April 2006 (Jana Andolan II) toppled the monarchy and led to the signing of the Comprehensive Pease Agreement in November 2006 and the election of the Constituent Assembly charged with the task of writing a new constitution for Nepal. While this is being done, the Nepal Army has been confined to its barracks and the PLA in cantonments.

The CPN (M) emerged as the largest political party in the Constituent Assembly Election held on 10 April 2008 and led the coalition government for nine months (September 2008 to mid-May 2009). At the time of writing, the ideologue of the CPN (M), Baburam Bhattarai, Finance Minister while presenting the country's budget for the fiscal year 2008/09 in the Legislature Parliament on 19 September 2008, identified some major challenges for the development of Nepal: (i) underdevelopment and absolute poverty; (ii) the stagnation of the agriculture sector, (iii) widespread unemployment and semi-unemployment; (iv) inequality and discrimination, (v) inadequacy of physical infrastructure, (vi) economic dependency, (vii) the deteriorating quality of public education and educational discrimination, (viii) corruption and (ix) very weak service delivery. These problems are widely cited to be the root causes of the armed conflict and livelihood insecurity of poor people of Nepal. Regarding underdevelopment and extreme poverty, the Finance Minister wrote:

> *Alarming figures of extremely low per capita income and more than half of population living below absolute poverty line present an awful image of the overall economic condition. Average growth rate of 2 per cent during the period of last fifty years clearly reveals that there is structural bottleneck in the economy. Therefore, breaking the vicious circle of poverty and underdevelopment through rapid economic growth along with its equitable distribution is the major economic challenge of the day. (MoF 2008)*

Identifying the problem is said to be half of the solution. Now it is up to the Government of Nepal to address this issue. In Nepal, challenges related to underdevelopment and poverty are well identified. The problem is lack of commitment, capacity and sincere efforts to address these issues. Similarly, the Government assessment of the stagnation of the agriculture sector is:

> *Despite agriculture sector being a source of employment for about 68 per cent of manpower, its contribution to Gross Domestic Product is only 32 per cent. Poverty is rampant among those engaged in agriculture because the per capita productivity is the lowest one. Our goal of rapid economic growth and poverty alleviation can never be achieved until we succeed to increase productivity of agriculture sector and shift the excess manpower from agriculture to the other sectors of economy by way of creating opportunities for gainful employment. Overall transformation of agriculture sector cannot take place without breaking the century-long feudal production relations rooted in the sector. Because of the feudal-based production relations, where peasants cultivating the lands do not have their ownership and those owning the land do not cultivate, productivity of agriculture is always low creating adverse impact on the economic growth. (MoF 2008)*

This is not an easy task for the Government, particularly with the deep tension between the major political parties over land related issues. Breaking the feudal relations of production means challenging the status quo, which is reinforced by most of the senior leaders of all the major political parties, as most of them come from either a feudal socio-economic background or from that mindset. The Maoist led government's assessment of the situation of unemployment and semi- unemployment was:

> *Unfortunately, our youth force is unemployed within our own country and are compelled to engage in painful foreign employment. Brain drain of educated and trained manpower is increasing. It has become a major challenge to create employment opportunity within the country for those youths who are marginalized from the mainstream of development, and make them participate in the process of building new Nepal. (MoF 2008)*

Addressing widespread semi-unemployment and disguised unemployment requires a holistic approach to development, and the institutional arrangements and procedural provisions are complicated. This presents serious problems in tackling unemployment, disguised employment and underemployment. Until there is a national consensus on addressing the root causes of the conflict, which is highly unlikely, achieving livelihood security and economic prosperity and social stability will be extremely difficult.

When the citizens of Nepal are engaged in democratic practices and when the state protects the human rights of its citizens, ensures social justice and promotes equity, livelihood security will improve. For that, economic development, political stability, lasting peace and inclusive democratic practices are required. The new constitution, to be framed by the 601 members of the Constituent Assembly, will hopefully ensure these conditions. The start is promising: the Constituent Assembly is the most diverse legislature in the history of Nepal, with as the 191 women and 49 Dalits, and numerous other previously marginalised and excluded groups finding representation. For the first time a broad cross-section of Nepal will be involved in writing a constitution to represent all of their interests. The livelihoods of the Nepalese people will be secure in the future if the new constitution: (i) ensures the participation of all members of society in decision making (ii) deals with some of the structural causes of poverty in Nepal, and (iii) addresses social discrimination. In addition, the state must provide a conducive policy framework and responsive institutional arrangements to ensure equity and livelihood security, and sincerely implement these mechanisms in the new Nepal.

Regrettably, the political environment seriously deteriorated in April and May 2009. The political parties, deeply entangled in their vested political interests and personal egos, have put aside the important components of a successful peace process such as constitution making, addressing PLA issues, restructuring of the state and delivering peace dividends. The termination of chief of the Nepal Army by the Government resulted in the collapse of the coalition government led by UCPN

(M) and a deep political divide and mistrust. The ousting of the UCPN (M) from the Government raised serious concerns among the Nepalese people about the potential for future conflict. Although, the senior leaders of the CPN (UML) are well known to be moderate politicians, and one of the few important players in the past peace process, Mr Madhav Nepal, was elected as Prime Minister with the support of 22 out of 24 political parties present in the parliament, the challenges ahead for him are serious given the seriously deteriorated relationship between the UCPN(M) and the CPN (UML).[5]

---

5 The UCPN (M) blame the CPN (UML) for the collapse of the UCPN (M) led coalition government as the CPN (UML) was second largest coalition partner. The UCPN (M) led government had a series of disputes with the Chief of Nepal Army (such as denial of entry of Defence Minister into one of Nepal Army Barracks in Chitwan, recruitment of Nepal Army personnel despite the disapproval of UNMIN and the coalition government, opposition of the discontinuation of Nepal Army Generals after their retirement, withdrawn of Nepal Army players from the national games due to participation by the PLA, resistance of Nepal Army Chief to the integration of PLA into the Nepal Army, submission of a complete draft of the constitution by Nepal Army Chief to National Interests Protection Committee of CA containing some provisions that contradict political agreements, labelling the CPA simply as a political document and not legally binding, and so forth etc.). Hence, the UCPN (M) wanted to remove the Chief of Nepal Army

2.6 Conclusions

Livelihood security cannot be achieved without addressing the problems of poverty, structural inequality, political and social exclusion, discrimination, and bad governance. The political change of 2006 paved the way for a federal democratic republic, but it also brought with it enormous challenges. The changed political context has provided a broader framework for change, but structurally embedded, pervasive socio-cultural and economic discrimination and inequality on the basis of caste, ethnicity and gender are still obstructing factors that must be overcome.

The livelihood basis and options of poor and marginalised people were severely affected during the decade of conflict in Nepal. State funds were diverted away from development to fight the insurgency. Damage to property and infrastructure during the armed conflict is estimated at 5 billion rupees, of which 3.8 billion rupees is required to reconstruct. Health, education, transport and markets were all severely disrupted. Food security in Nepal hit an all time low, with 60.2 per cent of households experiencing food insufficiency. The conflict also negatively affected agriculture processing and distribution systems, as well as investment in water resources. The serious violations of human rights committed by both the security forces and the insurgents created a culture of fear in which people were not able to freely engage in their usual livelihood activities. Conflict-induced internal displacement further disrupted livelihoods and left many villages without a male workforce. All of these factors severely disrupted livelihood security in Nepal.

---

from his post and sought approval from the main coalition partner CPN (UML), whose general secretary gave the go ahead before visiting China in late April 2009. But once the Government issued the termination letter to the Army Chief, the CPN (UML) withdrew from the coalition government and coordinated all other political parties to oppose the decision. They requested the President to keep the Army Chief in the post against the decision of the Government. Hence, the President issued a letter at midnight asking the Army Chief to continue in his position. Consequently, the UCPN (M) resigned from government.

Supporting people to achieve livelihood security should be a priority of the new government. The government should give priority to addressing the structural causes of the conflict (exclusion, discrimination and unequal distribution of resources). Changing existing power relations is an important structural means of enhancing the access of poor and marginalised people to alternate livelihood opportunities. Similarly, development strategies should consider the need to create livelihood security, which will also help to address the structural causes of the conflict, and strengthening peace and security.

A critical examination of the overall impacts of development programmes (Pandey 1999; Shrestha 1997; Upreti 2004a) raises the fundamental question as to why development has failed to address poverty and social exclusion in Nepal, the major structural causes of the conflict. The question directly points towards the performance of the government, the governing system and the development administration (proximate causes). The effective implementation of the Tenth Five Year Plan was severely affected during the period of the escalated conflict (2002–2006) and by malgovernance within the development administration of Nepal. Rural-urban inequalities, internal displacement and migration, the diversion of funds by the government to security and the fragile state of the private sector have held Nepal's development back and are jeopardising Nepal's prospects of achieving the Millennium Development Goals by 2015.

The people of Nepal lost trust in the political change of 1990 because of broken promises and failed delivery. They harbour a deep mistrust toward the Government and political parties because of their poor performance and many failures. Hence, the politicians and ruling elite that emerged after the political change of 2006 have to learn a lesson from the past. Many of the challenges faced by Nepal today are the product of the inherent weaknesses of the governing systems, social exclusion, the lack of public engagement in governance practices and failure to recognise pluralism in Nepali society. These issues need through consideration.

The main political actors and the government are still able to offer the Nepalese people a realistic hope of attaining a decent standard living. The poorest groups are entrenched in a deprivation trap – a cycle of social exclusion and poverty. This needs to be addressed or it will sow the seeds for future discontent and instability. Livelihood security is essential to lasting peace.

To ensure the livelihood security of the Nepalese people requires a radical shift in current thinking and practices. The principle of inclusiveness must be applied by civil society, political actors and other segments of society. A culture of tolerance, respect for diversity, inclusiveness and reconciliation must be incorporated into governance principles and practices. The root causes of conflict such as poverty, social and political exclusion and the marginalisation of ethnic minorities, discrimination, unequal access to resources, and bad governance need to be properly addressed to create lasting peace in Nepal. It is essential for all political and social actors to change their perceptions, shed stereotypes and promote tolerance and embrace inclusiveness. In essence, the current conflict should be used as an opportunity to broaden political and social reforms in Nepal. The armed conflict undoubtedly had many negative impacts, but it also contributed positively to altering the unequal social relations in Nepalese society. These gains must be consolidated, and Nepal must move forward to create a society in which all of its citizens can prosper and live in dignity.

Although Nepal has experience armed conflict for the past ten years (and suffered the causes of the conflict for a lot longer), there is a ray of hope emerging. After the defeat of the autocratic regime by the people's movement of April 2006, the new government and the Constituent Assembly are entering into serious political negotiations for the restructuring of the state and the establishment of an inclusive federal democratic republic. If the negotiations are successful, this nation will be transformed into an inclusive modern Nepal, where all citizens are represented. A Nepal where everyone has an equal right to dream, work and prosper.

References

Acharya KP. 1998. *A Review of Foreign Aids in Nepal.* Kathmandu: Citizens Poverty Watch Forum.

Aditya A, Upreti BR, and Adhikari PK. 2006. *Countries in Conflict and Processing of Peace: Lessons for Nepal.* Kathmandu: Friends for Peace.

AI [Amnesty International]. 2005a. *Nepal: A Long Ignored Human Rights Crisis now on the Brink of Catastrophe. 18 February 2005, ASA 31/022/2005.* London: Amnesty International.

AI [Amnesty International]. 2005b. *Nepal: Killing with Impunity. 20 January 2005, ASA31/001/2005.* London: Amnesty International.

Bhattarai BR. 2003. *The Nature of Underdevelopment and Regional Structure of Nepal: A Marxist Analysis.* New Delhi: Adroit Publishers.

Bhattarai BR. 2005. *Monarchy vs Democracy: The Epic Fight in Nepal.* New Delhi: Samakalin Teesari Duniya.

CBS [Central Bureau of Statistics]. 2004. *Statistical Pocket Book.* Kathmandu: Central Bureau of Statistics.

Chambers R and Conway G. 1992. *Sustainable Rural Livelihoods: Practical Concepts for the 21st Century, IDS Discussion Paper 296.* Brighton: Institute for Development Studies.

DFID [Department for International Development]. 1999. *Sustainable Livelihoods Guidance Sheet.* London: Department for International Development of UK.

Hachhethu K. 2003. *The Question of Inclusion and Exclusion in Nepal: Interface between State and Ethnicity.* Paper presented at 'The Agenda of Transformation: Inclusion in Nepali Democracy' on 24-26 April 2003. Kathmandu: Social Science Baha.

Hachhethu K. 2009. *State Building in Nepal. Creating a Functional State.* Kathmandu: Enabling State Programme.

Hutt M. 2004. *Himalayan 'People's War': Nepal's Maoist Rebellion.* London: Hurst and Company.

ICG [International Crisis Group]. 2003. *Nepal Obstacle to Peace- Report No 57.* Brussels/Kathmandu: International Crisis Group.

ICG [International Crisis Group]. 2005.*Towards a Lasting Peace in Nepal: The Constitutional Issues, Asia Report No. 99, 15 June 2005.* Brussels/Kathmandu: International Crisis Group.

IDD [Internal Displacement Division]. 2005. *Report on the Inter-Agency Internal Displacement Division Mission to Nepal.* Kathmandu: Internal Displacement Division.

INSEC [Informal Sector Service Centre]. 2005. *Human Rights Year Book.* Kathmandu: Informal Sector Service Centre.

Karki A and Seddon D. 2003. People's War in Nepal: Leftist Perspective. New Delhi: Adroit Publishers.

Kumar D. 2006. Proximate causes of Conflict in Nepal. *In:* Simkhada, SR and Oliva F, editors. *The Maoist Insurgency in Nepal (Monograph)*, pp 67-122.

Lawoti M. 2005. *Towards a Democratic Nepal: Inclusive Political Institutions for a Multicultural Society.* New Delhi: Sage Publications.

Mackinlay J and Upreti BR. 2003. The King and Mao. *In: The World Today.* London: Royal Institute of International Affairs, pp 26-27.

Mainali M. 2003. Development vs. the Maobadies. *In:* Thapa D, editor. 2003. *Understanding the Maoist Movement in Nepal.* Kathmandu: Martin Chautari, pp 125-127.

Manandhar N. 2007. *The Kathmandu Post.* 19 July 2007.

MoF [Ministry of Finance]. 2008. Budget for the fiscal year 2008/09 presented by the Finance Minister in the Legislature Parliament on 19 September 2008.

Nickson RA. 2003. Democratisation and growth of communism in Nepal. *In:* Thapa D, editor. *Understanding the Maoist Movement in Nepal.* Kathmandu: Martin Chautari, pp 2-33.

NPC [National Peace Campaign]. 2003. The Cost of War in Nepal. Kathmandu: National Peace Campaign, P. 23.

Onesto L. 2005. *Dispatches from the People's War in Nepal.* London: Pluto Press and Chicago: Insight Press.

Pahari A. 2003. *From Liberation to Insurgency: The Politics of Paradoxes in Nepal.* Paper presented at 'The Agenda of Transformation: Inclusion in Nepali Democracy' on 24-26 April 2003. Kathmandu: Social Science Baha.

Pandey DR. 1999. *Nepal's Failed Development: Reflections on the Mission and the Melodies.* Kathmandu: Nepal South Asia Centre.

Pokharel B. 2004. *Cost of Conflict in Nepal.* A Paper Presented at the Seminar of "Cost of Conflict in Nepal" on 9 June 2004. Kathmandu: Nepal Foundation for Advanced Studies.

Seddon D and Hussein K. 2002. *The Consequences of Conflict: Livelihoods and Development in Nepal.* ODI Working Paper 185. London: Overseas Development Institute.

Sharma S. 2003. The Maoist movement: An evolutionary perspective. *In:* Thapa D, editor. *Understanding the Maoist Movement in Nepal.* Kathmandu: Martin Chautari, pp. 362-380.

Sharma S and Rana RS. 2006. Development cooperation and conflict. *In:* Simkhada SR and Oliva F, editors. *The Maoist Insurgency in Nepal (Monograph)*, pp. 162-213. Geneva: International Institute of Graduate Studies.

Shrestha NR. 1997. *In the Name of Development: A Reflection in Nepal.* Kathmandu: Educational Enterprise.

Thapa D and Sijapati B. 2003. *A Kingdom under Siege: Nepal's Maoist Insurgency, 1996 to 2003.* Kathmandu: The Printhouse.

Thapa HB. 2002. *Anatomy of Corruption*. Kathmandu: Sangita Thapa.

Thieme S. 2006, Social networks and migration: Far west Nepalese labour migrants in Delhi. *Culture, Society, Environment – South Asian and South East Asian Studies*. Vol. 7. Münster: LIT Verlag.

UNDP [United Nations Development Programme]. 2004. *Nepal Human Development Report: Empowerment and Poverty Reduction.* Kathmandu: United Nations Development Programme, Nepal.

Upreti, BR. 2001. *Conflict Management in Natural Resources: A Study of Land, Water and Forest Conflict in Nepal.* Published PhD dissertation. Wagenignen: Wagenignen University.

Upreti BR. 2002a. *Management of Social and Natural Resource Conflict in Nepal: Realities and Alternatives.* New Delhi: Adroit Publishers.

Upreti BR. 2002b. *Nepal: A Nation in Search of Peace and Development. A Country Assessment Report.* Berne: Swiss Agency for Development and Co-operation.

Upreti BR. 2004a. *The Price of Neglect: From Resource Conflict to the Maoist Insurgency in the Himalayan Kingdom.* Kathmandu: Bhrikuti Academic Publications.

Upreti, BR. 2004b. Resource conflicts and their resolution practices in Nepal. *Mountain Research and Development Journal* 24(1):60-66.

Upreti BR. 2004c. Land conflict in Nepal: Peasants' struggle to change unequal agrarian social relations. *Journal of Community, Work and Family* 7(3):371-394.

Upreti BR. 2004d. Neglected reality: Resource governance and conflict in Nepal. *In:* Mukti Rijal, editor. *Readings on Governance and Development Vol. 3.* Kathmandu: Institute of Governance and Development, pp 95-111.

Upreti BR. 2005a. Human rights approach to conflict transformation: Ensuring respect and fulfilment of human rights in peaceful settlement of the armed conflict in Nepal. Paper presented at Human Rights and Peace Conference on 24–25 January 2005. Kathmandu: National Human Rights Commission.

Upreti BR. 2005b. *Working on Conflict: Peace and Conflict Impact Assessment of Commercial Agriculture Development Project in Eastern Nepal. Final Report.* Manila: Asian Development Bank.

Upreti, BR. 2006. *Armed Conflict and Peace Process in Nepal: The Maoist Insurgency, Past Negotiation and Opportunities for Conflict Transformation.* New Delhi: Adroit Publishers.

Upreti BR. 2009. *Nepal from War to Peace: Legacies of the Past and Hopes for the Future.* New Delhi: Adroit Publishers.

Upreti BR and Dhungana DN. 2006. Peace process and negotiation in Nepal: Revisiting the past and envisioning the future. *In:* Simkhada SR and Oliva F, editors. *The Maoist Insurgency in Nepal (Monograph)* pp 214-252. Geneva: International Institute of Graduate Studies.

Upreti BR. 2007. *Conflict Sensitive Development Policy in the changing context of Nepal. A Background Paper.* Kathmandu: Ministry of Peace and Reconstruction.

Upreti BR, Sharma SR and Basnet J, editors. 2008. *Land Politics and Conflict in Nepal: Realities and potentials for Agrarian Transformation.* Kathmandu: Community Self-Reliance Centre, South Asia Regional Coordination Office of the Swiss National Centre of Competence in Research (North-South) and Human and Natural Resources Studies Centre/Kathmandu University.

* * * * *

CHAPTER 3

Natural resources governance and livelihoods in Nepal: Political economy and political ecology perspectives

Netra Prasad Timsina

Abstract

In this chapter, the 'political economy' and 'political ecology' are used as conceptual frameworks for analysing the livelihoods of people who depend on natural resources in Nepal. The political economy takes into account the power structure of the society including the social relations in production and distribution. The political ecology accommodates ecological considerations, referring to the relationship between nature and society. This chapter combines these two concepts in analysing resource policies and, in particular, access to and control over natural resources for livelihoods. Land and forests are the most important natural resources in Nepal. The state has direct control over these resources through various policies, legislation and institutions. Although the Government has introduced participatory approaches in managing natural resources, particularly in the management of forestry resources, the outcomes have been variable depending upon the level of autonomy given to the local people. Forests, as common property resources, are easier to manage using a participatory approach than land. Nevertheless, even when forests are managed by communities, the interests of local elites and bureaucratic classes and existing policies and institutions continue to marginalise the natural resource dependent poor. Overcoming inequity in the distribution of resources is essential to ensure people's livelihoods. This requires a complete transformation of the natural resource sector to infuse inclusive democracy into the processes and institutions related to natural resource management.

3.1 Introduction

This chapter looks at natural resource governance and livelihoods in Nepal from the theoretical perspectives of the political economy and the political ecology. The political economy encompasses the power structure in society, which determines the institutions and policies that frame the allocation of access to and control over resources. The political ecology refers to the relationship between society and nature, and is considered here as an extension of the political economy in order to accommodate ecological considerations.

This chapter examines the political economic history of natural resource management (NRM) in Nepal, particularly of forest resources and, to some extent, of land resources, and analyses resource ownership, use and management over time. It also outlines how the Government maintains control over valuable forests such as the Terai forests. It is argued that conservation and elitist discourses sideline the needs and priorities of people in the name of participatory resource management. It is asserted that policies and institutions for natural resource management need a complete transformation, as existing institutions do not ensure the rights of people over natural resources. This chapter also recommends an organised social movement for a complete transformation of the institutions and policies in favour of the poor and marginalised sections of society.

The information in this chapter is primarily based on secondary data and a literature review. The author also draws on his several years' research experience in the field of natural resource management in Nepal. This is supplemented by observations gathered in interactions with a number of people involved in advocating for people's rights in relation to natural resources.

3.2 Political economy and political ecology

The concept of the political economy looks at two closely related questions: how politics determines economic aspects and how economic institutions determine political processes (Staniland 1985). Theoretically, the political economy begins only when someone's access to resources and the means of production are affected. It begins with the production system, which is based on the social division of labour and regulated by rules and regulations external to the will and consciousness of the individuals concerned. The production system in a definitive historical period and, under a certain set of conditions, determines the mode of distribution, thereby shaping the specific structure of a society. The issue of land distribution in Nepal is being debated to reduce class antagonism by giving a large proportion of people access to directly engage in small-scale agricultural production. Large-scale agriculture, such as in the large tea estates in Northern India, can lead to class antagonism as the elite class controls resources and receives most of the benefits/profits, while the working class provides the labour. With differences in the distribution of resources, class differences emerge in society between the privileged and the underprivileged, the 'haves' and the 'have nots', the exploiter and the exploited, and the ruler and the ruled (Engels 1880). The relations of production directly influence the use and management of resources, such as forests, in a society. It is, therefore, important to understand the different production systems determining people's relationships in a society. In this sense, production systems may serve as an entry point for understanding disparities within a society. Society has never been the mere sum of individual acts, but rather a totality of interacting individuals, facing one another in various relationships. Modern society did not emerge from a series of simple human relations among individuals, but instead arose out of an array of historically specific social and economic relations, such as those of capitalists to workers and landlords to tenants (Rodolfo 1975).

Individuals in society are embedded in particular class relations, with their own class interests. The determinants of class depend on the relations of production, which relates directly to the social division of labour and the political ideological superstructure. If capitalists and workers are defined by their position in production relation, the capitalists, as the owner of resources, exercise a definite power over the workers. Although Marx (1977) explained this phenomenon in relation to the industrialised 19th Century, it is equally applicable today in developing countries, as local elites/landlords exercise power over poor and marginalised people. The elites/ landlords become the ruling class in which 'class' is used as an economic term and 'rulers' as a political one. The phrase 'ruling class' thus contains the theory that an economic class rules politically (Bottomore 1993).

However, Marx (1977) explains that the given social relations can be changed by a militant class, which is conscious of its historic vocation and deliberately acts upon it. According to Marx, freedom for an individual must be achieved; his/her feeling of dignity, which transforms the society, must be respected. This dignity and freedom is achieved through widespread class-consciousness among the oppressed, which threatens the ruling class. In the case of Nepal, it is more relevant to understand the Maoist movement as an example of a class struggle. However, as Scott (1976; 1985) argues, a social relationship is not only determined by material conditions, it is also the product of the ideology of a group in society. This explanation applies to Nepalese rural society, which has hierarchies in a chain of relationships and an exploitative structure. The elite represent the formal power structure at different levels. There are the political elite, the politically elected representatives and the top civil servants. Social elites are those who control non-political organisations like businesses, professions and so forth. All the elites (politicians, bureaucrats, administrators, business people and landlords, etc.) whether local or national, share certain common ideologies and political positions, values and perspectives (Gough 1979).

However, the conventional concept of the political economy is criticised for being limited to economic reductionism. To avoid such a limitation, the political ecology approach emerges to internalise the sensitivity of the diverse socio-political forces and their relationship to environmental change (Bryant & Bailey 1997; Graner 1997). The political ecology can be understood as an extension of the political economy, which accommodates ecological considerations. Blaikie and Brookfield (1987) define the political ecology as follows:

The phrase 'political ecology' combines the concern of ecology and a broadly defined political economy. Together this encompasses the constantly shifting dialectics between society and land based resources, and also within classes and groups within society. (p 17)

Moreover, Guha and Martinez-Alier (1997) explain the concept of political ecology along the same lines as Blaikie and Brookfield that the political ecology deals with the relationship between society and nature and also with various socio- economic groups within society. Neumann (1992) takes land users and their social relationships in the context of a broader spatial setting and historical perspective as the main subject matter of the political ecology. The political ecology focuses on the political causes of environmental change and the struggle for access to, and control over, environmental resources (Paudel 2005). The idea of a politicised environment conceives the environment as the subject of intense struggle between different social actors in their efforts to meet their own interests (Ibid). Accordingly, Harvey (1993, p 25) says "all ecological projects (and arguments) are simultaneously political economic projects (and arguments) and vice versa".

3.3 Political economic history of natural resource management in Nepal

In Nepal, many people rely on natural resources for their livelihood. Land, forest and water are the major natural resources on which the majority of Nepali people depend. The following statement made by a farmer from Chitwan district to a researcher reflects the needs of a typical farmer in Nepal:

> *My land should be near a natural source of water, so that I can irrigate my rice fields. A bit of Sarhad (dry field) should also be available to plant mustard on. My land should be close to the forest, so that my cattle can graze there. I would like to be allowed to get everything I need from the forest, wood, grass, and reeds, fruits and vegetables. When I am not working in the fields, I would like to go fishing, so streams and rivers should also be close by. (Müller-Böker 1999, p 91)*

Until the 1950s, land and forest resources in Nepal, the major means of production and livelihood, were controlled by the ruling classes (Regmi 1978a; Malla 2001; Upreti 2004). Generally, the rulers granted land to the people who supported them in their campaigns for state expansion. Land was granted mostly by patronage to family members and local elites in the form of Birta (Regmi 1978a; 1976). In this way the ruling classes maintained control over resources located in distant places. Although the system of Birta existed before the Rana period, the control over forest resources by the Ranas accelerated in two ways. One, they gave land in the form of Birta to their own family members, patrons or relatives of the ruling classes. Two, the ruling classes received a significant amount of income from the export of timber from the Birta land to India (Regmi 1978a). The Ranas were excited by the handful of income received from forest products and promoted the slogan "Hariyo ban Nepalko dhan" (green forest, Nepal's wealth), a saying originally introduced by Prithivi Narayan Shah. However, the ordinary people rarely benefited from this notion of forest wealth. There were separate rules and regulations for the use forests by the general public, and Birta land was exempt from these rules (Mahat et al. 1986).

Other forms of land tenure in Nepal include Jagir and Kipat, which are also the product of the political and economic situation of the period (Regmi 1978a 1976). Land given to soldiers and government officials for their services and loyalty were called Jagir. The Jagir system, which was inherited from the previous Gorkhali rulers, was established due to a shortage of cash to pay lower ranking soldiers. The Rana rulers retained the Jagir system to make the Nepalese Army as attractive as the British Gurkha regiment, especially to lower ranks (Mahat et al. 1986). The Kipat system represented a communal form of land tenure. A tribe, village, community or family held land with individuals having defined rights of use (Regmi 1978a).

Among the land tenure systems, Birta was the most prominent from the time of Nepal's unification by Prithivi Narayan Shah in 1768 to the end of Rana period in the 1950s. According to Regmi (1978b):

> *Oligarchic regimes, such as those that governed Nepal prior to 1950, have always depended on a select class for the sustenance and continuance of the authority. Birta land grants to members of such classes ensured a regular stable income for them and thus left them free to indulge in war or politics in the interest of rulers.*

Under the Birta system, different forest management systems were in operation, among them, the Talukdari system and, in the eastern hills, the Kipat system. Talukdars were local functionaries of state and were responsible for revenue collection for the state. Most often, local landlords were appointed as Talukdars. Under the Kipat system, Jimmawals (local headmen) were recognised as tax collectors and were also responsible for forest resource management (Hobley & Malla 1996). Although, there was some sort of a two-way relationship between the people and the state functionaries, the latter exercised state power over the people as they were appointed politically by the state (Regmi 1978b). Most of the forests in Nepal were used under the Birta tenure system, before and during the Rana period, to maintain the loyalty of local allies to the Shah dynasty. This practice continued until the 1950s. In 1957, forests were nationalised with a view to putting an end to elite control of vital resources. However, after the dismissal of the elected government in 1960 and the introduction of the partyless Panchayat system, stringent regulations were enforced to protect forests from people who were thought of as enemies by the Panchayat elites and forest bureaucrats (Ojha et al. 2005).

During the Rana period, the Nepali timber market was expanded up to India. The Government encouraged the clearing of Terai forest for infrastructure development. Major deforestation of the Terai forest took place during the construction of the Koshi and Gandaki barrages, and the Sunauli highway, almost halving Nepal's Terai forest area. Terai forest destruction accelerated when the then King Mahendra decided to construct the East-West highway from the bottom of the Chure hills. At the same time, in 1963, King Mahendra invited non-resident Nepalese to settle on cleared Terai forestland. He also encouraged landless mountain people to resettle in the Terai by clearing the dense forest. Forest technocrats used landless people to clear the forest to earn money. Landlords competed to capture the fertile lands of the Terai by clearing the forests (Karki 2001).

In 1977, then Prime Minister, Kirtinidhi Bista, decided to clear the Sissau forest of Kapilbastu to sell to the Indian match industry, with a view to acquiring Indian currency. In 1979, when Surya Bahadur Thapa became Prime Minister, he invited the forest contractors to clear the forest (Nepal Weekly 2005). The money collected was used to defeat the multiparty democratic system and replace it with the partyless Panchayat system in a referendum held in 1980. At that time, government supporters could do whatever they liked to the forest if they committed themselves to vote against democracy. As an extra incentive, voters were also resettled inside the Terai forests.

In 1964, The Panchayat regime enacted the Land Reform Act with the stated objective to increase agricultural productivity through the distribution of land to the peasants who cultivated it. However, the cultivators, agricultural labourers and landless people did not benefit from this initiative. Instead, the ruling class and landlords legalised holdings of land that were above the legal land ceiling (maximum area of land that could be held by one family) set by the Act by registering the land in the name of their family members. Bribery and corruption in land transactions were rampant, and many landless and small farmers were provided with fake land certificates (Karki 2001; Upreti 2001).

As land is the principal economic resource for all categories of people, the elite and powerful captured most of the land and many poor peasants became landless. The political elites and the land owning classes continued to control the land in the same way as they did before the 1950s. These classes included ministers, members of parliament, high-ranking bureaucrats, as well as members of the army and the police. A significant area of arable land was (and still is) controlled by the members of the Royal family and the Ranas, the then rulers of Nepal. This became evident when the Ministry of Land Reform and Management made public the area of land registered in the name of Royal family (Kantipur Daily, 4 August 2006). These classes are usually absentee landlords. They do not live in the villages where their lands are situated, but extract the income from the land. Most of the cultivators, on the other hand, are landless and property-less, but are fully integrated within the wider economy and are important to labour relations in the village closest to their settlement (Ghimire 1998).

Dalits and some ethnic nationalities have been deprived of land ownership since the formation of modern Nepal. The struggle for land rights by landless peasants has increased over time, particularly since the 1950s. From time to time governments have brought in land reform programmes as a response to the land rights struggle. Since 1976 (and even after 1990), governments have consistently formed landless resettlement committees with the stated objective to solve the problem of landlessness. However, all these attempts have remained in rhetoric only. In practice, the land settlement and reform processes in Nepal, then and now, have served only to safeguard the economic and political interests of the ruling class, politicians and bureaucrats (Upreti 2004). This is a prominent area of class struggle in Nepal. Because the political elite formed the dominant segment of the landowning elite, the implementation of land reform policies and programmes was determined by the landowning members of the aristocracy and bureaucracy.

3.4 Participatory forestry in Nepal

The changes in the policies and programmes for forest resources over time have been slightly different than those concerning land, as forest resources are considered common property and also have a direct environmental significance. The 1970s were a 'push decade' for community forestry (CF) in Nepal from the point of view that external agencies were interested in being involved in the forestry sector as a strategy for environmental conservation (Hobley & Malla 1996; Graner 1997).

Worldwide, donor agencies started to pressure national governments to change their development and natural resource policies. As the environmental agenda became a prominent issue in the 1970s, external donors, alarmed by the perceived environmental degradation in the Himalayan region (Eckholm 1976), insisted that Nepal was among the most affected countries. Concurrently, a community-oriented group of foresters promoted the idea of working with local people in forest management.

In 1976, a National Forestry Plan was formulated, which made provision for the allocation of some forestland to village Panchayats. Under the plan, full power was given to the then Divisional Forest Officers (DFOs) to formalise the transfer of nationalised forestland to individual village Panchayats (Hobley & Malla 1996). Hence, the initiation of community forestry in Nepal was the product of both national and international efforts in this field.

Based on the National Forestry Plan, in 1978, Rules and Regulations were promulgated to manage local forests in the form of Panchayat Forests (PFs) and Panchayat Protected Forests (PPFs). Between 1978 and 1990, forestry development work in the hills had been strongly influenced by these Regulations, and much of the Government's and aid agencies' efforts have focused on the creation of PFs and PPFs (Gilmour & Fisher 1991).

The 1980s were a period of experimentation with different participatory forestry practices. The Government declared a forest sector policy for the first time in its Sixth Five Year Plan (1981–1985), emphasising the need for active community participation in the management, conservation and utilisation of forest resources (NPC 1985; NPC 1992).

The diverse experiences in community forestry led to the development of a 20- year Master Plan for the Forestry Sector (MPFS) in 1988. The MPFS formed the basis for forest policy and clearly articulated meeting local people's basic forest product needs through community forestry. The Forest Act 1993 identified six major forest management regimes, according to management responsibility. They are community forest, government managed forest, protected forest, leasehold forest, religious forest and private forest.

Community forestry in Nepal has been the 'mother programme' of all other participatory forest resource management programmes. In 2006, 20 per cent of the country's forest was under community forestry, with almost 35 per cent of the country's population participating in CF. Even though the donors supported CF as a programme of the government, it has been institutionalised at the community level and is one of the most successful community development programmes in Nepal (Ojha et al. 2005). CF established the rights of communities over forest resources. Many other programmes have adapted learning from the community forestry programme. Some of the lessons derived from the community forestry programme include:

- If communities are granted full power and authority over resource management, both the objectives of conservation and livelihoods can be achieved.
- CF encourages dialogue between the policy level and the practice level, which has allowed a number of innovations in forest resource management.
- CF has been a platform for the development of a critical civil society in Nepal, which has constantly advocated for decentralisation, devolution and people's rights in forest resource management.

Other forest management approaches have also been implemented in Nepal, and some have been in place for nearly two decades. These include leasehold forestry, buffer zone management, conservation area management, watershed management and collaborative forest management, all of which come within the larger framework of participatory forestry.

Leasehold forestry aims at supporting the poorest of the poor and has been the focus of national policies and programmes for poverty alleviation. Under this approach, the management of degraded land is handed over to a group of poor people for income generation from forestry activities. However, the programme does not appear to have benefited the poor. The programme has proved to be impractical in supporting the livelihoods of people.

The buffer zone management approach allows people who live around the national park to access forest resources, particularly grasses and reeds, from a 'buffer zone' around the park. However, the buffer zone management approach has also been criticised for not being participatory and accessible to people, particularly the poor (Paudel 2005; Soliva et al. 2003; Budhathoki 2003).

The conservation area management approach is being implemented in Nepal within certain protected areas and a number of community development activities, including conservation, have been carried out. This approach was first adopted in 1985 with the Annapurna Conservation Area Project (ACAP), which has had a mixed impact. Although ACAP has had a positive impact in promoting community development and conservation activities, it has been criticised for not addressing the livelihoods needs of poor people in the area.

Watershed management is an integrated development approach that looks at the landscape as a whole. The approach was first implemented in Nepal in the mid- 1970s and aims to increase the ecological and economic benefits to the people. The impact of this approach is yet to be assessed.

Collaborative forest management is currently being implemented in the Terai region of Nepal. The approach is modelled on the Indian Joint Forestry Management approach, and, although it is a participatory approach, it is not compatible with the long running and highly successful community forestry programme. Under CF, the community has autonomy over the management of forest resources, and benefits are channelled back into the community. In contrast, under collaborative forestry management, the government bureaucracy controls the forest management committee and 75 per cent of any revenue generated goes to the government.

Leasehold forestry, buffer zone management, protected area management and collaborative forest management are discussed and compared with community forestry in the following sections.

3.5 Competition between community forestry and other programmes: Issues of power and authority

As discussed above, various natural resource management approaches have been implemented in Nepal including leasehold forestry, collaborative forest management, buffer zone management and protected area management. Unfortunately, some of these approaches compete with community forestry. These approaches will now be compared with community forestry.

Although the rationale behind leasehold forestry is to enhance the livelihoods of the poor, the poor appear to have limited access to productive resources, including land and forests, under the approach (Thomas et al. 2003). Under community forestry, land is handed over to communities for an indefinite time period, ensuring their autonomy. Whereas under leasehold forestry, the community has limited autonomy as leasehold forests are handed over only for up to 40 years. Although the focus of leasehold forestry is on the poor, the way that it is structured and the actors involved make it unlikely to improve local people's livelihoods. In many cases, CF is in competition with leasehold forestry.

While the community forestry process has recognised CFUGs as autonomous institutions for local forest management, under buffer zone management, the buffer zone council has no autonomous decision making power. The park warden has the sole control over the buffer zone council. Centralised power and authority lies with the warden in the name of conservation, not with the community. Hence, the warden has the right to control land use within the buffer zone (Paudel 2005; Dhakal 2004; Soliva et al. 2003; Sharma & Shaw 1993).

Under protected area management, there is a provision to invest 30 to 50 per cent of park income in local development activities. However, the poor do not benefit from this provision as local elites have captured the benefits and used them to fulfil their political and economic interests. Nitya Nanda Khanal, a researcher of buffer zones, quotes a forest user, "Wild animals destroy our crops and harm us, but the development activities have been implemented somewhere else" (cited in Ojha et al. 2005). People have realised the economic value of conservation, but the process has yet to be made democratic and transparent. The park authority often denies people entry to the park to collect forest products, reducing their access to basic forest resources, which are essential for many poor people. This seriously affects the livelihoods of the local people (Budhathoki 2003; Heinen et al. 2000; Ghimire et al. 1997).

3.6 Terai forest management: Political and bureaucratic interests

Despite the progressive nature of the community forestry programme in Nepal, the national government and bureaucracy in Nepal have resisted the devolution of power and authority to communities for the management of Terai forest resources. So far, they have only agreed to hand over the hill forests, which are barren and degraded. When the Federation of Community Forest Users-Nepal (FECOFUN), a network of community forestry user groups (CFUGs) in Nepal, and some NGOs suggested the wider application of forest legislation to include Terai forests, the forest bureaucracy started to put constraints on the process of community forestry in Nepal.

Some donor agencies also have their own political interests in managing Terai forests. One such agency, Finish International Development Agency (FINIDA), initiated pilot projects in Bara and Parsa districts. FINIDA planned to hand over the Terai forest in Bara to a Finnish timber company, but their ill intention was exposed and vehement protests by FECOFUN and various NGOs resulted in the plan's withdrawal by the Government. However, the Government has continued to make plans for Terai forest management without consulting users and civil society organisations such as FECOFUN and NGOs. A resource inventory was carried out in the Terai to develop an Operational Forest Management Plan (OFMP), including a plan for the conservation of Churia forest in mid-1990s by the Department of Forest. In fact the OFMP led to the development of Terai forest policy in 2000. The Terai Forest Policy it introduced the concept of collaborative forest management, a regressive milestone in the history of community forest resource management in Nepal.

Collaborative forest management was developed as a sector-wide programme to sideline community forestry. The institutional structure of the District Forest Coordination Committee (DFCC) developed under this programme is undemocratic and centralised, providing limited space for civil society organisations to influence the decision making process. The Government developed guidelines under the Terai Forest Policy without consulting other stakeholders and has not moved ahead

towards any tangible outcomes. This is evidenced by result as collaborative forest management seems to be not moving forwards in terms of participatory forest management in collaborative forest management. Recent confrontations over the proper management of the Terai, inner Terai and Churia forest are a result of the tension between community forestry, promoted by civil society organisations and communities, and collaborative forest management, imposed by the Government (Bhattarai 2006).

From time to time the Government has imposed a number of taxes with the intention of controlling the Terai forest. Table 3.1 gives an overview of these provisions.

Table 3.1 Government orders for tax/revenue collection

Date	Government orders for tax collection	Remarks
May 2000	The Council of Ministers decides to collect 40% of the income from the sale of timber by CFUGs for commercial purposes.	FECOFUN challenges this decision in the Supreme Court.
March 2003	The Supreme Court finds that the Government's taxation of CFUGs is illegal.	MoFSC files a review petition to the Supreme Court but the Supreme Court rejects it.
July 2003	The Government includes a provision in the Finance Ordinance to allow it to collect 40% of all income received by CFUGs.	FECOFUN, civil society and the donor community oppose this provision.
August 2003	The Government publishes a notice to collect 40% of the revenue only from the sale of timber to the non-users of particular community forest for commercial purposes.	FECOFUN, civil society and the donor community oppose this provision.

Date	Government orders for tax collection	Remarks
January 2004	The Government amends the Finance Ordinance and includes a provision to collect 40% of the revenue from the sale of timber from two species, sal (Shorea robusta) and khair (Acacia catechu), and 10% from other species sold for commercial purposes to the non-users of particular forest.	FECOFUN and all stakeholders are not satisfied with this provision oppose it. CFUGs responding by not selling timber commercially.
July 2004	In the new Finance Ordinance, the Government inserts a provision that requires CFUGs in the Terai to deposit 15% of the revenue collected from the sale of two species of timber, sal (Shorea robusta) and khair (Acacia catechu) to the non-users of the particular CFUGs.	FECOFUN is still not satisfied with this provision.

Source: Adapted from Bhattarai and Khanal (2005)

3.7 Conservation and elitism: An example of aristocratic class interests

Although nature conservation has long-term benefits, it can create hardship for poor and marginalised people. Often, the economic and cultural rights/interests of people are ignored by national and international agencies working for nature conservation (Müller-Böker 1999). Conservation is an international discourse controlled by elite environmentalists. Environmental protection is considered a global issue. Environmentalism keeps people away from forests and water by restricting their access to these resources; people do not have access even to protect the environment the way they want to protect it. Thus, discourse about environmentalism prevents people from protecting the environment, although participatory approaches to protected area management have been introduced (Zimmerer et al. 2003; Paudel 2005). Nepal is no exception. For example, the Royal family set up a number of trusts for conservation (e.g., for biodiversity, heritage, etc.) and controlled their governance. Although the stated goal of the nature conservation trusts were to let local people benefit from biodiversity conservation, the unstated goal appeared to be to provided a centre for recreation for elites, primarily the Royal family and their allies. However, it is not only the intentions of the ruling elite that need to be critically examined; there is also a need to understand the intentions of international conservation organisations working in Nepal.

3.8 The struggle for rights over natural resources management

Both in Nepal and elsewhere, struggles between the government, bureaucracy, elite class, and forest and land dependent people over who should control natural resources are common. While the liberal development policies of capitalism have pressured the government to adopt people-oriented policies for natural resource management, there has not been any focus on the control and ownership of the resources by people themselves. Moreover, policies are rarely put into practice, and the rights of people, especially the poor and marginalised, are yet to be realised. There have been a number of recent struggles to establish the rights of people over natural resources, provoking resistance and class antagonism in response.

The cases below show how people are concerned to protect their class interests. Tension exists between the powerful and the powerless in relation to the control and ownership of natural resources. Environmental actors are vested with differing amounts of power and pursue differing interests, resulting in conflict over natural resources. Soliva et al. (2003) described the conflict as follows: "On one hand, the state may be responsible for nature conservation, on the other, it is interested in making money out of its natural resources".

3.8.1 Rights over forest resources

Case 1: FECOFUN's struggle to establish the rights of forestry user groups

Since its establishment, the Federation of Community Forest Users-Nepal (FECOFUN) has been struggling to establish the rights of forest users over local forest resources. Although many of the Government's policies, legislation and regulations appear to be progressive, their implementation has often been resisted, distorted and avoided by the forest bureaucracy and the Government, particularly in relation to valuable Terai forest resources. FECOFUN has been advocating that Terai forest management should be handed over to local users in the spirit of community based natural resource management. However, the Government and the forest bureaucracy appear to be reluctant to devolve power and autonomy to the people. Even after the people's movement in April 2006 (Jana Andolan II), the bureaucracy and Government have continually tried to undermine the achievements of more than 13 years of struggle to establish forest users' rights. For example, on 1 July 2006, the Ministry of Forest and Soil Conservation (MoFSC) responded to pressure by FECOFUN and agreed to implement a list of ten demands. However, only a few weeks later, the Ministry breached the agreement without consulting FECOFUN. Proponents of collaborative forest management lobbied against the agreement, gathering support from a few members of parliament, resulting in the Government backing out of the agreement. This indicates that the Government still does not want to devolve power to the local people and seems to be very much influenced by the interests of the bureaucracy and elite politicians (see Kantipur Daily 2 June 2006).

Case 2: Issues of impunity and injustice

A poor local Tharu resident of Chitawan living near the national park was detained by the park authority for illegally poaching rhino. He was beaten in detention and eventually died while undergoing treatment in hospital. The local people organised a mass rally of thousands demanding that action be taken against the perpetrators. The local administration took the responsible individuals into custody for investigation, but only because of pressure from the people. In response, foresters within the MoFSC and its departments and allies of the park authority expressed their solidarity with the staff responsible for the killing. They locked their own offices demanding the release of their colleagues. This conflict went on for months.

Case 3: Timber smuggling in Banke

In mid-2006, the illegal felling of sal trees in community forests and national forest areas in Banke district became a national issue. It appears that the District Forest Office in Banke gave timber contractors permission to fell sal trees from community forests, immediately after the forests were handed over to the community. A large number of trees were harvested against the approved plan of the community forestry users group. Local people suspected the DFO office of colluding with an alliance of timber contractors, elite members of the community and the CPN (M) (Kantipur Daily 1June 2006). The users of the community forests demanded action against those involved in the misuse of authority and power. The Government formed a probe committee, which was also blamed for siding with the illegal harvesters and smugglers. The dispute has not yet been resolved.

3.8.2 Movements related to land rights

In Nepal, movements for land rights are not new. The landless, including Dalits and indigenous people, have been struggling for land rights since the 1950s. Although dozens of policies and programmes are in place in the name of land reform, marginalisation and landlessness have continued. Indigenous minorities are particularly vulnerable to landlessness. The cases below highlight some of the issues facing marginalised and landless groups in Nepal.

Case 4: Farmers reclaim their land

About 35 years ago, a landlord, the then Chief District Officer, registered land under cultivation by the local farmers in his and his family members' names. The farmers were not informed that the land was registered by a powerful bureaucrat and were later removed from the land. In 2006, the farmers took back the land claiming that it belonged to them. The Government has remained silent on this and other prominent land rights cases (Kantipur Daily 5 July 2006), thereby protecting the interests of the land owning class.

Case 5: Protests by landless

On 4 July 2006, police destroyed more than 100 small huts built by landless people in the eastern Terai region of Nepal. The landless staged a protest against the Government's action in front of the District Administration Office. When the police tried to break up the protest some of the protesters were seriously injured (Kantipur Daily 5 July 2006).

Case 6: Kamaiya's movement for land rights

In 2000, the Government of Nepal freed a total of 35,621 Kamaiyas (bonded labourers) from their landowners. Now free from slavery, the Kamaiyas found themselves landless and without a source of livelihood. In 2006, the Kamaiyas staged a seven-day protest at Singha Durbar, the principal government secretariat in Kathmandu, demanding that the Government provide them with land and grant facilities. The Ministry of Land Reform and Management and the Kamaiyas reached an agreement that an all-party commission would be entrusted to make recommendations to the Government within 30 days (The Kathmandu Post 24 July 2006). Despite the Government's commitment in 2000 to provide them with land, over 19,477 Kamaiyas are still landless.

3.9 Politics of resource management and impacts on livelihoods

Poverty is compounded by the political economy (the production and distribution of power, wealth and knowledge) of communities, societies and nation states. The political economy determines access to and control over productive resources and the decision-making processes of people. Poverty is less concerned with how to manage forest resources or grow food crops, and more concerned with how people can derive benefits from forest resources, how arable land is distributed, and how entitlements over land and other productive resources can be ensured. Poverty in Nepal is closely related to the socio-political structure of society, which marginalises women, Dalits, Janajatis, disabled people, and other disadvantaged groups (GCAP-Nepal 2005).

Although participatory natural resource management has been widely applied in Nepal, the process of marginalisation of Dalits, women and Janajatis continues, and has even escalated. Property rights are denied to these groups and the development process has failed to address the key issues, working around the periphery of core issues and problems (DFID & WB 2005). Many excluded ethnic and marginalised groups live around large forests or along riverbanks. These groups are often denied access to the resources necessary for their livelihood by conservation laws and policies such as the National Parks and Wildlife Conservation Act and the Forest Act. For example, the Mushar (a so-called 'low' caste Terai group) are prohibited from fishing to earn their living because of conservation politics. Furthermore, wild animals trample local's crops and cause injury and even death, but it is an offence under these Acts to capture or kill wildlife. A local of Nawalparasi district resident pointed out:

> *Tigers are fed meat and other nutritious food, while the children of local people die of hunger. Birds are preserved for the sake of biodiversity conservation, and millions of rupees have been spent for their habitat, but local people are deprived of food and shelter in the same places and their habitats have been abandoned (pers. comm. with Kamal Bhandari, 5 May 2006).*

Conservation politics does not consider the issues of poverty and livelihoods as an urgent need to be addressed. The biodiversity conservation discourse appears to be so strong that the Government has a policy of expanding protected areas into human habitation, even though Nepal already contains a wide expanse of protected areas covering around 18.57 per cent of the total landmass. Attempts to exclude people from conservation benefits have undermined the livelihoods of people.

3.10 Incompatibility of policies and practices with people's livelihood needs

While many scholars and practitioners advise that policies need to be improved through trial and error (Lee 1993), politicians and bureaucrats take policy as a rigid instrument and do not adopt a process of learning and reflection. There are a number of policies in place related to poverty reduction and natural resource management in Nepal. But these policies have been formulated without consulting the poor. The elite politicians and bureaucrats develop these policies, and the priorities represented in the policies are largely set for them. There is no evidence that the poor have influenced the NRM policy process in any way in Nepal. Moreover, no policies have been developed yet to guarantee the land ownership and rights of small farmers and landless people in Nepal.

Even in the post-1990 democratic period, NRM was conceptualised within the broader framework of the liberal economy. Institutions in Nepal are built by transplanting the principals of liberal democracy upon the feudal social structure – without challenging the underlying ideology or practices of feudalism. This has resulted in the present crisis in the governance of the state, as well as in the governance of NRM (Ojha et al. 2005). The focus has been on the economic aspects of livelihoods, with less consideration given to the political processes. Although there are some good policies in place, institutions have not been transformed accordingly, and are therefore unable to implement them properly. Centralised, bureaucratic and hierarchal institutions are too rigid and exclusive (Timsina 2003 and 2002; Malla 2001) to facilitate a pro-poor development approach. Institutions for land resources are not sensitive to the needs of poor people. Such institutions mainly serve the interests of the powerful and rich, while Dalits, women and Janajatis are excluded.

3.11 A paradigm shift in natural resource management

To overcome the deprivation, destitution and oppression of the poor, women, Dalits, indigenous people and other marginalised groups, we have to recognise the role of freedom of different kinds. Individual agency is central to addressing these deprivations. Individual agency can be constrained by the social, political and economic opportunities that are available to individuals. The term 'agency' herein represents the autonomy and freedom of individuals (Giddens 1984); the degree to which they may act independently of, and in opposition to, structural constraints, potentially reconstituting the existing social structures through their freely chosen actions. For example, marginalised groups in Nepal have not been 'free' to earn a reasonable livelihood because their access to resources that form the basis of this livelihood has been constrained. It is important to recognise both the centrality of individual freedom and the forces of social influence on the extent and reach of individual freedom. Individual freedom needs to be considered as a social commitment (Sen 1999).

Under new concepts of development, the expansion of freedom is viewed both as the primary end and the principal means of development. Development, in this sense, consists of the removal of various types of bondage that leave people with little choice and little opportunity to exercise their reasoned agency (Sen 1999).

Economic and political freedoms reinforce one another, rather than conflicting (as is sometimes assumed). Institutions such as the state, the market, the legal system, political parties, the media, public interest groups and public discussion forums, among others, are important to ensure the livelihood rights of people. These institutions need to be seen as democratic ways of enhancing and guaranteeing the substantive freedoms of individuals (Sen 1999).

For example, Nepal's community forestry processes have entered the debate about social transformation towards a pro-poor, inclusive and more democratic social system (Timsina et al. 2004). The transformation process has to transform both the agency and the structures of society, which are historically constructed and embedded in social traditions, values and norms. In some of the community forestry user groups, the empowered agencies have changed the structure (norms, values and rules) to favour poor and marginalised users.

3.11.1 Transforming the mindsets of the rich to uplift the poor

Conventional development thinking defines equity as a problem of the poor. Mainstream development actors perceive the gap between the poor and rich as a deficit of the powerless, not as a fault of the powerful. They see a lack of education, access to credit or tools as the reason for the problem and advocate remedies to bring the poor up to par. They develop programmes for raising the living standards of the poor towards the level of the rich. In short, it is the poor who have to be developed in order to achieve greater equity. NRM strategies also usually aim at lifting those at the bottom, rather than transforming the mindset of the top. The wealthy and their way of exercising power remain entirely outside the spotlight, as always, in development discourse, and the burden of change is heaped solely upon the poor. However, from the perspective of poverty and livelihoods in a context of competing power for access to and control over resources, justice is also about changing the rich, not just the poor. Today, any debate on equity in natural resource management must first focus on transforming the top (Sachs 1999).

3.11.2 People's movements: A tool for social change

Making good policies is not sufficient to ensure people's rights over natural resources. There have been a number of good policies in place in Nepal, but, due to a lack of political will of the implementing politicians and bureaucrats, these policies have not been not implemented. Even where policies were implemented, most of them were distorted. Evidence shows that policies are often only implemented as a result of pressure exerted by public interest groups or people's movements. For example, FECOFUN's activities in ensuring forest users' rights have had an impact in Nepal. If the movement had not been launched by FECOFUN, the community forestry programme in Nepal would not have had such a significant impact. Similarly, land rights movements (organised by Dalits, women, ethnic groups and other marginalised groups deprived of land rights) have also exerted pressure on the Government and politicians. People's movements appear to be among the most powerful instruments for policy change and implementation.

3.12 Conclusions

The political economy and political ecology is a framework for the analysis of natural resource governance and livelihoods. Rights and ownership over natural resources are essentially a phenomenon of the political economy, especially when they involve the diverse interests of different individuals, groups and the state.

Tension between the state and communities in relation to NRM, especially in relation to the management of valuable resources such as forests and land, manifests in different ways. In the Terai and high hills, the state appears to be reluctant to hand over authority over forests to local people. This is due to the political economy (the relationship between production and distribution) of the highly valued forest resources. Similarly, the creation of landless people in Nepal resulted from the gradual evolution of land as a highly sought after commodity. Landlessness is the result of structural problems that have existed since state formation in Nepal.

However, as the development paradigm shifts over time, discourse on people's participation in NRM pushed the state to involve local people in the use and management of forest resources. Forest, as a common property resource, is easier to handle than land, when it comes to a participatory approach to its use and management. Community forestry has become a priority programme in NRM and is considered as the 'mother programme' of community-based natural resource management in Nepal. Nevertheless, given the resistance from the Government and bureaucracy to the devolution of power to communities and the antagonistic behaviour towards community forestry user groups, a constant interaction with the political process is needed to institutionalise these achievements.

While critically focusing on the prevailing inequity in Nepalese society, natural resource management needs to create opportunities for positive discrimination in relation to marginalised groups and the poor, such as providing them with the exclusive right to decide on the management of, access to and control over natural resources such as land and forests. A complete transformation of the natural resource sector is needed in the search for sustainable livelihoods, a transformation that ensures inclusive democracy in the processes and institutions related to natural resource management.

People's movements are a powerful instrument for change in NRM policies and to ensure proper implementation. The mobilisation of people through mass movement empowers individual agency and strengthens their ability to realise their rights. People's movements put aristocratic and bureaucratic classes under pressure and compel them to enter negotiations. In other words, people's movements help to break the present production relations, thereby impacting on the political economy. Organised and conscious movements are more relevant at the moment as Nepal is undergoing a process of state restructuring through the Constituent Assembly process.

References

Bhattarai AM and Khanal DR. 2005. *Communities, Forests and Law in Nepal: Present State and Challenges.* Kathmandu: FECOFUN.

Bhattarai B. 2006. Widening the gap between Terai and hill farmers in Nepal: The implications of the new forest policy 2000. *In:* S Mahanty, J Fox, M Nurse, P Stephen, L McLees, editors. *Equity in Community-Based Natural Resource Management in Asia.* Bangkok: Regional Community Forestry Training Centre RECOFTC.

Blaikie P and Brookfield J. 1987. *Land Degradation and Society*. London: Methuen.

Bottomore T. 1993. *Elites and Society.* London: Routledge. Ryant, R.L. and Bailey, S.1997. *Third World Political Ecology*. London: Routledge.

Budhathoki P. 2003. Nepal's Conservation in Crisis: Empowering People to Secure Natural Resources. *Journal of Forest and Livelihood. Vol. 2. No. 2. Pp. 72-76.*

DFID [Department for International Development] and WB [World Bank]. 2005. *Unequal Citizens: Gender, Caste and Ethnic Exclusion in Nepal (Summary).* Kathmandu: Department for International Development and World Bank.

Dhakal S. 2004. Crisis in conservation: Before or after insurgency? *Spotlight* 23(39):4.

Eckholm EP. 1976. *Losing Ground: Environmental Stress and World Food Prospects.* New York: World Watch Institute.

Engels F. 1880. Socialism: Utopian and scientific. *In:* SF Lewis, editor. *Marx and Engels: Basic Writings on Politics and Philosophy.* London: Collins, The Fontana Library.

GCAP [Global Call to Action against Poverty]-Nepal. 2005. *Whose Goals: Civil Society Perspectives on MDGs.* Kathmandu: Global Call to Action against Poverty- National Coalition Nepal.

Ghimire KB. 1998. *Forest or Farm? The Politics of Poverty and Land Hunger in Nepal.* New Delhi: Manohar.

Ghimire KB and Pimbert MP, editors. 1997. *Social Change and Conservation: Environ- mental Politics and Impacts of National Parks and Protected Areas.* London: Earthscan Publications Limited.

Giddens A. 1984. *The Constitution of Society: Outline of the Theory of Structuration.* Cambridge: Polity Publisher.

Gilmour DA and Fisher RJ. 1991. *Villagers, Forests and Foresters: The Philosophy, Process and Practice of Community Forestry in Nepal.* Kathmandu: Sahayogi Press.

Gough I. 1979. *The Political Economy of Welfare State*? London: Macmillan.

Graner E. 1997. *The Political Ecology of Community Forestry in Nepal. Saarbrucken:* Verlag fur Entwicklungspolitik.

Guha R and Martinez-Alier J. 1997. *Varieties of Environmentalism: Essays North and South.* London: Earthscan.

Harvey D. 1993. The nature of environment: Dialectics of social and environmental change. *In:* R Biliband, L Panitech, editors. *Social Register Vol 1.* London: Merlin Press.

Heinen JT and Mehta JN. 2000. Emerging issues in Legal and Protected Aspects of Buffer Zone Management with Case studies from Nepal. *Journal of Environ- mental and Development* 9(1):45-67.

Hobley M and Malla YB. 1996. From forests to forestry – The three stages of forestry in Nepal: Privatization, nationalization and populism. *In:* M Hobley, editor. *Participatory Forestry: The Process of Change in India and Nepal.* London: Overseas Development Institute, pp 65-92.

Kantipur Daily, 1 June 2006.

Kantipur Daily, 2 June 2006.

Kantipur Daily, 5 July 2006.

Kantipur Daily, 4 August 2006.

Karki AK. 2001. *The Politics of Poverty and Movements from Below in Nepal.* Unpublished PhD Dissertation. UK: University of East Angila.

Lee KN. 1993, *Compass and Gyroscope: Integrating Science and Politics for the Environment.* London: Island Press.

Mahat TB, Griffin DM, Shepherd KR. 1986. Impact on some forest of the middle hills of Nepal: Forestry in the context of traditional resource of the state. *Mountain Research and Development* 6(3):223-232.

Malla YB. 2001. Changing policies and the persistence of patron-client relations in Nepal: Stakeholders' response to changes in forest policies. *Environmental History* 6(2):287-307.

Marx K. 1977. Grundrisse *In:* D Mclellan, editor *Karl Marx: Selected Writings.* Oxford: Oxford University Press.

Müller-Böker U. 1999. *The Chitwan Tharus in Southern Nepal: An Ethnoecological Ap- proach.* Stuttgart: Steiner.

Nepal Weekly, 2005.

Neumann RP. 1992. Political ecology of wildlife conservation in Mt. Meu area of northeast Tanzania. *Land Degradation and Rehabilitation* 3(2):85-89.

NPC [National Planning Commission]. 1985. *Seventh Five Year Plan 1985-90,* Kath- mandu: National Planning Commission, His Majesty's Government of Nepal.

NPC [National Planning Commission]. 1992. *Eighth Five Year Plan 1992-97.* Kathman- du: National Planning Commission, His Majesty's Government of Nepal.

Ojha HR, Timsina NP, Khanal DR, Cameron J. 2005. Understanding environmental gov- ernance from deliberative democracy perspective: The case of forest policy making in Nepal. *Policy-Practice Outlook Vol. 1.* Kathmandu: Forest Action.

Paudel NS. 2005. *Conservation and Livelihoods: Exploration of Local Responses to Conservation Interventions in Royal Chitwan National Park, Nepal*. PhD Dis- sertation. Reading: The University of Reading.

Regmi MC. 1976. *Land Ownership in Nepal*. Berkeley: University of California Press.

Regmi MC. 1978a. *Land Tenure and Taxation in Nepal.* Kathmandu: Ratna Pustak Bhandar.

Regmi MC. 1978b. *Thatched Huts and Stucco Palaces: Peasants and Landlords in 19th Century Nepal.* Varanasi: Nath Publishing House.

Rodolfo S. 1975. *Social Classes in Agrarian Societies*. New York: Anchor Books.

Sachs W. 1999. *Planet Dialectics: Explorations in Environment and Development. London*: Zed Books.

Scott JC. 1985. *Weapons of the Weak: Everyday Forms of Peasant Resistance.* New Haven: Yale University Press.

Scott JC. 1976. *The Moral Economy of the Peasant: Rebellion and Subsistence in South- east Asia.* London: Yale University Press.

Sen A. 1999. *Development as Freedom.* New Delhi: Oxford University Press.

Sharma UR, Shaw WW. 1993. Role of Nepal's Royal Chitwan National Park in meeting the grazing and fodder needs of local people. *Environmental Conservation* 20(2):139-142.

Soliva R, Kollmair M, Müller-Böker U. 2003. Nature conservation and sustainable devel- opment. *In:* M Domroes, editor. *Translating*

Development: The Case of Nepal. New Delhi: Social Science Press, pp 142-177.

Staniland M. 1985. *What is Political Economy? A Study of Social Theory and Underdevel- opment.* London: Yale University Press.

The Kathmandu Post, 24 July 2006.

Thomas CA, Karmacharya MB, Karna BK. 2003. Exclusion is not easy: Lessons from a leasehold forest. *Journal of Forest and Livelihood* 2(2):48-54.

Timsina NP. 2002. *Political Economy of Forest Resource Use and Management: An Analysis of Stakeholders' Interests and Actions in Nepal's Community Forest Management.* Unpublished PhD Thesis. Reading: The University of Reading.

Timsina NP. 2003. Promoting social justice and conserving montane forest environment: A case study of Nepal's community forestry programme. *The Geographical Journal* 169(3):236-247.

Timsina NP, Luintel H, Bhandari K, Thapalia A. 2004. Action and learning: An approach for facilitating a change in knowledge and power relationship in community forestry. *Journal of Forest and Livelihood* 4(1):5-12.

Upreti BR. 2001. *Conflict Management in Natural Resources: A Study of Land, Water and Forest Conflicts in Nepal.* Wageningen: Wageningen University.

Upreti BR. 2004. Dynamics of resource governance, resource scarcity and conflict in Nepal. *Journal of Forest and Livelihood* 4(1):13-18.

Zimmerer KS, Bassett TJ. 2003. Approaching political ecology: Society, nature, and scale in human-environmental studies. *In:* KS Zimmerer and TJ Bassett, editors. *Political Ecology: An Integrative Approach to Geography and Environment- Development Studies.* London: The Guilford Press.

* * * * *

CHAPTER 4

Food insecurity, conflict and livelihood threats in Nepal

Jagannath Adhikari

Abstract

This chapter examines the food security situation in Nepal and the impact of the recent armed conflict on the food security situation. To begin with, the chapter discusses how food security or insecurity is understood in developing countries, in general, including in Nepal, specifically. The approaches used to analyse food security, particularly during times of crisis induced by civil war or violence leading to an increase in the risks associated with different aspects of food security (i.e., availability, access, utilisation and stability), are also briefly discussed. This chapter argues that food security is understood in different ways and that definitions have changed over time, as these definitions are influenced by different factors – both subjective and objective, and domestic and international. Our understanding of food security has also influenced, as in recent times in Nepal, policies and actions related to food security. Moreover, there has been difficulty in developing approaches to the investigation of 'food security' or 'insecurity', especially during times of crisis. The armed conflict in Nepal has made people vulnerable in different ways than previously, and the factors that determine vulnerability change frequently, making it difficult to define vulnerable groups and target them. The armed conflict has, generally, made the food security situation in Nepal worse, where both internal and external policies and practices had already made the situation precarious. Based on the analysis, some recommendations are made as to how to improve the food security situation in times of conflict, during normal times and in the context of globalisation.

4.1 Introduction

Nepal, an agrarian country, with a population of about 26 million in 2007, used to produce sufficient food at the aggregate level until the early 1970s, even though cases of food deficit and malnutrition were reported in the hills and mountains. The lack of infrastructure, mainly roads, connecting food producing areas like the plains in the south (Terai) with the hills and mountains, has affected the distribution and availability of food in many hill and mountain villages. Mountain regions, to a large extent, and hill regions, to a smaller extent, have been food deficit. The deficit was particularly high in the Mid-Western and Far West Development Regions of Nepal. The special trading practices (north-south trade involving Tibet, the mid hills of Nepal, the Terai region in Nepal, and India) ingrained in the local culture, which were developed to adapt to local ecological systems, had helped the local people to secure food. However, these practices have been largely eroded due to socio-economic changes, and particularly by restrictions in trade with Tibet. There have also been changes in people's food habits and increased dependence on food aid. The Karnali region, which is located in the mountains of the Mid-Western Development Region, suffered hunger deaths in 1997 when about 1400 people died due to famine. Food crises are still reported from time to time in this region. The Karnali is also the region that suffered the most from the armed conflict, which adversely impacted on the food security of this region. Urban areas were less affected by the armed conflict than rural areas. As a large number of people (almost 84%) live in rural areas in Nepal, the conflict had an impact on a large proportion of the population. Almost all village development committees (VDCs) suffered in one way or another from the armed conflict.

The armed conflict in Nepal started in 1996, when the Communist Party of Nepal (Maoist) [CPN (M)] resorted to armed struggle to bring about change in the political system. The Government also used the army to control the armed struggle of the 'rebels'. This so-called 'counter-insurgency' also created many problems for the people. In a way, the people were caught between the two armed struggles – that of the rebels and that of the Government. Many people lost their lives during the conflict (approximately 13,300 people). There were also frequent disruptions to transport; frequent strikes, *bandhs* (forced temporary closure of businesses and schools and the restriction of movement by vehicle) and blockades; the restriction of the movement of goods and commodities including food and people; the internal displacement of people (IDPs) and their mass out-migration from Nepal to India; and the destruction of property and infrastructure of the people, communities and the state. The other cost of the conflict is delayed development. Funds that could have been used for development were spent on the army and weapons. As a result, the budget for security has increased tremendously. For example, the defence or security budget was only NRs.5.16 billion in 1998/99, but increased to NRs.19 billion in 2003/04.

The overall impact of the conflict on food security is analysed in this Chapter, even though the conflict ended after the political revolution (Jana Andolan II) in April 2006. 'Conflict', for the purpose of this chapter, refers to the armed conflict between the CPN (M) and the Government from 1996 to 2006. This conflict was not only characterised by differences in the interests and objectives of different groups, but also by the violence unleashed by CPN (M) in the name of people's revolution, and by the Government in the name of counter-terrorism. This violence was mainly responsible for the adverse impact on the livelihoods and food security of the people. In this chapter, the term 'livelihood security' is used to refer to overall security in the means of securing sustenance (including food and other basic necessities), whereas 'food security' mainly relates to the different dimensions of food as a basic need (see below for further explanation).

4.2 Understanding food security

There is no common framework for understanding food security or insecurity. There is even more disagreement with regard to what action and approach to take to mitigate food insecurity problems. The approaches of different organisations and institutions to food insecurity seem to depend on various local, national and international factors including philosophy regarding the role of the market or trade, political and human rights, ecological sustainability, and national sovereignty with regard to food and food production, as well as larger political-economic interests. In the 1960s and 1970s, food security was understood more generally as the ability of a nation to meet its aggregate food needs in a constant manner. Accordingly, countries used to develop food balance sheets showing the aggregate supply and demand or requirement based on food requirement norms (like 180 kg food per capita per year in the past, and 200 kg now – this was particularly so in Nepal). The World Food Conference in 1974 identified sufficient food production, reliable supply and less fluctuating prices as crucial for meeting food security. Accordingly, technologies introduced with the green revolution, which contributed to increases in production, were emphasised to improve food security in developing countries. It was believed that the market will regulate supply and prices once food production has increased sufficiently. In the 1980s, with the seminal work of Amratya K. Sen (discussed below), which emphasised entitlements or access to food, the approach to food security shifted towards the 'demand side', i.e., providing individuals access to food through the market or social/political mechanisms. Lately, some concerns have also been raised by economists with neo-liberal principles over placing re-emphasis on the supply side (i.e., the production of food and productivity of resources). They have also focused on the role of technology. As a result, technology like genetic engineering or other forms of bio-technology have been promoted and used by multinational companies to increase the food supply. At the same time, social activists, mainly from developing countries, have expressed concerns about food safety and about the right to adequate food, right to feed oneself, the need for developing countries to have food sovereignty (i.e., control over the food chain so that they can make independent decisions on how to best meet their food security needs) and cultural suitability. Increased integration of different nations' economies associated with the processes of globalisation, as well as new international trade institutions, agreements and policies, such as those promoted by the World Trade Organization (WTO), have given rise to these new concerns.These concerns have also been vital in shaping the food security policies in developing countries, including Nepal. After the political revolution of April 2006 in Nepal, civil society activists have focused on the right to food and food sovereignty. These rights were enshrined in the Interim Constitution of 2007. In line with this, Nepal's Three-year Interim Plan (2008–2010) has, for the first, included a chapter on food security.

There are numerous definitions of food security, and the definition has changed over time and with changes in approaches to food security. Two definitions are given here that are influential in devising policies in developing countries.

> *Access by all people at all times to enough food for an active, healthy life (WB 1986).*

> *Food security means that food is available at all times; that all persons have means of access to it; that it is nutritionally adequate in terms of quantity, quality and variety; and that it is acceptable within the given culture. Only when all these conditions are in place can a population be considered 'food secure' (FAO, http://www.fao.org/).*

Of these two definitions, the Food and Agriculture Organization's (FAO's) definition seems more comprehensive. It focuses on four key components: availability, access, utilisation and stability. FAO considers these as the four pillars of food security.

4.2.1 Availability

Availability refers to the possibility of feeding oneself (individual, household or other units) either directly from productive land or other natural resources, or through distribution, processing and marketing systems that can move food from the site of production to where it is needed. At the international level, there is sufficient food available to feed about 6 billion people (Lappe et al. 1999). All nations can achieve and maintain a sufficient food supply for their population through domestic production, imports or a combination of both (Ibid). Hence, for sufficient availability, proper policies are needed regarding the production, distribution, processing and marketing of food. In Nepal, lack of infrastructure and marketing information and support, especially in the hills, often places constraints on the availability of food. The decade-long armed conflict has also led to increased food deficits, especially in hill and mountain districts.

4.2.2 Access

Access refers to economic and social access to food or purchasing and/or the food- gaining capacities of people (which include food prices in relation to wage rates, income opportunities, and social networks that provide food during times of distress, traditional safety nets, etc.). Each household/individual should have access to food. Sen (1981) used the idea of entitlement and endowments to explain how a person can have access to food. According to Sen, food availability in the market does not guarantee people's access to food for consumption. Therefore, individuals and households only have legitimate command over foods and other commodities if they have entitlement to a 'bundle of resources' such as land, capital, technology, skills, stocks and income. Sen later used the term 'expanded entitlement' to include social networks, kin relations and the like that help in receiving food, especially during times of stress.

4.2.3 Utilisation

Utilisation refers to the proper use of food, good food habits and the availability of culturally acceptable food. It also means the conversion of food intake into nutrition and into physical functions, which also depends upon other 'complementary factors' like safe drinking water, health protection and the like. Given that food is only valuable when it can be converted for bodily or metabolic use, its conversion into nutrition (utilisation) is essential. Therefore, it is important that each individual should have food utilisation capacity. Nutritional status (nutritional security) is an indicator of food security from the perspective of food utilisation. Another critical dimension of the utilisation aspect of food is food safety.

4.2.4 Stability

Food security also means a sustainable food system (production, distribution, consumption and waste management) at all levels – from the household to the national and international levels, and at all times. Therefore, stability means a food system that is able to meet the basic food needs without much fluctuation. To reduce fluctuation, availability and access to food must be ensured beyond the level required for mere subsistence.

There are also other dimensions to food security, which are usually not discussed in the literature of international agencies like FAO and World Bank. These include the control over food chains (production, distribution, processing, marketing and consumption) by a few transnational companies, changes in consumption behaviour and the role of media, the erosion of traditional or indigenous knowledge, and gender dimensions in food security. Women play an important role in every step of the food cycle in Nepal – from food production and gathering to food preparation and feeding. Women's lack of economic power at the household level and various socio-cultural taboos that deny women access to resources and a healthy environment mean that they face discrimination in access to food. For example, in Nepal, especially among the Hindus, women have to remain content with whatever food remains after all males are fed. They also have to follow difficult and torturous rules (e.g., staying in an animal shed while giving birth or during menstruation periods). These rules are still very common in the Mid-Western and Far West Development Regions, which suffer from food insecurity and malnutrition. Women in Nepal have ownership of only about ten per cent of the land holdings and about five per cent of the total cultivated land (Adhikari 2006a). The income of the household/family is generally controlled by males. This deprives women of their choice of food and from controlling food purchases. The media's role in changing food habits is also growing. Industrially produced food, which is often less nutritious in comparison to its price, is becoming popular (Adhikari & Ghimire 2006). For example, this can be seen in cases where rural farmers exchange a litre of milk for a small packet of biscuits or a bottle of Coca-Cola. The change in food habits is also considered to be one of the reasons for the growing food insecurity in the Karnali region of Nepal, where, as discussed above, hunger and death have been reported from time to time. Because of the new food habits of the lower hills and Terai (e.g., the consumption of rice) introduced in this region, local foods are now not grown and new generations have lost traditional knowledge about these foods. On the other hand, rice is not generally grown in the Karnali region, mainly due to climatic reasons. Jumla of Karnali is an exception to this and rice is grown in Tila and Sinja river-valleys using a technology that requires strict adherence to time-bound farm practices, especially in the growing of seedlings.

Until the recent past, 'food production' was generally equated with 'food security'. The assumption was that if a country produced enough food (food self-sufficiency) it would meet its food security needs. This assumption has been invalidated, even though 'production' is one factor in the availability of food and food self-sufficiency is important for various political and social reasons. Several studies have supported this finding. Some of the critical food insecurity situations that have resulted in hunger, malnutrition and death have occurred in periods where food production was above average. Therefore, even though food production is considered a prerequisite for food security, it is not considered a sufficient condition on its own (Sen 1981; Watt 1983). These research studies also consider the larger political- economic situation affecting distribution, entitlement and access to food as causes of food insecurity. Other causes are the breakdown of traditional food security mechanisms by external forces (colonisers, liberalisation and globalisation) and the lack of new measures to replace them. This fact has led to the conclusion that food security cannot sufficiently be examined only from a national perspective. Rather, one has to look into micro-level processes, encompassing the household level and, if possible, the intra-household level. The need to consider the intra- household level arises from the fact that the household is also a unit within which all forms of social injustice takes place. Discrimination against girls, women, elderly and the disabled is widespread in many developing countries. The predominantly patriarchal family system in Nepal, for example, creates such discrimination.

The new emphasis on 'access' to food has also led to changes in the measurement of food security. Now anthropometric measurements (like weight and height according to age, arm girth according to age), food and nutrition intake surveys (like food intake, calorie and protein intake, existence of symptoms of malnutrition like the protein-energy deficiency symptoms seen in cases of stunted growth), and socio- economic surveys (to gauge food security in indirect ways using various proxies like poverty, real wage rate relative to food prices, employment and demand on emergency food supply situations and the like) are also used to examine the food security situation. These measures usually measure the short-term crisis in food. But for 'security', which means a secured feeling of availability and access to food, a long-term perspective is necessary. Security also requires a lack of vulnerability in the long run. Therefore, vulnerability analysis is important. In this chapter, the food security situation in Nepal is examined from the above perspectives.

4.3 Vulnerability, access to resources and livelihood security: The political economy

As discussed above, sustainability and availability (i.e., stability in availability and access) are key components of food security. Because of this 'sustainability', the concept of 'vulnerability' has become important in the analysis of food insecurity. Individuals and households or communities and nations should not be vulnerable to food security. Freedom from fear of going hungry is also one of the criteria of food security, and, if there is vulnerability, fear will increase. This is also a condition of food insecurity. Because of the long-term focus, the livelihoods of individuals or households should be improved for sustainability in food security. 'Food First' programmes (programmes aimed at meeting nutritional requirements in the short term, without considering food production aspects), such as vitamin A programmes, food programmes for children and women, and food-aid in crisis programmes, which are generally implemented to improve the nutritional intake of women and children, provide only short-term solutions. Such programmes can be considered as an immediate form of food security, which, in fact, is not food security at all, because security requires a long-term perspective. But, unless livelihoods in general are improved, food security is not secured.

The term 'livelihood', as will be discussed below, refers to the different dimensions of securing sustenance. A secure and sustainable livelihood is considered to be a sufficient and necessary condition for food security. Therefore, food security depends on individuals and households having a reliable and sustainable source of livelihood. In line with this approach, the World Food Summit in Rome in 1996 emphasised the sustainable management of natural resources, elimination of unsustainable patterns of consumption and production, and equality between men and women as essential conditions for food security.

As livelihood improvement is an essential condition for food security, it is essential that its components are discussed, particularly the reasons for vulnerability. Livelihoods are generally defined as the means for living or sustenance. Blaikie et al. (1994, p 5) define livelihood as the "command an individual, family, or other social group has over an income and/or bundle of resources that can be used or exchanged to satisfy its needs". A livelihood is sustainable if it can bear the weight of present activities for a long period without compromising future prospects. The opposite way of looking at livelihood security is the analysis of 'vulnerability', a condition that has been defined in various ways. For example, Chambers (1989, p 1) has defined vulnerability as "the exposure to contingencies and stress, and difficulty coping with them". He goes on to say that "Vulnerability thus has two sides: an external side of risks, shocks, and stress to which an individual and household is subject; and an internal side which is defenceless, meaning a lack of means to cope without damaging losses" (Ibid). According to Blaikie et al. (1994, p 9), vulnerability describes "characteristics of a person or group in terms of their capacity to anticipate, cope with, resist and recover from the impact of natural hazards". In essence, vulnerability arises from two main factors – risk in securing the assets and capacities required for a livelihood and inability to cope with that risk. The risk could arise from various factors like natural hazards, market failures, a decline in the price of commodities sold, an increase in the price of commodities purchased, personal loss in the family, health problems in the family, loss of employment or wages, and the like. A decline in social insurance or safety nets provided in the society, on a traditional or formal basis, can be another cause of vulnerability.

There is, generally, a lack of theoretical basis for vulnerability analysis, despite some attempts by a few scholars. Bohle (1995) and Watts and Bohle (1993) have developed a three dimensional approach for mapping the space of vulnerability. They argue that the space of vulnerability is formed by three co-ordinates – risk exposure, coping capacity, and recovery capacity. Each of these co-ordinates has three dimensions – endowments, political ecology and empowerment. These dimensions are in a way linked to the political capacity to secure access to resources or the influence required for securing resources (from the society or the state). Two models developed by Blaikie et al. (1994) to explain the vulnerability of a particular individual or a household also centre around 'political power'. In the Pressure and Release (PAR) Model a disaster is located at the intersection of two forces processes generating vulnerability and physical exposure to hazards (Blaikie et al. 1994, pp 90-91). The forces or processes generating vulnerability are rooted in the socio-political and economic structure of the society. The root causes of vulnerability (which reflect the distribution of power in a society) put people in unsafe conditions. It is generally the powerless (economically, politically and socially) who are pushed into such unsafe conditions. When the hazard or accident takes place (e.g., drought), they are the ones who suffer the most as they are in the unsafe or hazard-prone situation. Moreover, these people lack the assets to cope with hazards and recover from them. Another model, called the Access Model (Blaikie et al. 1994) focuses on the way that unsafe conditions arise in relation to the economic and political processes that allocate assets, income and other resources in a society. The 'access' of an individual to resources is determined by political-economic processes and is linked to the social relations of production, gender, ethnicity, status and age. The Access Model takes into account the dynamic situation of the society, and, thus, is more capable of explaining the access position of households and their vulnerabilities. Concepts like FAD (food availability decline) and FED (food entitlement decline) (Dreze & Sen 1989), which are used to explain food insecurity and famine/hunger, are also linked to access. As the concept of entitlement includes production-based entitlement, trade-based entitlement, own-labour entitlement, inheritance and transfer entitlement, and other forms of expanded entitlement (Dreze & Sen 1989, p 10), the study of food security should also be concerned with the food system or food chain. The food system involves not only the system of food production, but also the degree of access to land and inputs, the operation of markets, and the ways in which food is distributed, transported and processed, how prices are determined, and how traders behave. The importance of a political and economic perspective (Fig 4.1) in the analysis of food (in)security has also been pointed out by Seddon and Adhikari (2003, pp 5-15). They suggest that the most effective approach is the one that begins with an analysis of the 'historical political economy' of food production, distribution and consumption, which is capable of providing a broad framework for examining and exploring key issues of unequal food availability and unequal entitlement to food. The historical political economy is concerned with how social-political and economic structures are developed and how they impact on the formation and functioning of institutions and organisations. This also influences trends and shocks. The other major component in the framework is 'assets'. The historical political economy impacts on the claims and entitlements of an individual, household or group to assets, which, in turn, shapes livelihood (natural resource-based or non-natural resource-based) strategies. These strategies then determine food security and insecurity. Seddon and Adhikari (2003) argue that "embedded within the political economy of food security should be a livelihoods analysis which enables us to appreciate the range of constraints and opportunities operating on the livelihood strategies of households and individuals, which, in turn, affect their ability to provide (or not to provide) a degree of security as regards access to food". Here, conflict (such as the armed conflict in Nepal) can increase 'shocks' leading to a decline in claims and entitlement to assets of all types, including natural assets like land and forests. This increases food insecurity.

Figure 4.1 Framework of food production, distribution and consumption

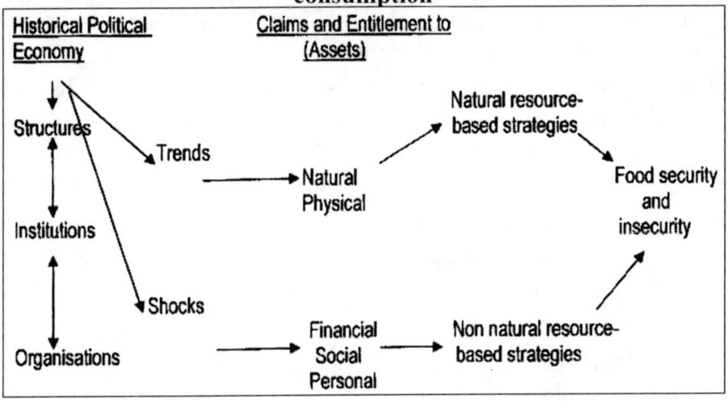

Analysing food security from a household perspective, the possession of assets is crucial to food security. Swift (1989) divides assets into three broad categories: investments, stores and claims. Here, investments include human (individual and collective) assets; stores include food stores and items of value, such as gold and money in the bank; and claims are potential assets to be obtained from others (loans, gifts and other forms of support and assistance). Ellis (2000) identifies five sets of assets or capital: natural, physical, human, financial and social. He notes, tellingly, that human capital is perhaps the most crucial to the poor: "...it is often said that the chief asset possessed by the poor is their own labour" (p 33). In a very real sense, for each individual, the most immediate and precious asset is that of health and wellbeing. Significantly, in their analysis of food security and how hill farmers cope in Nepal, Adhikari and Bohle (1999a) agree that:

> *[P]ersonal assets (health status, skill and physical power or fitness) and household composition were by far the most important factors in helping the households to cope with food deficiency. Other type of assets like land and forest were also found to affect food security, but their role was much less than that of personal assets and household structure. (p 16)*

The role of other factors like ownership of land and forest was low in food security because of the fact that land holdings are small and food self-sufficiency is low for most households, and because farming is difficult and labour intensive.

However, moving away from the individual and household level towards the community, regional or national levels, structural causes seem to be more important in food security. Claims and entitlement to food shaped by these structural causes also change as a result of changing power structures and definitions of eligibility. For example, a study conducted by Rural Reconstruction Nepal (RRN) and Action Aid Nepal (AAN) (2003, pp 33-34) has identified the following causes of food insecurity, which are, in general, linked to socio-economic, political and environmental factors (cited in Seddon & Adhikari 2003, pp 5-15):

Socio-political structures, which effectively prevent the rural poor from having equitable access to productive resources and community assets

- Persistent degradation of natural resources and community assets
- Policies and institutions that exclude small/marginal farmers and
- women from the benefits of development and public services
- Caste, gender and class based exploitation, violence, discrimination and marginalisation, that limit the access of these social categories to education, health and employment opportunities, and other basic human rights and justice
- Imperfect mechanisms for the distribution of goods and services,
- nationally, regionally and locally
- Low purchasing power of the majority of the population
- Gender discrimination in general
- Limited recognition of food security needs
- Lack of commitment on the part of governments to implement appropriate changes

During periods of conflict, the analysis of the political economy is important. The political economic perspective helps us to understand the 'claims and entitlement' structure. As the power relations change during periods of conflict, the entitlement matrix will also change. For example, the seemingly wealthy people who had more assets before the 'conflict' in Nepal were considered class enemies and displaced. Similarly, others not directly supporting the rebels were also displaced. As a result, their entitlement to food declined and they became vulnerable. Therefore, as explained above, conflict increases the shocks or risks to entitlement for certain categories of people, which can be poor as well as wealthy, placing them in a vulnerable position. A common approach to the study of livelihood security has been the Sustainable Livelihoods Framework (SLF) used by DFID (http://www. livelihood.org/), even though the approach has been criticised as inadequate for understanding vulnerability in a conflict situation. This approach (see Figure 4.2) is an analytical tool for understanding people's livelihood strategies as shaped by interactions between livelihood assets, vulnerability and transforming structures (institutions and processes), and for developing intervention mechanisms based on existing livelihood strategies (capacities).

Figure 4.2 Sustainable livelihoods framework

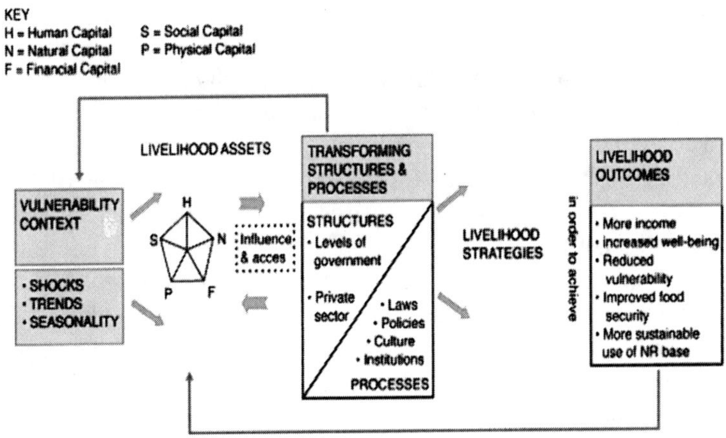

Source: DFID, http://www.livelihoods@difd.gov.uk

In this model, five livelihood assets (physical, natural, social, financial and personal) are considered central, but they need to be analysed in terms of the vulnerability context and transforming structures. The interaction of these three components shapes livelihood strategies to achieve the livelihood outcome. This tool is also used for research, evaluation, policy analysis and development. It is not a new approach, with its origins in the early 1980s at the Stockholm Conference on Environment and Development. It uses the key concepts discussed above, but integrates them in a simplified model. The focus of the framework is to improve livelihood strategies and the long-term viability of those strategies. This approach also puts people at the centre of the analysis and considers that their asset position is important when exploring options open to them. The other components of the framework are transforming structures and processes (now termed the 'rules of game' (http://www.livelihood.org/), livelihood outcomes and livelihood strategies. By analysing the assets and institutions and processes it is argued that one can link the micro-level situation with the macro-level policies.

By analysing food security situations during conflict (as is done in the later section in the case of Nepal), one can find various weaknesses in this approach for explaining food insecurity and in devising targeting mechanisms. For example, the approach is more concerned with the individual situation and is depoliticised, as it mainly aims to identify the efficient management of assets of the targeted people without much emphasis on the context or the circumstances. It also sets limits on the inclusion of factors to be considered and the relationships between these factors. The approach emphasises the role of social agencies, but undermines the role of the larger political economy. For example, the conflict in Nepal has its roots in unequal political-economic structures set by social relations among the variables of caste, class, region, gender, and so forth (Thapa & Sijapati 2003). Which factors are more important and how their importance changes over time cannot be analysed using DFID's Sustainable Livelihoods Framework. Similarly, the threat to food security by globalisation and the control of food chains by a few multinational companies is not explained very well by this approach. The external environment like agricultural subsidies from developed countries and the use of political and economic power by developed countries in negotiations (e.g., negotiations by the WTO) are affecting agriculture in developing countries. These are the main factors in determining how developing countries meet food security needs and in generating a situation of food insecurity. Even though these are major events or processes, they are narrowly included under the vulnerability context. For example, the international context affecting food production caused food prices to increase in 2008, leading to food riots in the Philippines and in some African countries. Such global socio-political and economic structures and their impacts are not explained by this framework. The opportunities available at the global level are also not explained by this model. The role of culture and traditions, like changes in food habits, which has caused severe food security problems in the Karnali zone, is also important. Such changes are also taking place at an increasing rate among young people in urban areas. DFID's SLF has no specific place for these cultural aspects, but deals with them as part of the vulnerability context.

The 'livelihood approach', as used in SLF model, does have some advantages in analysing food security. For example, Young et al. (2003) argue that the livelihood approach is useful in understanding short-term as well as long-term food security/ insecurity. In this approach to food security, the severity of food security is gauged by its impact on people's ability to feed themselves in the short term (risk to lives), and on livelihood and self-sufficiency in the long term (risk to livelihood) (Young et al. 2003). The risk to lives can be understood by studying the food consumption pattern. If there is significant change in the major exchange entitlement to, or sources of, food, and if this impacts on the nutritional status of people, then we can say that there is risk to lives requiring immediate attention from the state and responsible agencies and individuals. Risk to livelihood is understood by studying the vulnerability, risk and coping strategies of the livelihood groups, i.e., people adopting different means for their sustenance. In essence, the livelihood approach helps in "finding out the food availability, ability of people to feed themselves and how different groups of people gain access to food, risk to lives and risk to livelihoods" (Young et al. 2003). Conflict increases these risks.

4.4 Conflict, livelihoods and food security

The livelihood approach became popular after Sen's study of famine (discussed above). Sen considered that the exchange entitlement (or the livelihood sources) reflects the ability of the individual/household to acquire food. The livelihood of a person is a combination of exchange entitlements. Risks to livelihood occur when there are vulnerabilities, threats and a lack of coping mechanisms. Various risks can erode exchange entitlements, as discussed above. This can lead to a reduction in sources of food and an inability to make up the difference or deficiency, malnutrition and the over extension of coping abilities leading to the destruction of livelihood assets. Then the real case of food insecurity occurs requiring immediate help in the form of 'food aid'. If food aid is required, then it is necessary to understand the following things: How much food aid is necessary and what type of food? Who needs food aid and why? How long food aid is required and the point at which the need for food aid is reviewed? Whether or not there are locally available resources and capacities to transport, store and distribute food? In a conflict situation, it is difficult to identify the target group based on the SLF approach as vulnerability conditions can vary for different groups. Even the wealthy and those with enough livelihood assets can become food insecure if their entitlement to food declines. Moreover, during periods of conflict, it is difficult to physically provide food aid; food meant for the target group can end up in the hands of the groups causing the food shortage.

The entitlement approach that is central to livelihood analysis and to understanding famine or food insecurity, gives little attention to conflict, violence and political factors. Sen (1981) views famine and food insecurity as economic disasters. The impact of conflict and violence are not examined because Sen's analysis is of the exchange entitlements that take place within the legal regime. However, during periods of conflict, this legal regime is ineffective, and food is illegally and forcefully transferred from one group to another (Young et al. 2003). As violence and food insecurity are closely associated, one cannot dismiss violence (caused by conflict) as something illegal. This political vulnerability is not adequately dealt with by Sen's (1981) analysis. During periods of violence and conflict, food transfers take place from one group to another, but are outside the legal boundaries. Even though the livelihood approach, and, in particular, the SLF of DFID, has been refined to take into consideration crisis situations (such as drought in Africa), it has some limitations when analysing food insecurity during periods of conflict.

In general, there is still a lack of conceptual approaches for studying and analysing the impact of political instability or conflict on food security and livelihoods. The genesis and impact of conflict on food security in Nepal is not dealt with in detail here, only the conceptual approach to examining this impact is discussed. Generally, models of food security and livelihood analysis take political instability and conflict as a type of shock or stress, and, hence, see it in neutral terms. Seddon and Adhikari (2003, pp 10-15) argue that in any political conflict, like that of the Maoist insurgency in Nepal, there will be 'sides', and that there will be those who are directly and deeply implicated, and there will be those indirectly and less deeply implicated. This will have significant implications for the nature and distribution of effects and consequences – and, hence, for the differential impact on different social categories. This explains how the kind of conflict affects different social categories differently. From a theoretical point of view, a political insurgency or revolution like the Maoist insurgency should have direct adverse impacts on what they term as 'class enemies' or the 'ruling class'. Therefore, the components of the economy (like infrastructure) that have been beneficial to these people are disrupted. But there are also unintended consequences of any revolution, however pure the motives may be. The actions taken by the opposite parties (both supporters of the conflict and those who oppose it) in the conflict need to be analysed. Accordingly, the impact of the actions taken by the parties who oppose the conflict (in Nepal, the ruling class and the state and its security and administrative forces) need to be examined to determine how they have affected food security. In a way, those agencies opposing the conflict are also part of the conflict. On the other hand, although the parties supporting the conflict (e.g., Maoist insurgents) say that they are working for the food security of poor and marginalised people and communities, their actions can adversely impact on the food security of the people they want to help. Moreover, the actions of these insurgents also push previously food secure or well-off households (who the insurgents call 'class enemies') into a precarious position as these households are also obstructed from using their various assets. Therefore, the 'entitlement' approach is more suitable in conflict situations for analysing food security and identifying the target group. An understanding of this requires a political-economy perspective. As the power position changes, the use of livelihood assets may be disrupted with the aim of harming certain groups of people. Hence, the entitlements of people shift considerably during periods of conflict. However, overall risks increase for all groups due to unintended impacts.

One common way of analysing the impact of conflict is to disaggregate the different components of food security as discussed above and then examine the impact on these components (see also Seddon & Adhikari 2003). The various components of food security include entitlements and claims (production, exchange, social safety nets and political support like government supply, which includes the transportation and storage of food) and how they impact upon availability, access, utilisation, acceptability, and adequacy of food and food systems. The approach of capital or assets may also be combined by analysing which assets are lost by an individual, household or community due to conflict. In general, conflict may have an adverse impact on food security in the following ways.

- Food production may decline.
- Exchange entitlement to food may decline.
- Overall physical availability of food may decline.
- Access to food may decline.

- Political claims on government or public resources (like food supply and medical services by the government, NGOs and other agencies) are reduced.
- Overall capacities, and, especially, the personal assets, of
- individuals and families may decline due to malnutrition and injuries
- caused by the conflict.
- Lack of security generally, combined with food insecurity, can also lead to large-scale internal displacement and involuntary migration within Nepal and to India. These displaced people are not able to use their assets (like natural resources such as land, forest, water and so forth) for food-security related activities.

These are also the ways in which food security has been impacted in Nepal, and will be discussed in more detail later on.

4.5 Food security: A basic human right

Increasingly, food security is seen as a basic human right, and as a means of achieving other human rights. In 1953, the United Nations specified twelve elements for 'living', of which, food, nutrition and food security were the main elements (see Adhikari 2004). This is now being advocated mainly by NGOs and INGOs. Food security is considered a part of people's economic rights. 'Freedom from the fear of hunger' is basic to all political and social freedoms of individuals. Considering food security from this perspective, it is the obligation of national governments and international agencies to provide adequate food for the people. However, this has not been the approach of most of the bilateral and multilateral agencies like the World Bank. These agencies still subscribe to the idea that the market regulates food availability and ensures 'food security' to the people. On the other hand, these agencies still focus on the 'production' of food despite the fact that the world has more than enough food to feed its population. Bio-technology, including the production of genetically modified organisms (GMOs), has been promoted with the aim of producing more and nutritious food. However, this technology and the current free trade in agricultural products have led to the increased control of multinational and transnational companies (MNCs or TNCs) on food production and the consequent decline in food security and food production at the household (farm) and national levels in poor and developing countries (ActionAid 2005). This is also illustrated in Table 4.1.

There has been a decline in the share of developing countries in the international food trade in the last 30 years. They have become net importers of food, and their imports are increasing (FAO 2001). The price of the food stuff they export has been declining and fluctuating, creating hardships. As a result, their income, which could also be used to pay for food imports, has been declining. The increased control of the food system by a few multinational companies is creating a crisis in food security. The existing neo-liberal policy initiated in World Bank circles in the 1980s, and the other policies linked to that, represent the main political economic sphere worldwide; this has helped multinational companies to expand their tentacles around the world.

Table 4.1 Concentration of corporate power: Control of top 10 companies of world market share (in 2005)

Sector	Top 10 companies (in descending order of economic power)	Control over market share (by top 10 companies)
Pharma	Pfizer, GlaxoSmithKline, Sanofi-Aventis, Johnson & Johnson, Merk & Co., AstraZeneca, F. Hoffman-La Roche, Novartis, Bristol-Meyers Squibb, Wyeth	59% market share of world's 98 drug firms
Animal Pharma	Pfizer, Merial, Intervet, DSM, Bayer, BASF, Fort Dodge, Elanco, Schering-Plough and Novartis.	55% of the US$ 20,255 million world's veterinary pharmaceutical market
Bio-technology	Amgen, Monsanto, Genentech, Serono, Biogen Idec, Genzyme, Applied Biosystems, Chiron, Gilead Sciences and Medimmune.	75% of the global market

Sector	**Top 10 companies (in descending order of economic power)**	**Control over market share (by top 10 companies)**
Seeds	Monsanto (with Seminis), Dupont, Syngenta, Groupe Limagrain, KWS AG, Land O'Lakes, Sakata, Bayer Crop Science, Taikii, DLF-Trifolium, Delta and Pine Land.	About 50% of US$ 21,000 million commercial seed market
Pesticides	Bayer, Syngenta, BASF, Dow, Monsanto, Dupont, Koor, Sumitomo, Nufan and Arysta	84% of US$ 29,566 million global pesticide market
Food retail	Wal-Mart, Carrefour, Metro AG, Ahold, Tesco, Kroger, Costo, ITM Enterprises, Albertson's, and Edeka Zentrale	24% of US$ 3.5 trillion global market
Food & Beverage Processing	Nestle, Archer Daniels Midland, Altria Group, PepsiCo, Unilever, Tyson Foods, Cargill, Coca- Cola, Mars Inc and Groupe Danone	24% of an estimated US$ 1.25 trillion global market of packaged food

Source: Based on ETC-group (2005, pp 1-10)

To achieve food security, it is also essential that basic human rights are respected. In a place where there is no repressive regime, people can organise themselves and demand food or other basic facilities from the state. In such a place, the media can report on impending problems like famine. There will be public pressure to take decisions and steps taken to solve problems. However, these political actions are not possible in dictatorial or undemocratic countries. For example, famines have drastically declined in India since independence (Dreze & Sen 1990). The main reason for this, as argued by the authors, was the lack of political or public action taken during colonial times. Moreover, the colonial government destroyed the agricultural system and resource base that supported the food security of the people.

The growing realisation of the 'right' to food security has also been impacting on the policies of nation states, including Nepal. After the April 2006 revolution, social activists promoted the 'right to food' approach, in which the state is generally made responsible for protecting its citizens' right to food/food security. Generally, the state's role is to respect, promote and protect the right to food security of each and every citizen in the country. Accordingly, Nepal's Interim Constitution 2007 has enshrined this right and it is reflected in the Interim Three Year Plan (2008–2010) of the Government. This makes the Government of Nepal responsible or liable (theoretically) if there is any individual who is food insecure.

4.6 Globalisation, food sovereignty and food security

Globalisation has made food security a complex problem. Its consequences can be seen in many different forms. Recent globalisation, aided by information technology and bio-technology, has led to the corporatisation of agriculture, which means the whole food chain has been increasingly controlled by the corporate sector. This has slowly destroyed local food systems. Firstly, because of globalisation, food systems have been increasingly controlled by TNCs (here TNCs and MNCs are taken interchangeably) through their direct control over resources like seeds and inputs (see Table 4.1) and through their farming (direct or through contracts) in developing countries. Through this process, TNCs seem to control valuable resources like productive land and water. This production is targeted mainly at exports and cash income, which often compromises local food security. Secondly, the vulnerability of local farmers in developing countries is increasing as they are more exposed to, or affected by, the decisions taken in the world's city centres, which control information, finances and political power and which are also the seats of international organisations and TNCs. These agencies are not accountable for the adverse impact they create as they themselves do not bear the burden of their decisions (for details see Yamuna Ghale's chapter in Adhikari & Ghimire 2006 [2063 BS]). Different features of globalisation, like changes in food habits, the media and advertising, the development of technology, which favours the wealthy, state subsidies that support wealthy farmers and the corporate sector in a hidden manner, fashions and fads discouraging local products and the like, are also linked to the food insecurity of poor people. As a result of all these changes, the 'terms of trade' for products from the agricultural sector in developing countries are declining, as compared to those products from developed countries. In general, developing countries, including Nepal, have become increasingly dependent on developed countries for food. In particular, Nepal's dependency on India for food is growing. As the food brought from India is cheaper because it is subsidised, it is also contended that it has been helping the food security of the poor. However, this chapter argues that such a dependency is detrimental to food security in the long run. When global food prices increased in early 2008, India imposed restrictions on the export of food to Nepal. The restriction was imposed because of declining production and food shortages in India. This clearly demonstrates that dependency on other countries for food is not beneficial in the long run. Hence, the concept of 'food sovereignty' has been promoted, under which it is argued that a country should have the right to decide on the total food system and food security mechanisms. Total control over food production, resources (like seeds and inputs), processing and trade should remain within the country. Unless there is food sovereignty, the food security situation will not improve in a sustainable way. The focus on the right to food security must be combined with the right to feed oneself.

Globalisation has also led to the promotion of neo-liberal economic principles, in which the market is given a free hand and the larger corporate world is promoted. Under such policies, trade is expected to provide food security and the self-sufficiency of a country in terms of food production is not considered to be important. Most bilateral and multilateral agencies like World Bank, FAO and WTO now promote 'trade' as the main mechanism for meeting food security needs. As a result, liberalisation policies have been followed in the agricultural sector in Nepal, as is evident in the Agricultural Perspective Plan (APP). However, civil society, including NGOs and community based organisations (CBOs), now feel that trade alone is not sufficient to ensure food security, and the concept of 'comparative advantage' does not hold good, at least not in the food sector, because it is related to people's lives. The following reasons have been put forward to argue against the principle that trade is the best way of solving food security problems.

- If a country depends on the international market for food, what will happen in a situation of war, accidents and artificial shortages created by businesspeople?
- Dependence on the international market for food means that people will lose the culture of farming and skills and knowledge about genetic and other resources (like seeds, terraces, irrigation, etc.). This culture or resources cannot be developed in a short span of time or when they are immediately needed.
- The world is divided into two main groups in terms of food trade: food exporting countries (a few developed countries) and food importing countries (mainly poor and developing countries, which are many and where a large part of the world's population lives). The ability of the later to produce food and export it has been consistently declining. The terms of trade for the products of these countries have also been declining. If this situation persists, these countries will become poorer and their food production capacity and food security will be further reduced.
- Food related local cultural patterns and biodiversity will be lost. The changes in food habits requiring food that is not produced locally will undermine food security.

For the above reasons, it can be argued that it is too risky for a country like Nepal to totally depend on the international market for food security. Internal food self- sufficiency is also important. Some of the components of the local food system that assist in increasing food security – like community control over resources, the production of a variety of foods within the home farm or community, easy access to seeds, an integrated and diversified farming system, cooperation within communities for resource management, and social safety nets – help to reduce vulnerability during times of crisis and increase food security (Adhikari 2000).

Globalisation is also affecting food security by creating employment opportunities in certain locations, for example, in urban areas, and in certain countries. As a result, people are increasingly moving to these locations. In Nepal, and other countries in South Asia, it is mainly the males that move out for such employment opportunities. The farming is then left in the hands of the women. As a result, the feminisation of agricultural is occurring. At the same time, the marginalization of women is also slowly growing as their control over the household economy is declining. The agricultural sector has also lost its vibrancy and productivity, further marginalising women. Women have become more disempowered than before in a real sense because society and families in rural South Asia now see less use for women in terms of economic rationality. This is one of the reasons for the declining population of women in areas (especially in India) where the green revolution has been successfully implemented. Dreze and Sen (1989) and Sen (2000) have written extensively on these issues in the context of India. How far this is happening in Nepal is difficult to analyse, but the tendency to migrate, internally as well as internationally, is also growing in Nepal. This migration is again male- specific. For example, the Nepal Living Standards Survey conducted in 2003/04 revealed that urban wages are higher than rural wages; hence, those who are able to migrate to urban areas have been able to reduce their poverty level (CBS 2005) (Thieme 2003). Food insecurity is one of the primary reasons for this migration. This is particularly true in the Mid-Western and Far West Development Regions of Nepal, from where there is a large movement of people to India for temporary and seasonal work. Migration to the Gulf countries and Malaysia is also growing due to both push and pull factors. This type of foreign labour migration seems to generate about NRs.75 to NRs.125 billion (US $1 to 1.3 billion) in remittances annually (Adhikari 2005). How far such employment opportunities will sustain and be beneficial to the Nepalese people is yet to be seen. However, studies have revealed that the poor people, who have not been able to fulfil their food security needs, have also not been able to migrate for foreign employment (Seddon et al. 2001). They go to India, instead (Thieme 2003), where they also do not find many remunerative opportunities. Their strategy is, again, basic livelihood security, rather than an accumulative strategy.

Out-migration, which globalisation has made easy, may be taken as a way of solving problems related to poverty and food insecurity. Nepal also seems to have benefited tremendously from remittances. For example, the Nepal Living Standards Survey of 2003/04 reported that there has been a reduction in the poverty rate by 11 per cent in a period of 8 years (from 42% in 1995/96 to 31% in 2003/04), mainly due to remittances from formal as well as irregular migrants. But this study also revealed that the poorest 20 per cent of households have not been able to benefit from this opportunity as they lack the various resources (money, social networks and the like) to migrate for employment. Some of the poorest people may have succeeded in migrating to India, but they, in all likelihood, have not generated remittances as they are also marginalised there. A large proportion of migrants to India use all of their earnings just to live (see Adhikari 2006b). Moreover, reducing poverty may be one way to increase food security, as previously poor people can have income if they are moved out of poverty, which may enable them to purchase food, if not to produce it. The other way to improve food security in a sustainable way is to develop a sustainable food system, in which everyone has access to healthy and culturally/individually suitable food. This food system may benefit from links to the global system, but, at present, globalisation seems to pose more problems than solutions. The provisions in the WTO and the present trend of TNCs and MNCs controlling various inputs and technology, the denial of farmers' rights in developing countries, bio-piracy, the commercial use of the resources of poor farmers, and so forth are posing problems for the development of sustainable local food systems.

Nepal became the 147th member of the WTO in April 2004. The Agreement on Agriculture (AoA) in the WTO is contentious with regard to food security and agriculture in developing countries. Nepal will also have to abide by the AoA, which limits the domestic support that a member can provide to the agriculture sector, except for some exceptions like 'Green Box' subsidies and support to low income resource-poor farmers. To date, Nepal has not been able to use the limit for domestic support to agriculture (i.e., the AoA provides that 10% of agricultural gross domestic product [AGDP] can be given as domestic support and Nepal gives only 1.3% of AGDP for this purpose); hence, there is an argument that this will not hinder agricultural development in Nepal (see ActionAid and SAWTEE 2004). AoA impacts can be seen in terms of the impacts and consequences of the opening of the domestic market, market access, and export subsidies. As 83 per cent of the population in Nepal are involved in farming for livelihoods, the question arises as to how to protect them from providing market access to products from other countries. Cheap imports of food (as there will be no barriers created by tariffs), in the absence of other meaningful employment or income earning opportunities, will endanger farmers' livelihoods. One can argue that Nepal can also benefit from market access in other countries; but there are so many other barriers (mainly non- tariff barriers like quality requirements) to access to markets in developed countries that Nepal has not been able to take advantage of this. The subsistence nature of farming in Nepal and lack of competitiveness is clearly a disadvantage in the new WTO context. This is one of the most crucial factors that will hamper Nepal and its food security in the future.

The overall impact of the AoA will be seen when the subsidies are removed from this sector in developed countries. This will mean increases in the price of food produced in developed countries, which will give developing countries such as Nepal an incentive to increase food production and sell it in the markets of developed countries. This will create employment and increase wage rates in the farming sector, which will also enable labourers to purchase food, even if food prices increase. However, this does not appear to be a likely scenario as there has been disagreement on this issue until now.

The Agreement on Trade Related Aspects of Intellectual Property Rights (TRIPS) is another contentious issue within the WTO. TRIPS has violated many areas of farmers' rights in developing countries. Under intellectual property rights, the person or agency that develops a new idea (product, technology, etc.) has the right to use it commercially, and others must pay to use it. If this is implemented, developing countries and their farmers will have to pay to use technology (including seeds and other) developed in advanced countries or by any individual or agency. Moreover, some of the modern technology developed in agriculture, especially in relation to seeds and other inputs, comes from the traditional knowledge and resources (e.g., local seeds, genotypes or biodiversity) conserved by farmers for generations. This is a gross violation of their rights. It will also limit farmers' access to and ability to use modern technology and, as they are already dependent on these technologies, this inaccessibility will displace them from farming. As they do not have other opportunities for income or employment, their food security will be threatened. This is a violation of basic human rights – the right to become a farmer and to feed oneself (Action Aid 2005).

The impact of TRIPS and the control of modern seeds by the corporate sector is now clearly visible in developing countries like India. In Nepal, the effect has been less visible as commercial farming has not been that extensive in major crops. In India, a recent report stated that more than 600 farmers in one district (Vidarbha) of Maharastra state committed suicide in a year (June 2005 to June 2006) because of loans and use of modern GMO cotton seeds from Monsanto Company. In Maharastra state alone 4,100 farmers committed suicide in 2004, while government officials reported that more than 8,900 farmers did so in four states since 2001 (The Himalayan Times, 21 July 2006). The basic reason is that farmers were encouraged to grow GMO cotton using seed from Monsanto, and then, in one year, the seed price increased four times. Other costs also increased. Farmers took loans from banks and private sources to meet their expenses, but the price of cotton declined, which caused heavy indebtedness. In Nepal, the use of hybrid seeds is growing, mainly in vegetable production. Very recently, hybrid rice seeds have also become popular in the Terai. There are long queues of farmers desperate to buy these new seeds coming from India. Similarly, farmers also buy many other inputs like fertilizers and pesticides. They know that the yield of the paddy from this seed will be high, but the plants from this seed do not produce seeds. This essentially means that in a few years time, local seeds will be lost and farmers will be dependent on seeds from India. If seed prices increase, which is also very likely, the scenario seen in India could be repeated in Nepal.

4.7 Food security in Nepal

4.7.1 Availability of food

For the past several years, Nepal has not been self-sufficient in food, as its production growth rate is slower than the population growth rate. This is also evidenced by the food balance sheets of the country, and the country's net import of food grains and food items. As a result, food insecurity is the prime problem of the country, but it has not received the emphasis it deserves. Several reasons have been identified for the lack of sufficient food production in Nepal. The productivity of the land, reflected in the yields of food grains, has declined for some crops (especially in the hills and mountains) and stagnated for most crops. This should be viewed in the context of increased use of fertilizers, pesticides and other inputs. Lack of proper infrastructure like irrigation facilities and roads is blamed for the lack of improvement in agricultural production, but there is also a social reason for this. Agriculture, as a profession, now receives the least prestige (Adhikari 2000). It is a job for those who cannot find other types of work. Lately, it has been the work of the elderly and uneducated. This has resulted in a lack of innovation in agriculture. Because of the lack of good returns and the backwardness of agriculture, educated people are not interested in this profession. People are also hesitant to invest in the development of the agricultural sector. The increased labour migration of young and able-bodied persons has also contributed to this situation (Seddon et al. 2001).

The subsistence nature of agriculture is also blamed for the lack of rapid growth in agricultural production. From the perspective of food security, there is no problem with subsistence production. Rather, this form of farming system is considered beneficial for sustainable food security as it is least affected by market failures and the vagaries of prices and marketing conditions. Therefore, subsistence production is somewhat proofed against these problems, which can led to food scarcity and death from hunger. But the problem with Nepalese agriculture is that it is not subsistence in the true sense. The subsistence nature of agriculture has been eroded, as it is not able to feed most households for more than six months of the year. This is especially so in the hills. Landlessness, fragmentation of land, lack of irrigation, the improper use of inputs and environmental degradation are some of the reasons for the decline or stagnation in production.

Political instability and disharmony in recent times is also one of the reasons for food insecurity in Nepal. Due to political conflict, food production has severely declined in the hills and some mountain areas. A large number of young people have been displaced from their place of origin, caught in the conflict. Most of the food insecure districts are also conflict-affected districts. These districts, being the hilly and mountainous districts, have been facing food deficits for a long time. But other income/livelihood opportunities like the trading of products made from local resources (like herbs, woollen clothes and other handmade goods, forest products, dairy products and the like) and seasonal migration had been helping to offset the accelerating deficits in food production. In addition, the supply of food through government channels (through Nepal Food Corporation [NFC]) and other development projects) had also been increasing to some extent.

Another major source of local income for these people is the wage employment created by development initiatives. This income had helped some groups to increase their entitlements. In a peaceful environment, there were no problems with transportation; therefore, food was available in the market centres. But, with the Maoist insurgency and the possibility of being caught between the CPN (M) and the military and with the regular *bandhs* and road blockades leading to the disruption of movement of goods and commodities, the whole system of supplying food and increasing entitlement was disrupted. Even though no data is available in this regard, various newspaper reports support the fact that the food insecurity problem is particularly severe in conflict-affected districts in Nepal. In general, food insecurity is growing all over Nepal.

Food insecurity in Nepal is not a new thing. It existed even when there was enough production. However, previously, insecurity was seen mainly in the form of malnutrition. Lately, it has been seen in the form of hunger deaths. There are several reasons for the decline in food security in Nepal. These include, among others, a decline in agricultural output per capita because of the growing population, limited supply of resources like land, lack of basic infrastructure like irrigation and transportation facilities, and limited research and other services from the Government. A country which was a net exporter of food until the early 1980s now imports food. At present, it is estimated by the World Food Programme (WFP) that Nepal can meet only about 80 per cent of its food requirements. However, the Government estimates that food production in Nepal can meet the basic requirements of food for its population (see discussion below). Food production fluctuates depending upon the weather situation, and it has become a cause for concern. Lately, increased incidence of drought is leading to severe food insecurity. In early 2009, it was estimated by WFP that about 2.2 million people in Nepal, particularly in the Far Western and Mid-Western Regions, will face food problems, mainly because of the drought. Agricultural productivity has also been declining because of the unbalanced use of chemical inputs. On top of this, the conflict has exacerbated food insecurity in villages as it adversely impacted on both the production and distribution of food.

Extent of deficit in food production

Nepal was considered a food secure country until the mid-1980s. This conclusion was drawn because food self-sufficiency was considered a criterion of food security by policymakers and planners in the past.

Since the beginning of the 1990s, the proportion of the population experiencing food deficit has grown rapidly. Koirala (1992) estimates that 47 per cent of the population in the hills was under supplied (Koirala 1992) 23 per cent in the Terai and 31 per cent in the mountains. The high population density and the degradation of land and forest resources were considered as the main reasons for food deficits in the hills.

In 2002/03, government records on food balance by district showed that 43 of the total 75 districts of Nepal were not able to produce sufficient food to meet the minimum requirements of the people in these districts (Table 4.2). This shows that food production is a general problem. During this time, food insecurity was exacerbated by the conflict, especially in remote districts like in the Karnali zone (Adhikari 2008). Inaccessibility means that food prices are much higher, normal marketing channel non-existent and transportation often extremely difficult in these remote districts. During the armed conflict, the food security situation further deteriorated as food availability was obstructed due to restrictions on food transportation and distribution. The decline in availability caused an increase in food prices. The conflict resulted in a 30 per cent increase in the normal prices in the Karnali (Adhikari 2008).

Food deficits are high in Nepal in the mountain districts and the Mid-Western and Far West Development Regions. These regions are also the traditionally food deficit districts. Out of 16 districts in mountainous regions, 13 were food deficit in 2002/03. In the hilly regions, 24 out of 39 districts were food deficit. In the Terai, there are 20 districts, and only six were food deficit. This shows that food deficiency is most severe in mountain regions, followed by the hills (Table 4.2). The average amount of food deficiency is also highest in the mountain regions, where it is estimated that in 2002/03 the region suffered a food deficit of 39 kg per capita. In the hills, this figure came to about 24 kg per capita. In Terai, overall, food was produced in surplus (of 34 kg per capita (Table 4.3). The impact of conflict was also high in the mountain region, where local food production is generally not sufficient.

Table 4.2 Food deficit districts in 2002/03

Ecological belt	Eastern region	Central region	Western region	Mid-Western region	Far West region	Total
Mountain	1 (3)	2 (3)	2 (2)	5 (5)	3 (3)	13 (16)
Hills	3 (8)	6 (9)	6 (11)	5 (7)	4 (4)	24 (39)
Terai	0 (5)	4 (7)	0 (3)	1 (3)	1 (2)	6 (20)
Total	4 (16)	12 (19)	8 (16)	11 (15)	8 (9)	43 (75)

Note: Figures in parenthesis are total districts in each region/belt.

Source: (DoA 2004, pp 189-191)

Table 4.3 Belt-wise food availability and requirement of cereals 2002/03 (in MT)

Ecological belt	Total population	Total available	Total requirements	Balance
Mountain	1,728,288	262,764	330,102	- 67,338
Hills	10,568,028	1,867,328	2,124,176	- 256,648
Terai	11,665,965	2,511,374	2,111,542	399,832
Total for Nepal	23,962,281	4,641,466	4,565,820	75,646

Source: DoA (2004, p 188)

Food production, requirements and deficits in Nepal from 1990/91 to 2004/05 are given in Table 4.4. Considering the five main crops in Nepal, food availability in edible form (which essentially represents production) was declining in comparison to food requirements until 1998/99. Accordingly, food deficits were occurring and growing until then. The food deficit as a percentage of requirements fluctuates as it is also dependent on climatic conditions. In some years, favourable climate conditions lead to a bumper harvest, and, in other years, unfavourable conditions lead to a meagre harvest. Even in the past, when Nepal was a net exporter of food grains, it used to suffer from occasional food deficits. For example, in 1972 there was a severe drought, which led to very high prices for food grain.

This happened again in the 1980s. This fluctuating production is another cause of food insecurity. As is seen in Table 4.4, the deficit reached 12.5 per cent of the requirements in 1994/95, or 485,155 metric tons. Food deficits in the early 1990s (1991/92 to 1994/95) were generally higher than in the latter half of the 1990s. On average, the deficit as a percentage of requirements during the period from 1991/92 to 1994/95 was 7.7 per cent, but from 1995/96 to 1998/99 it averaged only 2.8 per cent. For the years 1999/00 to 2004/05, there was a surplus production of 1.5 per cent to 4.4 per cent. Again, favourable weather conditions are considered responsible for this increase in food production.

Table 4.4 Nepal's food requirements and production of edible food grain (in MT)

Crops	1990/91	1991/92	1992/93	1993/94	1994/95	1995/96	1996/97	1997/98
Production Rice	1892105	1738013	1393697	1827110	1577820	1949761	2002747	2035725
Maize	877075	836564	1100452	837653	883267	929513	894779	940767
Wheat	651956	603592	595998	687426	709304	786936	827438	806849
Millet	190177	187700	194407	224958	219262	236478	236982	233764
Barley	7642	7579	7572	7965	8107	11190	10641	10244
Total production	3618955	3373448	3292126	3585112	3397760	3913878	3972587	4178077
Total requirement	3486776	3561838	3633724	3723722	3882915	3948229	4079135	4178077
Balance	132179	-188390	-341598	-138610	-485155	-34351	-106548	-150729
% Deficit/ surplus	-	- 5.3	- 9.4	- 3.7	- 12.5	- 0.9	- 2.6	- 3.6

Crops	1998/99	1999/00	2000/01	2001/02	2002/03	2003/04	2004/05
Production Rice	2074193	2259393	2356646	2294205	2271914	2455971	2358540
Maize	920094	1007178	1001478	999831	1059751	1082455	1186840
Wheat	55647	934559	914885	1008827	1069257	1105087	1151282
Millet	238968	242331	231915	231714	231931	232373	237778
Barley	8710	8478	8255	8472	8613	8485	8113
Total production	4279491	4451939	4513179	4543049	4641466	4884371	4942553
Total requirement	4279491	4383443	4430128	4463027	4565820	4671344	4779710
Balance	-181876	68496	83051	80022	75646	213027	162843
% Deficit	- 4.2	+ 1.5	+ 1.8	+ 1.8	+ 1.6	+ 4.4	+ 3.3

Source: DoA (2006,pp 202–207)

Even though recent trends (1999/00 to 2004/05) show improvement in food self- sufficiency at the national level, the urban areas and food insecure areas continue to be dependent on Indian markets. In a study of urban food security, it is revealed that urban areas in Nepal (Kathmandu and Pokhara) depend heavily on Indian markets for all types of food grains, vegetables, fruits and other food products. Moreover, the distribution of food is controlled by a handful of businesspeople. The supply of food from government sectors in these towns where non-food producers live is almost negligible. Most people living in urban areas depend on income and employment for food security. For them 'income security' is most important, and there should also be the free flow and smooth marketing practices with regards to food. But, due to the current oligopoly in the control of food, food shortages could also result from artificial shortages created by businesspeople. Kathmandu experienced such situations in 1982. Dependency on India for food may also make the urban population vulnerable to the vagaries of international politics and production conditions (Adhikari & Bohle 1999b; Adhikari 2006c). This was very well observed in Kathmandu when there was a strike in the Terai by Madheshi people in the second half of February 2008. On the other hand, the conflict-affected regions (like the Karnali) were impacted differently. There, the supply of food from outside was curtailed by the CPN (M) through the imposition of strikes and blockades and the extortion of both food and cash.

4.7.2 Access to food and its utilisation: Food consumption and nutritional status

One of the main features of food security, as discussed above, is the access to sufficient food by all people at all times. To examine whether this situation exists or not, surveys like health surveys, nutritional surveys or even food consumption surveys are conducted. The analysis of food consumption (or nutritional status) is more important than the analysis of food availability, as households not producing food may be consuming sufficient food through other exchange systems, like purchase, exchange of food for labour or other assets/property, member of a kinship group or other social groups having access to food, or by borrowing food or money to purchase food.

Various nutritional surveys conducted in Nepal reveal that the nutritional status of people, usually of children, has been deteriorating. A national survey conducted in 1975 revealed that 48.1 per cent children suffered from chronic malnutrition and 6.6 per cent children suffered from acute malnutrition. A survey conducted in 1995 revealed that 63.5 per cent of children suffered from chronic malnutrition and 6 per cent from acute malnutrition. The Nepal Family Health Survey (NFHS) conducted in 1997 revealed that 48.4 per cent of children suffered from chronic malnutrition and per cent from acute malnutrition. The Nepal Multiple Indicator Surveillance (NMIS) conducted in the same year found the figures to be even higher than this: 53 per cent for chronic malnutrition and 16 per cent for acute malnutrition.

Nutritional surveys conducted in Nepal in 2001 and 2006 also reveal that nutritional status of people, especially of children, has been deteriorating. The recent surveys that are worth mentioning are the Nepal Living Standard Survey (2003/04) and Demographic and Health Survey, 2006. These identify the groups of people suffering from various problems related to food insecurity, mainly nutritional problems (see Table 4.5). Table 4.5 shows that about 40 per cent of people consume less than the required energy (2240 calories per day) in 2003/04. Stunting among children (below 5 years) remained more or less same in the period from 2001 to 2006, but the incidence of underweight declined significantly, from 45 per cent to about 37 per cent. However, the incidence of wasting grew significantly during this period. There is also a variation in the type of malnutrition according to ecological region and development region. In terms of calorie intake and stunting, Himal and hill regions suffer more. But in terms of wasting, the Terai seems to have the most severe problem. Similarly, the problem in Mid-Western and Far Western Regions is far more serious than in other regions.

Table 4.5 Poverty and food (nutritional) insecurity according to ecological and development regions

Region	Poverty Rate (%)	Population not consuming minimum calories (%)	Stunting among children below 5 years (low height for age) (%)		Underweight among children below 5 years (low weight for age) (%)		Wasting (low weight for height) among children under 5 years age (%)	
			2001	2006	2001	2006	2001	2006
Nepal	30.8	39.9	50.4	49.3	45.2	38.6	9.6	12.6
Ecological zone								
Himal	32.6	45.2	61.4	62.3	45.1	42.4	5.3	9.4
Hill	34.5	41.8	52.4	50.3	41.4	33.2	5.9	8.4
Terai	27.6	37.4	47.3	46.3	48.4	42.3	13.3	16.6
Development region								
Eastern	29.3	37.6	47.6	40.3	43.4	32.9	9.1	10.1
Central	27.1	39.9	50.0	50.0	44.7	38.2	10.8	13.8
Western	27.1	37.2	50.1	50.4	43.4	38.5	8.9	10.9
Mid-Western	44.8	44.3	53.9	57.9	49.0	43.4	8.8	11.6
Far Western	41.0	44.9	54.0	52.5	48.9	43.7	8.8	16.7

Source: CBS, WFP & W B (2006); USAID, New Era, MoHP (2007)

The nutritional security or the status of nutrition among children is also dependent on many social factors, including the status of women and girls in society. This status is the accumulated effects of various other factors like violence against women and illiteracy, which in turn affect access to health and sanitation knowledge, the decision-making role of women, intra-household food distribution practices and fertility rates. The cultural practices that put women in a lower position reduce their empowerment within the family. Thus, they have less access to food and other resources. This leads to low health and food security for women. The children of such mothers also suffer from health and food insecurity.

Poverty, food insecurity and their determinants

Poverty and food insecurity are interdependent. Poverty erodes entitlement to food, and, as a result, food insecurity may result, even if there is sufficient food. Employment and income opportunities can reduce the food insecurity of an individual.

In the context of globalisation and free trade, income security is also considered important for food security. But the question arises as to whether or not trade is fair and free and whether or not there is a perfect market. Lack of free trade and various interventions in the market and its control by a few oligopolists have led to many unfavourable situations with regard to food security. Moreover, food is also a political weapon that can be used against a country that is not self-sufficient in food.

Poverty in Nepal, measured by different indicators, is widespread, even though its concentration varies from one geographical region to another and from one group of people to another. Based on the data collected for the recent Nepal Living Standards Survey (2003/04) it is estimated that poverty has decreased by 11 per cent over a period of eight years (from 42% in 1995/96 to 31% in 2003/04), mainly due to remittances, increases in real wages in agricultural and non-agricultural sectors, and urbanisation (CBS 2006; Table 5). However, it should be noted that remittances have been mainly enjoyed by wealthier households. The poorest 20 per cent, whose income has not increased in recent decades, do not have access to remittances. Therefore, food security may not have improved for these poorest 20 per cent of households. Between 1995/96 and 2003/04, the incidence of poverty declined by 8 per cent in rural areas (from 43% to 35%) and by 12 per cent in urban areas (from 22% to 10%). During this period, expenditure inequality widened. The income inequality between the rich and poor as measured by the Gini coefficient rose from 0.34 in 1995/96 to 0.41 in 2003/04. This indicates a sharp rise in inequality. The main reason for this growing disparity in income is the lack of access to remittances by the poorest 20 per cent of households, which is the main factor responsible for the overall increase in average per capita income of people, but which has happened due to a rapid increase in the income of wealthier households. The consumption expenditure of the bottom 20 per cent of people increased by only 22 per cent, whereas that of the upper 20 per cent of people increased by 64 per cent. In 1995/96, the bottom 20 per cent of households constituted 8 per cent of total consumption expenditure, compared to 43 per cent by the upper

20 per cent. In 2003/04, these figures were 7 per cent and 49 per cent, respectively – revealing a growing gap.

The income poverty discussed above has many dimensions, including food insecurity. Food insecurity is the most common expression of poverty for the majority of households in Nepal. Despite the label of 'subsistence agriculture', most households do not derive their full security from farming. Therefore subsistence farming and the consequent subsistence affluence is a myth in the context of Nepal. Food poverty is widespread in Nepal and reaches an annual peak during the 'hungry season' of April to July.

The spatial dimensions of poverty in Nepal also need attention. In line with the distribution of poverty, food security is also different in the different development regions. The most food insecure region in the country is the Far West Development Region, especially the Karnali zone, where hunger deaths in the late 1990s drew the attention of policymakers (1400 died during a famine in 1997). This incident also heralded the failure of development initiatives in the country. The districts, in which hunger deaths and food insecurity are chronic, also have the lowest human development index (HDI) in the country. As a matter of fact, there is a direct and rough correlation between food insecurity and HDI in the districts of Nepal.

Table 4.6 Poverty scale in Nepal in 1995/96 and 2003/04

Regions	**Poverty headcount rate**		**Distribution of poor**		**Distribution of population**	
	1995/96	**2003/04**	**1995/96**	**2003/04**	**1995/96**	**200304**
Nepal	41.8	30.8	100.0	100.0	100.0	100.0
Urban	21.6	9.6	3.6	4.7	6.9	15.0
Rural	43.3	34.6	96.4	95.3	93.1	85.0
Kathmandu	4.3	3.3	0.3	0.6	2.6	5.4
Other urban	31.6	13.0	3.3	4.1	4.4	9.7
Rural western hills/mountains	55.0	37.4	32.7	23.6	24.8	19.4
Rural eastern hills/mountains	36.1	42.9	19.4	29.4	22.4	21.1

Regions	Poverty headcount rate		Distribution of poor		Distribution of population	
	1995/96	2003/04	1995/96	2003/04	1995/96	200304
Rural western Terai	46.1	38.1	18.4	18.9	16.7	15.3
Rural eastern Terai	37.2	24.9	25.9	23.5	29.1	29.1
Development Regions						
Eastern	38.9	29.2	21.0	23.4	22.5	24.7
Central	32.5	27.1	26.9	32.2	34.6	36.6
Western	38.6	27.1	18.7	16.7	20.3	18.9
Mid-Western	59.9	44.8	18.5	17.7	12.9	12.2
Far West	63.9	41.0	14.8	9.9	9.7	7.5
Ecological belts						
Mountains	57.0	32.6	10.7	7.5	7.9	7.1
Hill	40.7	34.5	41.9	47.1	43.0	42.1
Terai	40.3	27.6	47.4	45.4	49.2	50.8

Source: CBS (2006)

The determinants of poverty and food insecurity at the household level in Nepal vary, and they are also complex. In addition, these determinants do not act alone. The combination of these determinants may vary from one household to another and from one region to another. A study on the determinants of food security in rural Nepal revealed the following determinants (Adhikari & Bohle 1999a).

- **Access to resources:** Access to land and water was the main factor affecting the risk exposure of households. Access to irrigated lowlands suitable for paddy cultivation was found to be most important. As the size of household landholdings is declining because of increases in population, and a large proportion of households already have small landholdings, other factors related to off-farm activities determine their ability to secure food.
- **Ecological setting:** The ecological setting determines the type of resources available in a certain locality. Harsh environmental conditions put people in a vulnerable position.

- **Accessibility:** Settlements in accessible areas have relatively better food security. Inaccessible areas face higher food prices. They were also found to be politically weaker, and, hence, unable to put pressure on the government and media for relief measures when faced with landslides and floods.
- **Marketing opportunities:** In areas where marketing opportunities exist to sell or exchange things that villagers produce, food security was comparatively better.
- **Availability of common property resources:** Common property resources like forest and pasture helped poorer households to derive a livelihood. In areas where common property resources existed, people were less vulnerable to various external and internal shocks like flooding, landslide and famine.
- **Family size and composition:** Family size is strongly correlated with the consumption of food. Families with proportionately more children, and with sick and elderly people, were found to be in a more vulnerable position, i.e., consuming less food.
- **Ethnicity:** Particularly members of the occupational caste (Dalits) were found to be in a vulnerable position as they face discrimination, not only in their work, but also involving food preparation and access to resources.
- **Gender:** Various cultural and political practices were found to make girls and women vulnerable to food insecurity. Lack of mobility, lack of access to education and family property, and customs those place women in a lower position than men make them vulnerable to food insecurity.
- **Social network:** Families without membership in well-to-do households are particularly vulnerable. Social networks were found to be important for obtaining relief during times of distress, and for access to off-farm job opportunities, both within and outside the country.

- **Education:** People with higher educational level were found to be relatively secure in food as they know about food and its availability, have knowledge about health and sanitation, and have information about the political process for obtaining food. Education was also found to increase the income of people and they had greater resilience to shocks and risks because of their knowledge and access to information.
- **Political assertiveness:** Areas with high level of political assertiveness were found to receive various facilities from the government and were relatively food secure.

Even though the above determinants were directly related to food security at the household level, they are also the result of the national economic, social and political conditions. At the national level, economic growth rates have been rather slow to generate employment and income opportunities for poor people. Whatever has been generated has been mainly taken by higher-class people. During the period from 1976/77 to 1995/96, the overall growth rate (GDP) was about 4 per cent, a rate that only marginally exceeded the population growth rate of 2.37 per cent. During the same period, the growth rate in the agricultural sector was even smaller, less than 2.5 per cent and over the years has shown very inconsistent behaviour (Sharma 1994). However, it should also be noted that growth rates in total GDP and in agriculture have not been consistent. For instance, in the 1990s, the annual growth in real GDP varied from a low of 2.72 per cent in 1997/98 to a high of 7.90 per cent in 1993/94 (Ibid). But in 2001, GDP grew by only 0.8 per cent. While the growth of the non-agriculture GDP (NGDP) always remained positive, less variable and greater than the population growth rate, until 2000; negative growth rates have been recorded since then. This is partly linked to the political unrest created by the Maoist insurgency. The decline in the export opportunities for carpets and readymade garments is also equally responsible for this sorry state of affairs. Growth rates in agriculture GDP (AGDP) were negative in three out of eight years in the period 1993 to 2000, and had a higher variability and were less than the population growth in five out of these eight years. Growth rates in agriculture vary because it is influenced by rainfall patterns, and a large area still lacks year-round water supply. The low and declining productivity of the land, the high population growth rate, and deteriorating environmental conditions are other reasons for the slow growth rates in agriculture. Despite these problems, the income from remittances has been propping up village economies. This income has acted as a main force to balance the current account deficit of the country. The income from remittances is estimated to contribute from 15 to 25 per cent of GDP, and, in 2001, approximately NRs.77 billion to NRs.110 billion is estimated to have entered Nepal (Graner & Seddon 2004, pp 29-54). But the conflict led to a lack of economic activities within the country, leading to the unemployment of many young people. Overall, the decline in agricultural production activities, transportation blockades, restrictions on trade, the restricted movement of food from one part of the country to another, blockades on selling village products to the cities leading to a lack of income for poor and marginal farmers, unavailability of food, increases in the prices of food, and the like were the results of the conflict that are directly related to food security.

Wage rates and food security

The wage rate in relation to food prices is one indicator of food security. As argued by Sen (1981), falling wage rates in comparison to food prices put wage earners and marginal farmers not producing enough food in a vulnerable position. These people now dominate Nepali society. Therefore, it is important to examine wages rates in relation to food prices and inflation.

In 2008, prices of food increased tremendously all over the world. It was a global crisis. Prices of food also increased at a high rate in Nepal. Prices of basic food items like rice, wheat flour and cooking oil skyrocketed. The price of cooking oil increased by about 50 per cent and the price of rice by 30 per cent in this period. As the poor already spent more than 75 per cent of their income on food, the increase in price directly reduced the amount of food and other non-food essentials they could purchase. As the expenditure on food increased, poor households had less to spend on other activities like healthcare and children's education (Adhikari 2008, p 4).

At the same time, the wage rate did not increase. Instead it fell because of unemployment and surplus labour. Because of this, people could buy less food. This increased the burden on elderly and children, which was seen in the form of their participation in workforce to generate extra income for food purchases. Poor parents took their children out of school to take part in income earning activities.

One of the reasons poor households felt the immediate impact of price rise was that they did not have the capacity to stock food. As a result, fluctuations in the price of food affected them.

During the conflict (1996-2006), a similar kind of impact was seen. The conflict resulted in the increase of the prices of food because it imposed many risks on transportation. Businesspeople added all the potential risks and actual losses (like looting of food, taxes on trade imposed by Maoists, forced donations, etc.) onto the price of food. In the Karnali region, the prices of food were estimated to have increased by 30 per cent. At the same time, because of unemployment, in many places, the wage rate, in fact, declined absolutely.

Even at present (2010), inflation of food prices continues in Nepal, even though it has declined drastically in other countries like India. Nepal faced a whopping 13 per cent increase in food prices in the first half of 2009. But wages have not increased at the same rate. Except for the minimum wages imposed by the Maoist's trade union, wage rates have not increased significantly. In the informal sector, wages have not increased at all. As a result, most people complain about food being expensive in the market; the food crisis seems to be growing.

4.8 Impact of conflict on food insecurity in Nepal

The armed conflict in Nepal, which took place from 1996 to 2006, led to the destruction of basic infrastructure, the internal displacement of people; the death of about 15,000 people; regular strikes (*bandhs*) and blockades of transportation, schools, offices, industry and trade; restrictions on the movement of people, goods and commodities; the extortion of money, food and other things from individuals and businesses, and the conscription of young people to serve in the rebel army. The main targets of the insurgents (people on whom these difficulties were imposed) were, of course, their political opponents, who were generally the wealthy/ruling class (class enemies). But as the conflict was guided by political ideology, the victims were all those who opposed their political thinking or those who did not support the rebels or the CPN (M) party (now the UCPN [M]). Even though, the 'revolution' was meant to benefit, in theory at least, the poor or the working class, it seems that they also suffered much in the process. The severity of the problems experienced differed for different groups and regions. As the areas most affected by the conflict were already food insecure areas, it is difficult to separately evaluate the impact of the conflict. Nepalese society has always been impacted by violence of different types including gender violence, caste violence and other violence ingrained in the society (i.e., structural and cultural), which adversely impacts on food security, particularly of women, children and so-called lower caste groups. The different types of conflict and violence were working together, even during the armed conflict. However, attempts have been made to identify the problems added by the armed conflict with regard to food security. Nepal suffered from food insecurity, even before the armed conflict. The added impact of the conflict on food insecurity is primarily discussed here.

There is only scant information on the consequences of the conflict on food security. Anecdotal evidence and observations made during visits to rural areas reveal some trends with regard to food insecurity. The primary information presented here is mainly drawn from author's visits to rural areas during the conflict. The districts covered were Chitwan and Ramechhap (in Central Nepal) and Dailekh and Banke (in Western Nepal). The secondary information used here comes from various reports published in newspapers in the form of reports from the field.

Even though all seem to suffer from the conflict, it is mainly the poor, indigenous people (ethnic groups), elderly, children and women, and people in remote areas, especially the Mid-Western and Far West Development Region, who suffered the most from the conflict. Food insecurity caused by the conflict affected these people disproportionately. There was a variation in the intensity of the conflict from one region to another. Especially the hill and mountain villages in the Mid-Western and Far West Development Regions were adversely impacted as the rebels established their centres there. There is also a hypothesis that more Dalits and Janajatis were killed then other groups largely because their participation in People's Liberation Army (PLA) was disproportionately high as compared to other ethnic/caste groups. The counter insurgency unleashed by the Government security forces also adversely affected these regions. In general, urban areas suffered less because the rebels had no base in these areas, and they were also not in direct contact with the people in urban areas. However, cases of cash extortion were numerous in urban areas. In rural areas, people had to provide shelter, food and labour for the rebels. The armed conflict affected food security in a number of ways including:

- Decline in production
- Decline in income and employment opportunities
- Loss of household members or their productivity
- Displacement
- Decline in food stock and other assets
- Reduced mobility of people, goods and services, and increases in food prices
- Increase in child malnutrition
- Destruction of infrastructure and reduced basic services
- Decline in natural assets and income from common resources
- Decline in community trust and social safety net
- Reduced access to food and services from government and non- governmental agencies

These impacts are discussed in the following sections.

4.8.1 Decline in production

Food production in Nepal has declined for various reasons related to the armed conflict. Direct threats and attacks (by the CPN [M] or the security forces), insecurity, and diminished access to land and other inputs have reduced the ability to undertake normal farming activities and have led to involuntary migration. Estimates of internally displaced persons vary from 50,000 to 400,000. It can be assumed that the land they left behind is underused, if not left fallow. Reduced availability of inputs and the increased cost of inputs have also reduced the production of food. Similarly, livestock production has also declined substantially due to the conflict. A study (sample study of displaced persons from different regions of Nepal) estimates that there has been a drop of 35 to 60 per cent in production on bigger farms and between 5 and 30 per cent on smaller farms since the conflict (Dixit & Sharma 2003, p 29). The same study revealed that 31 per cent of the *khet* (lowland, paddy land) was left fallow by displaced persons, whereas no *khet* was left fallow during peaceful times. Regarding *khet* (wet land), 46 per cent of displaced persons left *khet* to remain fallow, whereas in peaceful times only 1 per cent did so. With regard to *pakho* (dry land), 58 per cent of displaced persons left it fallow, whereas before only 0.2 per cent did (Ibid, p 22 and 23). Before displacement, 89 per cent of households raised cows, 80 per cent raised buffaloes, 44 per cent raised oxen and 70 per cent raised goats. After displacement, this number reduced to 29 per cent, 30 per cent, 13 per cent, and 24 per cent, respectively (Ibid, p 25). Similarly, there has been decline in agro-industries by almost half since the conflict. In Chitwan district, which is known for commercialised farming, regular *bandhs* and blockades made it difficult to transport goods to the market. *Bandhs* or blockades sometimes lasted weeks and there were a number of instances where farmers spilt their milk and a large volume of vegetables on the road in protest and in desperation. Poultry production was also severely damaged by the conflict. Once, when there was a long blockade in Chitwan, the price of chicken meat and eggs fell substantial in the local market. As Chitwan normally supplies these products to many places throughout the country, local demand alone was not sufficient to consume all of the produce. In Ramechhap district, farmers stopped doing various farming activities like weeding and hoeing for maize crops, because of labour shortages, as many young people had fled the villages. In Kailali and Bardia district, for example, the CPN (M) captured more than 1500 *bigha* of land, which they allowed squatters to cultivate. But the squatters were too afraid to actually cultivate the land because they feared that the security forces might take action against them believing them to be CPN (M). As a result, this land has been left fallow (Chaudhary & Bhandari 2005, p 18).

4.8.2 Decline in income and employment opportunities

Because of the conflict, there has been a general decline in income and employment opportunities. Regular blockades, which prevented food supplies from reaching markets, especially district headquarters, reduced marketing opportunities, lack of mobility for trade and wage employment during farm off-seasons, reduced developmental activities, and reduced construction of infrastructure and houses has meant a decline in income and employment opportunities. The study conducted by Dixit and Sharma on displaced persons revealed that, on average, before the conflict, respondents employed farm labourers for 25 labour days (13 male and 12 female) in a normal year. After they were displaced, respondents employed only 5 labour days (2 male and 3 female). This means that displaced landowners reduced labour employment by 20 labour days a year (Dixit & Sharma 2003, p 17). The study reports that 67 per cent of the agricultural workforce had become jobless in the Far West Development Region and 10 per cent in the Mid-Western Development Region. Because of the high presence of Maoists in the Mid-Western and Far Western Development Region, labourers had cultivated the land (in the absence of landowners and often forced) and paid half of production to the local office of CPN (M) (Ibid, p 19). Before displacement, 78 per cent of landowners paid wages in cash, but after the conflict and displacement, only 32 per cent of the displaced paid wages in cash (Ibid, p 19). This essentially means a reduced ability to purchase food.

Wage employment opportunities have declined in general because of the decline in investment in agriculture, trade and commerce, development projects and infrastructure. As young men move away from the villages (IDPs are usually men), it is the women who have had to look after the children, run the farms, and deal with the problems created by the CPN (M). In some cases, women have had to voluntarily donate labour to the CPN (M) cause. Even those people who were not directly targeted by the rebels as 'class enemies', had to donate labour in the form of carrying goods and arms, and for development related works like road building.

For the poorest of the poor (who usually have no assets including land or who are marginal farmers), employment-based entitlements are the main source of food security. These entitlements in rural Nepal come mainly from farming. As farming were disrupted during the conflict, such employment opportunities have declined. Farming, as a whole, also declined because of external factors like international trade. On the other hand, even those who were carrying out farming as a way to utilise resources, reduced farming activities in the face of conflict and violence.

4.8.3 Loss of household members or their productivity

The death of about 15,000 during the conflict, most of whom were income-earning adults, is a big setback for their households. In addition, the number of disappeared and injured has increased the dependent members in a household. Those widowed and orphaned by the conflict must have experienced significant personal trauma, as well as threats to their livelihoods. Households with this problem not only lose income, they also have to shoulder the additional burden of looking after the sick and injured. In 2004, the author conducted a study on the impact of the conflict on general livelihoods in Ramechhap district. It was reported that there were more than 300 women widowed by the conflict. In general, widows (conflict related widows are generally young) were found to leave their husband house after some time.

They face problems related to farming, child welfare and the inheritance of property. Family property generally goes to the son, and, if the son dies, to his widow. However, especially young widows find it difficult to assert their rights over the property of their husbands. Although she is legally entitled to her husband's share of the family property, other family members fear that young widows might remarry and take their share of the family property to another man. Therefore, other family members create problems in sharing the family property. To escape this, young widows usually go back to their parent's family, if they have parents. But here they also cannot remain for long because the families of her brothers may not like her or may see her as a burden. There is also the possibility that these young widows may bring perceived shame to their parents and kin members by developing extra- marital relations. Because of all these problems, these conflict-affected women often run away from their families and communities to live in places where they are not known. They usually end up in Kathmandu working in some degrading job, especially in the 'entertainment' industry, for which no skills are required.

4.8.4 Displacement

The conflict has led to the displacement, not only of landlords (usually from the fear of CPN [M]), but also of poorer people (caught between the Government security forces and the Maoist). These include both families and individuals (usually male and politically active). The total number of internally displace persons (IDPs) is unknown, but some estimates suggest very large numbers indeed – possibly as many as 400,000 (e.g., Dixit & Sharma 2003) – and anecdotal evidence suggests that thousands a day crossed the border into India through checkpoints in the mid western and far western Terai in 2002. These figures seem exaggerated, but there is no basis for reliable estimates (Seddon & Adhikari 2003). The scale of the phenomenon is such, however, that it must have had some impact on farming in the areas, districts and villages from which these internally displaced/involuntary migrants have come.

Box 4.1 Internally displaced families in Nepalgunj

Kitthe Lohar, a blacksmith of Khamle-2, Mugu, was asked by the CPN (M) to leave his sick wife at home and work for them. Kitthe fled the village carrying his sick wife (in a bamboo basket) on his back and a child on his chest. Walking eight days he reached Mangalsen and then went on to Nepalgunj. Now living in a hut, he is still facing the problem of his wife's illness. The child does not eat anything. He had left behind two cows, two oxen, a buffalo and a field production of a few Muris paddy. Now he does not have anything to eat. He does not know how to treat his wife. His loan has amounted to NRs. 1,370.

There are 216 families displaced from the Bheri-Karnali that are now (2005) living in Nepalgunj. Most of them have no means of feeding their families. Among them is a 65-year old lady Nandakala Budha who escaped with her son by walking at night. Most of these families are not able to secure their basic food requirements. Somewhat earlier, the Nepal Red Cross Society had distributed 135 quintal of rice to 141 families living there.

Among these 216 displaced families, 73 are from Mugu, 63 from Dailekh, 40 from Jajarkot, 23 from Surkhet, 9 from Kalikot, 4 from Jumla, 2 from Humla, 1 each from Salyan and Bajura. Among them, 135 moved out as a direct result of the conflict and 81 because of social and economic pressure, an indirect result of the conflict. The Nepal Red Cross is of the opinion that these displaced people should be returned to their original villages instead of giving incentives to live in displaced camps. Because of the rumour that one can live in the camp with free meals, more and more people are coming to live in the camps. But the displaced persons say that they will be killed if they return. They do not believe that there will be peace in the villages (Gautam 2005, p 1).

Displaced people have also been fleeing to India, where they have created effective competition among themselves. As a result, they have had difficulty in getting employment. Wage rates are said to have dropped by about 25 per cent because of the competition. Moreover, most displaced Nepalis end up in slums, where there are already so many problems.

Displacement coupled with migration has adversely affected farming in the villages. The displacement and migration induced by the conflict is male specific, because it is politically targeted. As it was mainly men who were politically active, it was mainly men who had to leave the village because of the conflict. This resulted in the feminisation of farming. From time to time, there are reports of women doing farming activities that are ritually denied to them or that had been considered too hard for women. For example, ploughing (culturally considered to be a man's job) or roofing the house (which is physically difficult), and the like. Women have taken on these tasks out of necessity to grow crops for their family, the alternative being hunger.

4.8.5 Decline in food stock and other assets

It is a common fact that the CPN (M) and the Government security forces have extorted food from households. Extortion by the Maoist was more common than by the security forces. CPN (M) not only demanded food grains from households, but also lived in family homes in large numbers. This caused the depletion of household food stores, leading to food insecurity.

4.8.6 Reduced mobility of people, goods and services, and increases in food prices

A major impact of the conflict was the reduced mobility of people; restrictions on the transportation of food and goods; and reduced availability of other services. The result has been a decline in income (as mobility for wage employment and trade is one source of income) and an increase in the price of food stuffs. The usual flow of imports into the rural areas, including, notably, imported food stuffs, has been hampered by restrictions of various kinds imposed by both the security forces and the CPN (M), and by general insecurity. The CPN (M) taxed the flow of commodities and, in some cases, looted food stuffs being transported. Both the Government and other public agencies (like NGOs/INGOs and international agencies) as well as private traders stopped or reduced supplies of food to conflict-affected areas, which also happened to be food deficient districts in normal times. These districts (mainly in the Far West and Mid-Western Development Regions, particularly the upper Karnali), which used to depend on imported foods, experienced severe problems in obtaining food from Government stores and shops.

In Ramechhap district, for example, the conflict caused food insecurity. There were constant blockades of the district headquarters to increase the pressure on the Government. During the blockades, goods could not be supplied to markets, particularly headquarters. Similarly, goods from the markets could not be distributed to customers in the villages. Because of this, farmers were not able to sell their goods from time to time. In this district, farmers had kept dairy animals (cows and buffaloes) for the production of milk, which was sold in a co-operative. The co-operative then supplied the milk to Kathmandu. But because of the frequent strikes, people could not sell raw milk to the co-operative. As a result, they started producing ghee from the milk, as ghee can be stored for a long time. Profit from ghee was low compared to that from the sale of raw milk. Similarly, small farmers and poor people have been discouraged from increasing the production of goats, vegetables and other produce because of transport strikes. In Ramechhap, strikes and blockades were more frequent than in other places. The CPN (M) did not have good relationship with the only transport company that ran in the area, which failed to meet the CPN (M's) demands for donations. This resulted in frequent blockade and the destruction of vehicles. It is reported that the CPN (M) demanded NRs. 1 lakh per vehicle per year, which was considered too high by the company. It is mainly because of the conflict that prices of food grains increased. The WFP monitor in Ramechhap reported that 18 of the 55 VDCs in the district have faced chronic food insecurity. These monitors also record food prices. At the time of the survey, food prices had increased in Ramechhap because of blockades in Sindhuli, which supplied food to Ramechhap. For example, the price of rice was NRs.115 per pathi (normal price was NRs.80-90), maize NRs.60 per pathi (normal price was NRs. 35-40), wheat NRs.40 per pathi (normal price was NRs.25-30). A similar situation was also seen in Dailekh. At one time there was a continuous blockade for two-months, which led to significant price increases. At that time, the price of a 30 kg bag of rice increased to NRs.840 from NRs.640; dhal to NRs.60 per kg from NRs.35; kerosene to NRs.50 per litre from NRs.25 per litre; and sugar to NRs.45 per kg from NRs.35 per kg. The blockades also caused problems in the supply of products from villages to markets like Dailekh bazaar. Farmers were not able to sell perishable products like vegetables and milk. As food could not go from the bazaar to the villages, there was no option except to buy food from local landlords. From time to time, the Government security forces also imposed restrictions on the supply of goods to the villages. A villager could only take a pair of batteries and 15 kg of food to the village. This was done to curtail supply to the CPN (M), but it also created shortages.

Box 4.2 Food shortages in Diktel

Diktel residents have not been able to come to terms with the attack on the headquarters of Khotang district. They fear another attack by the CPN (M). Residents also fear food shortages and the high prices of commodities. Now (2005) the CPN (M) do not let them bring foods and other things from the villages to the headquarters and there are problems in transporting goods and food, it is done only by porters as there is no road from Gaighat. Thus, food is becoming scarce. The Nepal Food Corporation has not been able to supply enough food to the people. Those who come to the headquarters with a gunny bag for the collection of food, return home empty handed. There is famine in the village. It is expensive to buy food. The Government quota is just wishful thinking. Nowadays, people from the villages do not come to town, and even if they do come, they don't stay. There are no business activities, as in the past. Now it is difficult to survive. The town is depopulated as entrepreneurs and businesspeople have deserted it. There are only four telephone lines from which one-way communication is made. Very occasionally helicopters come. There are about a thousand porters and eight hundred donkeys for transportation. They are also stopped on and off by the rebels. As a result, food has become expensive. The price of food (NRs. per kg): rice – 80, maize, millet and wheat – 35, dhal – 90, salt – 30, mustard oil – 120, and kerosene – 70. At present only about 15 per cent of the food is being transported, compared to normal times.

Source: Magar & Rai (2005, p 1) – an article in Kantipur Daily, 20 July 2005

4.8.7 Child malnutrition

Nutrition experts have been concerned that the conflict has worsened the state of child malnutrition. The constant migration and displacement of villagers has made the problem worse. The children of displaced people need to cope with new food, and it is difficult for them to adjust. Displaced people are generally not able to afford green vegetables or enough rice and feed their children dry, non-nutritious foods lacking vitamins and protein. In conflict-affected areas, food insecurity and deficit consumption has adversely affected children. It is reported that about 90 per cent of children in conflict-affected areas (i.e., defined by the government as areas intensively affected by the armed conflict) suffered from chronic malnutrition. The problem got worse because whatever nutrition projects were operating in conflict areas were gradually phasing out as more organisations shifted towards conflict related humanitarian and relief work (Newar 2005, p 11). In Nepal, 70 per cent of child deaths are indirectly a result of malnutrition. Protein-energy malnutrition affects 63 per cent of Nepali children, which means they do not get enough food to maintain normal physical and mental functions. More than half the children have stunted growth (see Table 4.5). These children may also suffer from learning disabilities. A report indicates that the above stated problems, along with other problems like underweight among the children had increased among the conflict- affected families (Newar 2005, p 11).

4.8.8 Destruction of infrastructure and reduced basic services

During the armed conflict, infrastructure like bridges, community buildings (especially VDC buildings), and government offices were destroyed. Government staffs providing services to the people were displaced to district headquarters. Banks and financial institutions closed their operations in rural areas and moved to urban areas. Villagers were then deprived of all types of services – financial, health, security, agricultural extension, veterinary services and the like. As the moneylenders were also displaced, loans were not available in rural areas. People in general did not extend loans. The lack of services caused problems for many people. For official work (e.g., to meet the VDC secretary), one had to travel to the district headquarters, which meant spending one or two days and staying in a hotel. This increased the burden on people. Money which could have been used for food was diverted to such wasteful activities. It is difficult to objectively verify how much these things happened, or estimate the cost of such inconveniences and hardships. Some attempts were made in the past to measure the economic cost of the infrastructure damage. Karki and Bhattarai have estimated that about 8 to 10 per cent of GDP has been lost (Karki & Bhattarai 2003, p xiv). This could be roughly US $ 694.44 million. Another estimate revealed that the cost of repairing infrastructure damaged during the 15 months of the emergency alone is about US$ 30 million (Grosney 2003). Still another estimate claimed that the conflict or the 'people's war', as it is generally called, led to loss of 2 per cent in economic growth rates.

4.8.9 Decline in natural assets and income from common resources

During the armed conflict, the condition of community forests declined. This was driven by both the rebels and the Government security forces. The rebels disturbed the activities of community forestry by forcefully taking the income from forests. Many community forest groups were pressured by the rebels to fell trees and the income would go to the rebels. The Army also destroyed the forest so that they could have a better view of the rebels. In areas where Army camps were located, the Army feared that the forest in the vicinity would provide shelter for the rebels, so they destroyed the forest. Again, this is based on anecdotal evidence and observation; there is no objective data to support this fact.

The other common process through which poor people, especially in the hills and mountains, suffered is due to the rebels' control of non-timber forest products (NTFPs), especially herbs. The rebels either collected valuable herbs by themselves or charged a heavy duty on the collection of herbs by the people. Access to herbs had been a source of 'exchange entitlements to food' for the people, but this was reduced tremendously during the armed conflict. NTFPs were one of the main sources of income for the rebels. In districts like Mugu, Dolpa, Jumla, Bhajhang and Humla where NTFPs were available, the rebels' main concern was to control NTFP collection and trade.

4.8.10 Decline in community trust and social safety net

The activities of the rebels, and their indoctrination about class interests led to the decline of many forms of community based cooperation and social safety net mechanisms. The traditional moral economy was largely seen as a mechanism to exploit the underclass. There was suspicion about who was working for the rebels and who was working for the Army. This suspicion was the main reason for the decline in cooperation. As a result, the maintenance of traditional irrigation channels, trails, water sources, forests and pastures was not done. Villages started to look deserted. Landlords stopped traditional relations of *bista* (long-term labour employment relations). The micro-credit associations stopped functioning. People divided what was saved and the co-operatives were dissolved.

4.8.11 Reduced access to food and services from the government and non- governmental agencies

The conflict-affected areas were also food insecure areas even before the conflict. There were a number of programmes to help people secure food and improve nutritional standards. The Government's main institution for supplying food to people was the Nepal Food Corporation (NFC). Since the 1990s, it had continued providing transportation subsidies in remote districts not touched by roads. Even though its activities were reduced due to the Government's economic liberalisation policy, it had continued to supply some food to these areas. But the conflict led to the ceasing of its operations in these areas. Food was transported to the target area through local means (such as porters or pack animals like donkeys) and surface transportation. This was cheaper than airlifting the food. The general practice was to transport food by vehicle as far as possible and then use either porters or donkeys. But this system was vulnerable to hijacking by the rebels. After a few cases of food looting by the rebels, the Government started to airlift food. This increased the cost of food supply, and, thus, reduced the total volume of food supplied to remote areas. This was also the case with the various programmes launched by NGOs, INGOs, donors and UN agencies. When the staff of such agencies were killed or tortured, these agencies pulled their programmes from conflict-affected areas. In general, many donor agencies reduced their programmes in the conflict zones because of the risk to personnel working in such areas. This reduced the services and support (including food) available from government and other agencies. As a result, people's entitlements to food declined.

4.9 Government responses to food security needs

The concept of food security has only recently been introduced in government policies and programmes. This lack of emphasis on food security is linked to the assumption held until recently that food production would lead to food security. Accordingly, policies in the past aimed at increasing the production and productivity of crops. Accordingly, until the 1970s, the words 'food security' do not appear in the government reports and documents. In the late 1970s, Nepal adopted a policy of providing basic needs to the people. Since the 1980s, the concept of food security has gained momentum. It is now increasingly used in development discourse and in practice. But, at the same time, the liberalisation policy adopted in the mid- 1980s and emphasised since the 1990s reduced the scope of some of the public food distribution mechanisms (i.e., NFC) for food security. This seems against the spirit of the 1990 Constitution, which envisions Nepal as a welfare state, and in its directive principles the Government of Nepal is supposed to work for the welfare of people, which also includes meeting their food security requirements. During the armed conflict, the Government had no special plan to meet the food security needs of conflict victims. There was some support for internally displaced people, but this again went to the politically powerful. The Government was wary of the fact that food security programmes in conflict-affected areas gave the rebels access to food. As a result, there were restrictions on the transportation of food to conflict areas. Even during the conflict, the Government continued with the liberalisation policy pursued since the early 1990s.

The full impact of liberalisation principles can be seen in the Ninth Five Year Plan (1997-2002), which embraced the APP as the strategy for agricultural development and food security. This plan aimed to bring about a broad-based growth in the economy and to reduce poverty and food insecurity. The long-term concept of the Government in the Ninth Five Year Plan regarding food security through government support includes:

- To create an environment for the regular, adequate and accessible supply of essential goods
- To monitor the quality, availability and price of essential goods to protect consumers' rights
- To make arrangements for food security through maintaining the buffer stock of food at the regional level
- To prevent black marketing, creation of artificial shortages and profiteering on consumer goods in general and essential goods in particular

The policies adopted in the Tenth Five Year Plan (2002-2007) seem to be a continuation of the Ninth Five Year Plan. The main objective of this plan is to reduce poverty through broad-based economic growth. In agriculture, this has been emphasised by following the APP. Apart from mentioning that the Government would continue to supply food, salt and sugar to remote areas, there is no specific policy related to food security. Similarly, this plan aims at reducing the burden of subsidies in remote areas by improving agricultural production, resource management, skill development and employment opportunities. The Government also has a plan to encourage the establishment of cheaper stores through people's co-operatives.

Despite a clear lack of an action plan, there are, however, some governmental and non-governmental programmes to provide some targeted food security measures. These are discussed here below.

4.9.1 Transport subsidy are food grains for people in remote areas

The NFC is mainly responsible for providing food to remote food deficit areas. The Government provides a transport subsidy for this work. NFC was developed from an institution created to supply food to the security forces; later, it supplied cheap food to civil servants. In 1972, when there was famine in the Karnali region, this institution (under a different name at that time) was given the special task of airlifting and distributing food in that region. In 1974, the NFC was created and the task of supplying food (with transportation costs subsidy) was expanded to other food deficit districts. The Government earmarks part of the budget every year to NFC (via the Ministry of Supply) to provide transport subsidies. Until now, the NFC has been providing food (subsidised) to 38 remote districts. The main concern with the NFC is that it is neither cost effective nor do its services reach the neediest people. The liberalisation policy adopted since the 1990s has also reduced the scope of the NFC's work.

4.9.2 Food-for-work programme

The Rural Community Infrastructural Works (RCIW) programme is a major programme that provides food for labourers working to develop infrastructure required for the community. The RCIW helps in creating seasonal employment for villagers. Beneficiaries are employed in developing sustainable infrastructure identified as necessary by the communities themselves, particularly the poor and women. Literacy and other social activities are also carried out in order to empower people and improve the management of infrastructure. This is done to improve the participation of people, because it is generally felt that food-for-work is a service delivery programme. It is estimated that every year about 30,000 unskilled labourers participate in this programme. They are paid food rations and some cash for the work performed. About 10,000 metric tons of food is provided annually through this programme. This programme is being implemented in 25 districts. In recent times, some donors (particularly DFID) have withdrawn support for the Food-for-Work programme, claiming that the infrastructures developed by local people are generally of poor quality. As a result, the coverage of this programme has been reduced.

Even though the Food-for-Work programme is primarily helpful in meeting short- term food deficits, like that of the NFC's food supply, the RCIW also assumes that its programme will lead to long-term food security. Increases in accessibility due to road construction, conservation of resources like prevention of river cutting, the protection of land and the like, will lead to food security in the long run. Even though the programme is criticised for undermining self-help initiatives, it provides a useful service to the poorest of the poor who basically become paid volunteers under the programme.

Other programmes incorporating the principle of 'food for work', whether paid in cash or in food, have been implemented in the country. They are, in general, small and scattered in different places. A few programmes of this nature have also been implemented in conflict-affected areas, but their impact and coverage has been minimal.

4.9.3 Other programmes

Programmes like 'school feeding' and 'relief and emergency operations' have been implemented as a part of food security for children and to reduce vulnerability during the crisis in Nepal. The World Food Programme provides support for the school feeding programme in 12 food deficit districts, in which the Government is also implementing the Basic and Primary School Programme. During emergencies created by natural disasters, food is also provided to the victims under the 'relief and emergency operations' programme.

There was no specific programme to help improve food security in conflict-affected areas. Rather, the conflict became an excuse to reduce programme activities. For example, international agencies suspended supplying food to the areas because the CPN (M) looted their supplies. The Government turned a blind eye to the food insecurity problems caused by both sides of the conflict (the security forces and CPN [M]). Programmes designed for normal circumstances faced problems in reaching needy people during the conflict. The food distributed often did not reach the target groups. If targeting is not good, there are problems in improving access to food. Targeting can be done at different geographical levels – from the region and the district to the VDC and settlement levels. Different indicators need to be developed and regularly updated to target different food insecure geographical units. At present, the NFC uses the accessibility criteria for targeting. In accessible areas (by road), the NFC does not provide any subsidy for transportation. In 2007, WFP developed a programme to improve food security in areas previously affected by the conflict.

Increasing food production by marginal or landless farmers has also been one of the approaches to reducing food insecurity. This production could be for home consumption or for sale. There are different programmes in Nepal aimed at achieving this. These programmes include the APP-SP (Agriculture Perspective Plan-Support Programme) and activities to increase access to land initiated by various INGOs and NGOs like Plan International and the Government's Poverty Alleviation Fund (PAF), Community Self-Reliance Centre (CSRC). PAF has received support from various bilateral and multilateral organisations like the World Bank. In the APP-SP, small and marginal farmers are organised into groups and grants are given for small infrastructure and support. Similarly, other programmes help women, poor, and marginal and landless farmers to form groups and lease land and provide other support for farming, mainly vegetable farming. Various NGOs have also been implementing these types of activities. However, these activities have not achieved much success because the land they lease is not their own so they do not want to invest in it.

4.9.4 New emphasis on food security, especially for conflict victims

Since the *Jana Andolan* in April 2006, the popular revolt that led to political change and the signing of the Comprehensive Peace Agreement between the Government and the rebels in November 2006, more emphasis has been given to food security. The increase in the influence of civil society in policy making and the Government's commitments in international agreements to recognise food security as a basic human right have effected a policy change in this area. 'Food security' is now considered a basic human right. The Interim Constitution 2007 and the Interim Three Year Plan 2008-2010 have given priority to food security. The Interim Three Year Plan aims to meet the food security targets envisaged in the Millennium Development

Goals, i.e., reduce the number of food insecure people by half in 15 years (by 2015). This Plan has called for an increase in investment in food security. However, there is still no concrete action-plan and resource allocation to meet this target. Since the signing of the Comprehensive Peace Agreement, the international community (and in particular the WFP) has also shown concern to meet the food security needs of conflict-affected people.

One of the main aims of donor activity in food security is to meet short-term needs related to food. This approach generally avoids the 'livelihood approach' to meeting food security. This means that sustainability in food security in conflict-affected areas (which are also traditionally food insecure areas) is still in question. The short-term concern of the donor agencies is not helping the sustainable food system; as a result, food deficit area's dependency on external food aid is growing. At the same time, more and more people are now facing food security problems. In 2009, about 2.2 million people were reported to be facing food security problems (The Kathmandu Post 3 June 2009, p 1 and 25 May 2009, p 7).

4.10 Conclusion and recommendations

Food insecurity has been a major problem in Nepal, even before the armed conflict. The structural violence rooted in Nepalese society has put people from certain geographical areas, women, Dalits (so-called low caste), and some indigenous peoples in a vulnerable position. The conflict accelerated the food insecurity already existing in the country and among insecure groups. Even though the rebels intended to create problems only for certain groups, especially those considered to be 'class enemies' and those not supporting rebels activities, the conflict also impacted directly and indirectly on already food insecure groups. These groups became more vulnerable during the conflict. In addition, new groups who were previously relatively well off in terms of food security, became vulnerable and food insecure during the conflict. Moreover, the conflict had a disproportionate impact on different geographical areas. The impact was more severe in remote and isolated areas (like the Mid-Western and Far West

Development region, where the Maoists had their stronghold), as compared to urban and more accessible areas.

The chapter concludes that there is insufficient empirical information and theoretical understanding to explain food security/insecurity during the armed conflict. The 'livelihood approach' seems useful as it focuses on both short-term (risk to lives) and long-term (risk to livelihoods) vulnerabilities. But this approach is also incapable of understanding food security during the armed conflict as it does not adequately take into account illegal activities and changes in people's entitlements due to changes in their social-political and economic positions. In such a situation 'vulnerability' is better understood in terms of which individuals or groups have entitlements at a particular time. Conflict also increases risks generally and different groups bear these risks differently. Accordingly, their entitlements are also affected according to the risks they bear. But conflict periods also fluctuate widely, and this requires constant monitoring of the entitlement situation. Accordingly, 'food aid' should target those who lose entitlements. Asset position or ownership of assets may not be sufficient criteria for targeting the beneficiaries of such aid. However, asset position may be a good indicator of who may be able to cope with and recover from the shocks of conflict once the conflict is ended, i.e., when people are capable of using their livelihood assets. In normal conditions, however, the 'livelihood approach' of focusing on improving the livelihoods of people is valuable. Improved livelihood conditions reduce vulnerability and, thus, lead to sustainable food security.

Food security is a complex phenomenon, and it is essential to pay attention to the different dimensions of food security. Accordingly, there is no single solution to the problem of food insecurity. In Nepal, food security has been adversely affected by a host of interrelated factors, of which the armed conflict was one. Its impacts are still seen today, even though the conflict has ended. However, there are other types of conflict and violence ingrained in Nepalese society. Food security will continue to be affected by other types of conflict. Therefore, an understanding of how to work for food security during times of conflict is necessary. With regard to Nepal, other factors also need to be understood. At present, both agricultural production and food security are affected by events and processes at the international level. This is the result of globalisation. Local food systems that use diverse technical, social and economic resources need to be reinforced to improve the availability and accessibility of food produced on a sustainable basis and to ensure that it is distributed to all as a part of the 'right to food' and 'right to life'. There is also a need to interlink these local food systems at the global level, in a way so as not to abolish local systems, but to mutually support each other. Citizens should be able to participate in shaping the food system and ways of consumption of food so that it expresses family and community values and culture. Accordingly, the following steps need to be taken for food security.

- During times of conflict, risks to entitlements increase depending upon socio-economic and political configurations. As a result, groups seemingly food secure because of their asset position may also become vulnerable. Therefore, the entitlement position of all groups of people needs to be monitored and those at risk should be supported by various means. Food aid meant to help vulnerable people is also disrupted during times of conflict. Making food security a basic human right to be respected by all parties during conflict would help in providing food aid.
- During normal times, the sustainability of food security depends upon improved livelihoods. In this situation, the livelihood approach is important in analysing the status of livelihoods. Existing food security programmes in Nepal, especially those of the donors, take a short- term 'risks to lives' approach. This is a temporary, stop-gap approach. Emphasis needs to be given to improving the overall livelihoods of people. This also means adopting mechanisms to reduce vulnerability and increase the ability to cope with the risks. While short-term solutions are important during crisis periods, they should be complemented with, or backed by, programmes aimed

at livelihood improvement and creating social, economic and physical infrastructures helping to produce more and distribute food to the needy. Measures like local social safety nets may provide a solution in situations where there are 'risks to lives' or a short-term mechanism to avoid crisis. Food banks (indigenous systems like *dharma bhakari* or formal institutions like food banks) and other community assistance programmes should be developed and used as emergency measures. In Jumla in the Karnali zone, traditional *dharma bhakaris* were established and every household used to donate food on moral grounds depending upon their capacity. This food was distributed to households and individuals suffering from food crisis. It should be noted that the Karnali zone had (and has) a high vulnerability to food insecurity, partly due to climatic and geographic reasons. The formal forms of these traditional institutions could be food banks. These banks can help low-income consumers and distribute surplus food in the community. Structural measures (like land reform or guaranteed employment and increased access of poor and marginalised to resources) are needed to provide long-term food security. Similarly, to increase the access of women, children and the elderly within households, and to increase the role of women even in changed political context, gender empowerment, equity and equal access to resources and property are important. These long-term aims improve the livelihoods of vulnerable groups.

- To reduce the adverse impact of globalisation on agricultural production and food security, it is important to reinforce or develop local food systems that interlink all the resources available within the region or locality. The food produced and distributed from such a system is hygienic, fresh and culturally acceptable. The employment or the work generated by such a system increases or retains the income within the locality. The local biodiversity and ecosystem is preserved by this system, providing more choices of food to all, including the poor and marginalised. Moreover, such a local food system also increases the control of a community or household over resources, including seeds, and is helpful in using existing local knowledge. The power of MNCs and TNCs is also reduced by promoting local food systems. The problem of food unavailability will also be less in times of crisis (like conflict) if a large proportion of the food needs are met by the local production system.

- A strong research base is required to examine and analyse new risks and potential conflicts that could happen from time to time. At present, climate change is also emerging as a new risk and a factor in new types of conflict. Climate change is expected to have an immense impact on food security and the displacement of people. Research- based policies are important to enable us to act proactively to face these new risks and conflicts.

References

ActionAid. 2005. *Power Hungry: Six Reasons to Regulate Global Food Corporations.* Johannesburg: International Secretariat, ActionAid.

ActionAid and SAWTEE [South Asia Watch on Trade, Economics and Environment]. 2004. *Nepal in the WTO: Livelihood and Food Security Perspectives.* Kathmandu: ActionAid Nepal and South Asia Watch for Trade, Economics and Environment.

Adhikari J. 2008. Food crisis: How the country will feed its poor. *The Himalayan Times Daily,* 1st May. International Media Network Pvt. Ltd, p 4.

Adhikari J. 1996. *The Beginnings of Agrarian Change: A Case Study in Central Nepal.* Kathmandu: TM Publication.

Adhikari J. 2000. *Decisions for Survival: Farm Management Strategies in the Middle Hills of Nepal.* Kathmandu: Adroit Publications.

Adhikari J. 2004. Food security in the context of globalization [In Nepali]. *In:* Chene M and Onta P, editors. *Nepalko Sandarvama Samaj Satriya Chintan.* Kathmandu: Social Science Baha, pp 217-249.

Adhikari J. 2005. Foreign employment and poverty reduction: Possibilities and challenges [In Nepali]. *In:* Adhikari J, Gautam B, Basnet P, editors. *Nepal Ma Gareebeeko Bahas.* Kathmandu: Martin Chautari, pp 223-243.

Adhikari J. 2006a. *Land Reform in Nepal.* Kathmandu: NIDS [Nepal Institute of Development Studies (Unpublished report).

Adhikari J. 2006b. *Securitizing the Migration: A Case of Migration between Nepal and India.* A report submitted to Refugee and Migratory Movements Study Unit. Dhaka: Dhaka University.

Adhikari J. 2006c. Urban food security – Kathmandu context [In Nepali]. *In:* Adhikari J, Sharma P, editors. *Urbanization and Urban Livelihoods in Nepal.* Kathmandu: Martin Chautari (Unpublished).

Adhikari J, Bohle HG. 1999a. *Food Crisis in Nepal: How Mountain Farmers Cope.* New Delhi: Adriot Publications.

Adhikari J, Bohle HG. 1999b. Urbanization, government policies and growing food insecurity in Kathmandu metropolis. *Studies in Nepali History and Society* 4(1):191-246.

Adhikari J, Ghimire S. 2006. *Changing Food Chain* [In Nepali]. Kathmandu: Martin Chautari.

Blaikie P, Cannon T, Wisner B. 1994. *At Risk, Natural Hazards, People's Vulnerability and Disasters.* London and New York: Routledge.

Bohle HG. 1995. The Geography of famine and food crisis research. *International Geographical Union Bulletin* [Vol. 45], pp 5-12.

Bohle HG, Watts M. 1993. Hunger, famine and space of vulnerability. *Geo Journal* 30(2):117-125.

Carney D. 1998. Sustainable Rural Livelihoods. What Contributions Can We Make?' Paper presented at the DFID's Natural Resources Advisor's Conference. July 1998. London: DFID [Department for International Department].

CBS [Central Bureau of Statistics]. 1996 and 1997. *Nepal Living Standards Survey Report–1996 and 1997* (Main Findings: Volume One and Two). Kathmandu: Central Bureau of Statistics, His Majesty's Government of Nepal.

CBS [Central Bureau of Statistics]. 2002. *Statistical Pocket Book.* Kathmandu: Central Bureau of Statistics, His Majesty's Government of Nepal.

CBS [Central Bureau of Statistics]. 2005. *Nepal Living Standards Survey Report– 2003-04* (Main Findings: Volume One and Two). Kathmandu: CBS [Central Bureau of Statistics], His Majesty's Government of Nepal.

CBS [Central Bureau of Statistics]. 2006. *Resilience Amidst Conflict. Assessment of Poverty in Nepal 1993/94 and 2003/04.* Kathmandu: CBS, ADB [Asian Development Bank], WB [World Bank] and DFID [Department for International Development].

CBS [Central Bureau of Statistics], WFP [World Food Programme],WB [World Bank]. 2006. *Small Area Estimates of Poverty, Calorie Intake and Malnutrition in Nepal.* Kathmandu: CBS [Central Bureau of Statistics], WFP [World Food Programme] and WB [World Bank].

Chambers R. 1989. Vulnerability, coping and policy. *IDS Bulletin* 20(2):1-7.

Chaudhary G, Bhandari D. 2005. Farmers in problem. *Nepal National Weekly* 24 July, 2005, pp 18.

Dixit P, Sharma S. 2003. *Impact of Conflict on Agricultural Production and Small Landowners in Nepal.* Kathmandu: Centre for Economic and Social Development (CESOD).

DoA [Department of Agriculture]. 2000. *Agricultural Marketing Information Bulletin* [Special Issue], DoA, MDD [Market Development Directorate], Ministry of Agriculture, His Majesty's Government of Nepal, p 102.

DoA [Department of Agriculture]. 2004. *Agricultural Marketing Information Bulletin* [Special Issue]. Kathmandu: DoA [Department of Agriculture], MDD [Marketing Development Directorate], His Majesty's Government of Nepal, p 189-191.

DoA [Department of Agriculture]. 2006. *Agricultural Marketing Information Bulletin* [Special Issue]. Kathmandu: DoA [Department of Agriculture], MDD [Marketing Development Directorate], His Majesty's Government of Nepal, p. 207.

Dreze J, Sen A. 1989. *Hunger and Public Policy.* Oxford: Clarendon Press.

Dreze J, Sen A, editors. 1990. *The Political Economy of Hunger.* Oxford: Clarendon Press.

Ellis F. 2000. *Rural Livelihoods and Diversity in Developing Countries.* Oxford: Oxford University Press.

FAO [Food and Agricultural Organization]. 2001. *The State of Food Insecurity in the World 2001.* Rome: Food and Agricultural Organization (FAO).

Gatlung J. 1990. Cultural violence. *Journal of Peace Studies.* 27(3):291-305.

Gatlung J. 2003. Rethinking Conflict: The Cultural Approach. Speech delivered at the informal meeting of European ministers responsible for cultural affairs, Council of Europe. Strasbourg (17-18 February). Accessed via www.coe.int/T/E/ Cultural_Co-operation/ on 8 August 2006.

Gautam M. 1993. *Food Security, Nutrition and Hygiene in Nepal.* Kathmandu: The World Bank.

Gautam S. 2005. Difficulties to meet food for displaced [In Nepali]. *Kantipur National Daily,* 22 July 2005. Kathmandu: Kantipur Publications, p 1.

Gersony R. 2003. Sowing the Wind. History and Dynamics of the Maoist Revolt in Nepal's Rapti Hills. A report submitted to Mercy Corps International, Washington DC.

Graner E, Seddon D. 2004. Nepal's remittance economy: A decade of change (1996- 97 to 2003-04). *In:* Dahal, MK, editor, *Nepalese Economy: Towards Building a Strong Nation State.* Kathmandu: Central Dept of Economics, Tribhuwan University and New Hira Books Enterprises, pp 29-54.

The Himalayan Times, 21 July 2006, 'Farmer Suicides Reach Decade-High in India' (AFP), p 8.

INSEC [Informal Sector Service Centre]. 2005. *Nepal Human Rights Statistics, 2005.*Kathmandu: INSEC.

Karki A, Bhattarai B. 2003. *Whose War?* Kathmandu: NGO [Non-government Organization] Federation.

Karki A, Seddon D. 2003. People's War in Historical Context. *In:* Karki A, Seddon D, editors. *The People's War in Nepal: Left Perspective.* New Delhi: Adroit Publishers, pp 3-48.

The Kathmandu Post, 3 June 2009, p 1.

The Kathmandu Post, 25 May 2009, p 7.

Koirala G. 1992. Proposed Approaches to Poverty Alleviation in Nepal. A paper presented at National Seminar on 'Poverty Alleviation and Human Development'. Kathmandu: National Planning Commission.

Lappe F, Moore JC, Rosset P. 1999. Beyond guilt and fear. *In:* Boucher, DH, editor. *The Paradox of Plenty: Hunger in a Bountiful World.* California: Food First Books, pp 4-60.

Magar U, Rai DS. 2005. Diktel has become a Karnali of the east' [In Nepali]. *Kantipur Daily.* July 20. Kathmandu: Kantipur Publications, p 1.

Mikesell SL. 1993. The paradoxical support of Nepal's left for comrade Gonzalo. *Himal.*March/April. Kathmandu: Himal Media Pvt Ltd.

Mishra C. 2001. *Country Report Nepal (IDT/MDG Progress on International Millennium Declaration Development Goals).* Kathmandu: United Nations Development Programme.

Newar N. 2005. Underfed and under-funded: Seventy per cent of child deaths in Nepal are indirectly a result of malnutrition. *Nepali Times.* 15-21 July, 2005, Kathmandu: Himal Media Pvt. Limited, p 11.

Nickson RA. 2003. Democratisation and growth of communism in Nepal. *In:* Thapa D., editor. *Understanding the Maoist Movement in Nepal*. Kathmandu: Martin Chautari, pp 2-33.

Onta P. 2004. Democracy and duplicity: The CPN (M) and their interlocutors. *In:* Hutt M, editors. *Himalayan 'People's War': Nepal's Maoist Rebellion.* London: Foundation Books, pp 136-151.

Pantha R, Sharma BR. 2003. Population size, growth and distribution. *In:* CBS [Central Bureau of Statistics]. *Population Monograph of Nepal.* Kathmandu: Central Bureau of Statistics, pp 37-86.

Pfaff-Czarnecka J. 2004. High expectations, deep disappointment: Politics, state and society in Nepal after 1990. *In:* Hutt M, editor. *Himalayan 'People's War': Nepal's Maoist Rebellion.* London: Foundation Books, pp 166-191.

Pyakuryal B. 2004. *Nepal's Conflict Economy: Costs, Consequences and Alternatives.* Kathmandu: Nepal Economic Association.

RRN [Rural Reconstruction Nepal]/AAN [ActionAid Nepal]. 2002. Food Security in Nepal: The Civil Society Perspective. Brief Report of the Consultation Workshops on Assessment of Commitments and Plan of Action of the World Food Summit, 1996. RRN Report Series 2002. Kathmandu: Rural Reconstruction Nepal and Action Aid Nepal.

Scoones I. 1998. *Sustainable Rural Livelihoods. A Framework for Analysis.* IDS [Institute of Development Studies] paper No. 72. Brighton: IDS.

Seddon D, Adhikari J. 2003. *Conflict and Food Security in Nepal: A Preliminary Analysis.* Kathmandu: Rural Reconstruction Nepal.

Seddon D, Adhikari J, Gurung G. 1998. Foreign labour migration and the remittance economy of Nepal. *Himalayan Research Bulletin* 17(2):3-11.

Seddon D, Adhikari J, Gurung G. 2001. *The New Lahures: Foreign Employment and Remittances Economy of Nepal.* Kathmandu: NIDS [Nepal Institute of Development Studies].

Sen AK. 1981. *Poverty and Famine: An Essay on Entitlement and Deprivation.* Oxford: Clarendon Press.

Sen AK. 2000. *Development as Freedom.* New York: Anchor Books.

Sharma S. 1994. *Economic Liberalization and Agricultural Development in Nepal. International. Policy Analysis in Agriculture and Related Resource Management.* Research Report Series No.26. Kathmandu: His Majesty's Government of Nepal, Ministry of Agriculture / Winrock.

Shiva V. 1998. Overview of Globalization and Impacts to Food Security – The Global Perspective. *In: Proceedings of the Forum on 'Land, Food Security and Agriculture'.* 11-12 November. Kuala Lumpur, Malaysia.

Swift J. 1989. Why are rural people vulnerable to famine? *IDS [Institute for Development Studies] Bulletin Vol 20.* 2-April, pp 8-15.

Thapa D, Sijapati B. 2003. *A Kingdom under Siege: Nepal's Maoist Insurgency, 1996 to 2003.* Kathmandu: The Printhouse.

Thieme S. 2003. *Savings and Credit Associations and Remittances: The Case of Far West Nepalese Labour Migrants in Delhi, India.* Geneva: International Labour Organization (IOL), Working Paper No. 39.

Upreti B. 2004. *The Price of Neglect: From Resource Conflict to Maoist Insurgency in the Himalayan Kingdom.* Kathmandu: Bhrikuti Academic Publications.

USAID [United States Agency for International Development], New Era, MoHP [Ministry of Health and Population]. 2007. *Nepal Demographic and Health Survey*, 2006. Kathmandu: USAID, New Era and MoHP (Ministry of Health and Population).

Watts M. 1983. *The Silent Violence: Food, Famine and Peasantry in Northern Nigeria.* Berkeley: University of California Press.

Watts MJ, Bohle HG. 1993. The space of vulnerability: The casual structure of hunger and famine. *Progress in Human Geography* 17(1):43-67.

WFP [World Food Programme]. 2001. *Nepal Food Security and Vulnerability Profile 2000.* Kathmandu: World Food Programme.

Young H, Jaiper S, Brown R, Frize J, Khogali H. 2001. *Food Security Assessment in Emergencies: A Livelihood Approach.* ODI Working Paper. London: ODI [Overseas Development Institute].

* * * * *

CHAPTER 5

Corporate globalisation: Hunger and livelihood insecurity in Nepal

Yamuna Ghale

Abstract

This chapter deals with hunger and livelihood insecurity in the face of corporate globalisation. It argues that hunger and livelihood insecurity are a manifestation of structural causes that determine access to and control over means of production and participation in decision-making processes. It specifically argues that hunger is an even more complex phenomenon, determined not only by the availability, access and affordability of food, but by the meaningful participation of producers in production, value chain and decision-making processes, and influenced by the socio-political context and global economic forces. The concentration of resources, knowledge and power in the hands of multinational corporations as part of corporate globalisation is posing new challenges in the fight against hunger and livelihood insecurity, as well as threatening national food sovereignty. In addition, climate change and the promotion of bio-fuels worldwide have implications for food availability and an inherent relationship with trade and food prices, also affecting hunger, livelihood security and national food sovereignty. These issues have the potential to impact on the effective implementation of the Millennium Development Goals.

The right to be free from hunger is enshrined in various international instruments. However, corporate globalisation, liberalisation and privatisation have drastically altered the dynamics of the food production system and market processes. Hunger and food security in developing countries is impacted by global forces. Developed countries and international financial institutions, therefore, have a role to play in assisting developing countries to meet their international obligations to provide food security by increasing both technical and financial support.

Among the food insecure groups, economically poor and socially excluded groups are the most vulnerable. Hunger and livelihood insecurity have to be looked at within a broader framework of a livelihoods approach to ensure that vulnerable groups are protected. Developing countries such as Nepal must take advantage of the opportunities presented by international trade agreements, while protecting against threats posed by such agreements. In particular, farmers' rights must be protected to ensure the establishment of equitable and just production relations, and to promote conservation and the sustainable utilisation of natural resources, while at the same time promoting bio-prospecting, fair trade and the equitable sharing of the benefits of bio-prospecting through effective and inclusive policies and programmes.

Hence, it is clear that hunger and livelihood insecurity have multiple dimensions. These dimensions require closer analysis and commitment to understand the causes, contexts and implications of hunger and livelihood insecurity. If ignored, persistent hunger can result in starvation and even political and economic destabilisation.

5.1 Introduction

This Chapter establishes a relationship between corporate globalisation and hunger and livelihood insecurity, and examines these issues in the Nepalese context. Corporate globalisation, for the purpose of this Chapter, is looked at within the broader framework of economic, political and ecological aspects.

The conventional school of thought on hunger focuses on short-term measures to facilitate and alter the state of hunger and livelihood insecurity, emphasising service delivery as a response to the 'symptoms' of hunger. This school of thought is prevalent in the policies and practices of developing countries. However, there is a new school of thought that sees hunger as a political issue caused by the structural denial of access to and control over means of production within a feudal socio-political context, compounded by economic deprivation. The persistent denial of access to and control over means of production paralyses the production and purchasing capacity of people, especially of disadvantaged groups (DAGs)[1]. Advocates of the right to food and livelihood around the globe are demanding the unconditional implementation of the state's responsibility to adhere to basic principles to respect, protect and fulfil, and to realise its citizens' right to food. These principles secure people's right to organise themselves, to make informed choices, and to mobilise resources for sustained food sovereignty, and enable people from socially and economically disadvantaged groups around the globe to earn a dignified livelihood (AAI 2005).

Livelihood insecurity, for the purposes of this Chapter, refers to hunger, food insecurity, and the overall exclusion and denial of an individual's need for and right to a dignified life. The term 'livelihood', in contemporary development discourse, has strong inter-linkages with physical, natural, socio-political and financial assets, as well as an interface with human capital. Over two billion people around the world are engaged in agriculture for their livelihoods, but the majority of small producers and those dependent on the agriculture sector are systematically denied access to and control over means of production, excluded from decision-making processes, and, thus, rendered largely powerless. As a result, small farmers and disadvantaged groups are the hardest hit by hunger and livelihood insecurity in Nepal, and worldwide. Resource politics and the increasing influence of the global market economy pose new challenges and opportunities in promoting livelihood security for these groups. Hence, the central focus of this Chapter is on hunger and livelihood insecurity and their relationship with the structural causes of resource- based discrimination and unjust production relations. This Chapter

---

[1] Groups those are economically poor and socially discriminated.

analyses the causes and effects of hunger and livelihood insecurity to contribute to meaningful discourse in order to change societal attitudes and public policy for socio-economic transformation.

5.2 Corporate globalisation, hunger and livelihood insecurity: A conceptual framework

5.2.1 Corporate globalisation

Globalisation promotes the greater integration of national economies into the global system through the free movement of goods, services and capital. There is no agreement on what globalisation means or when it started; however, the first expansion of European colonialism in the 15th Century is generally considered the first period of globalisation. The roots of globalisation go back to the style of mercantilism practised in the 15th Century, which lasted until the 19th Century. Privatisation and liberalisation, based on classical economic theory (e.g., the theories of David Ricardo and Adam Smith), which firmly believe in economic growth-based poverty reduction, are leading the globalisation process today (Jawara & Kwa 2003). Friends of the Earth, an international organisation working on environmental issues for a healthier and more just world, considers ‘economic globalisation’ as a form of corporate globalisation that promotes the free movement of capital, the growth of multinational corporations (MNCs) and the integration of national economies into the global system. The threat of corporate globalisation is seen as its influence over state policy and people’s autonomy due to its large and expanding stake in national economies. It is feared that control by MNCs over the free trade system will lead to greater inequality between and within nations, worsening the livelihoods of the poor both in terms of assets and activities, and to the massive depletion of the natural and social environment (Friends of the Earth 2003). Globalisation, with its focus on economic reform through privatisation and liberalisation, is further criticised by those working in the fields of food security, agriculture, the environment and human rights, who interpret globalisation as a capitalist process that is unreasonably dominated by corporations and banking institutions, and which is largely unaccountable to democratic processes and national governments.

The process of globalisation is largely driven by the understandings and agreements made by the World Trade Organization (WTO). In principle, resource- poor member countries of the WTO are granted special and preferential privileges based on their 'non-reciprocity value'[2], in acknowledgement of their resource-poor condition, weak economic status and low trade competence. Non-reciprocity is one form of acceptance by developed countries of the need to support resource- poor countries to enhance their trade competence and to create a level playing field. This principle is believed to benefit all member countries of the WTO and other trade agreements by facilitating the free movement of goods, services and capital. However, globalisation today, which is predominantly led by corporate motives, controls global trade, the movement of goods, services, information, and technology, and the process of intellectual property rights. In the process of liberalisation and privatisation, unfair competition is escalating, and there is little possibility of equitable benefits to countries with poor economies.

In development discourse, there are many critiques of corporate globalisation due to its functioning mechanisms and negative impacts on the livelihoods of economically poor and socially discriminated people. The domination by corporations of the production and consumption of goods and services weakens state power and marginalises people's rights. In this process, the one-size-fits-all concept of profit-making corporate globalisation through liberalisation and privatisation has gradually encroached on basic services such as drinking water and health, and on food production, the value chain and marketing system. Farmers' organisations, civil society and environmentalists are urging nation states to be more cautious in regulating MNCs and to

---

2 Part IV of GATT under enabling clause there are three major provisions: i) preferences will be granted to developing countries, ii) can grant extensive and deeper preferences to LDCs, iii) S&DT provisions are hortatory not legally enforceable.

ensure that MNCs are accountable to the people and environment. The concept of corporate social responsibility is, thus, introduced as a way of mitigating environmental damage and to ensure improved livelihoods for poor and disadvantaged people. However, due to the voluntary nature of corporate social responsibility, many corporations still remain unaccountable to the people and society. Farmers' and land rights movements such as Via Campesina claim that economic globalisation driven purely by economic motives is undermining local and national sovereignty. Organisations like Via Campesina claim that production factors and the system should be controlled by local people and the state, rather than profit-oriented corporations. The seven principles of food sovereignty adopted by Via Campesina are presented in Box 5.1.

Box 5.1 Seven principles of food sovereignty adopted by Via Campesina

1. Food: A basic human right

Everyone must have access to safe, nutritious and culturally appropriate food in sufficient quantity and quality to sustain a healthy life with full human dignity. Each nation should declare that access to food is a constitutional right and guarantee the development of the primary sector to ensure the concrete realization of this fundamental right.

2. Agrarian reform

A genuine agrarian reform is necessary which gives landless and farming people – especially women

– ownership and control of the land they work and returns territories to indigenous peoples. The right to land must be free of discrimination on the basis of gender, religion, race, social class or ideology; the land belongs to those who work it.

3. Protecting natural resources

Food sovereignty entails the sustainable care and use of natural resources, especially land, water, and seeds and livestock breeds. The people who work the land must have the right to practice sustainable management of natural resources and to conserve biodiversity free of restrictive intellectual property rights. This can only be done from a sound economic basis with security of tenure, healthy soils and reduced use of agrochemicals.

4. Reorganising food trade

Food is first and foremost a source of nutrition and only secondarily an item of trade. National agricultural policies must prioritize production for domestic consumption and food self-sufficiency. Food imports must not displace local production nor depress prices.

5. Ending the globalization of hunger

Food sovereignty is undermined by multilateral institutions and by speculative capital. The growing control of multinational corporations over agricultural policies has been facilitated by the economic policies of multilateral organizations such as the WTO, World Bank and the IMF. Regulation and taxation of speculative capital and a strictly enforced Code of Conduct for Trans-national corporations is therefore needed.

6. Social peace

Everyone has the right to be free from violence. Food must not be used as a weapon. Increasing levels of poverty and marginalization in the countryside, along with the growing oppression of ethnic minorities and indigenous populations, aggravate situations of injustice and hopelessness. The ongoing displacement, forced urbanization, repression and increasing incidence of racism of smallholder farmers cannot be tolerated.

7. Democratic control

Smallholder farmers must have direct input into formulating agricultural policies at all levels. The United Nations and related organisations will have to undergo a process of democratization to enable this to become a reality. Everyone has the right to honest, accurate information and open and democratic decision-making. These rights form the basis of good governance, accountability and equal participation in economic, political and social life, free from all forms of discrimination. Rural women, in particular, must be granted direct and active decision making on food and rural issues.

Source: http://www.viacampesina.org/

The threat to people's rights and national sovereignty, as outlined above, is ever increasing. Global trade forums, like the WTO, and regional trade agreements (RTAs) are being used to promote privatisation and liberalisation based globalisation. Therefore, it is important to analyse how corporate globalisation affects smaller economies through the accumulation of resources, monopolisation of knowledge and concentration of power (see Figure 5.1).

Figure 5.1 Encroachment of corporate globalisation on resources, knowledge and power

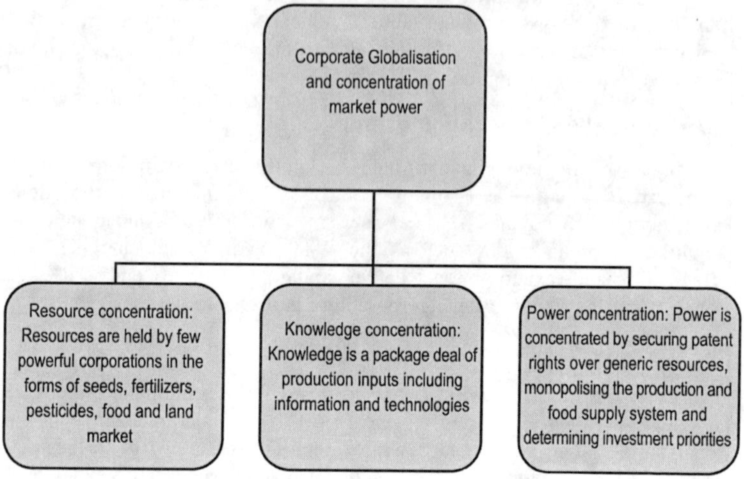

Resource concentration

The liberalisation and privatisation of goods and services requires a reliable and regular supply of primary resources and an adequately skilled workforce. It also requires a favourable policy framework and effective implementation mechanisms. In theory, privatisation does not necessarily imply that all MNCs are profit motivated. The process of globalisation can be regulated in a more inclusive and equitable manner to ensure the efficient provision of services, without losing the economic value of investors. However, in practice, this has not been the case. Concerns have been raised about the equitable distribution of resources, the existence of opportunities for all global trading partners and about the ability of benefit sharing mechanisms to deliver equitable benefits. The increasing concentration of power over market forces through the acquisition and merger of corporations at the international level impact on the ability of states to regulate trade and jeopardise local and customary practices in relation to resource distribution, governance and mobilisation. Economically weak countries face a dilemma as to how to reap the benefits of globalisation. Likewise, regional trading forums have not been effective in addressing the needs and concerns of developing countries, and specifically least developed countries (LDCs) and land locked developing countries (LLDCs). Despite the emergence of global trade forums like the WTO, Regional Trade Agreements are increasingly being activated in recent decades. According to the United Nations Conference for Trade and Development (UNCTAD), there were almost 300 Free Trade Agreements (FTAs) in existence in 2008, and an increasing proportion of world trade is governed by these agreements (UNCTAD 2005). FTAs heavily affect the agriculture sector, which is the basis of the livelihoods of rural poor in many developing countries. Commercial agriculture increasingly demands the intensive use of external resources to be competitive enough to meet national requirements and for export. This has led to the consolidation and concentration of productive land, privatisation of water resources, and the establishment of monopoly rights over genetic resources. In the same way, research and development priorities are determined by the interests of investors, who mostly prefer to promote lab-based technology development on market-led products. The sustainability of production resources is being encroached upon and threatened by the accumulation of bio-resources, the development of genetically modified plants, land acquisition, corporatisation and a high level of investment in profit-oriented crop development, processing and marketing, which is almost exclusive promoted by developed countries.

Knowledge concentration

The majority of people in developing countries still adopt agriculture as their livelihoods strategy. They possess a vast amount of associated traditional knowledge and skills in conserving, promoting and using bio-resources. Centuries- old customary rules and practices help in maintaining the balance between cultural values, social norms, livelihoods options and the sustainable use of bio- resources.

Investment patterns in the agriculture sectors of developed and developing countries vary greatly. Recently, there has been a steady trend of huge investment in agriculture sector protection and technology enhancement in developed countries.

Unfortunately, technology transfer mechanisms for the benefit of developing countries are either not in place or not effectively implemented. Developing countries are still struggling to develop crop varieties and livestock breeds within their public research systems. While there has been significant investment by private corporations in research and development in the food and agriculture sector, it has been of limited benefit to developing countries. Today's corporate globalisation is highly concentrated on high-tech information and technology, which carries a high risk of knowledge accumulation at resource rich laboratories. This has contributed in creating dependency in developing countries on resource rich countries and corporations. The trend of growing genetically modified (GM) crops is an example of how life science companies in the developed world are controlling resources and production systems. The cultivated area for GM crops is greatly increasing in developing countries, without understanding the long-term implications. According to International Service for the Acquisition of Agri-biotech Applications (ISAAA), who is monitoring the GM coverage worldwide, the number of countries growing GM crops rose from 6 in 1996, to 25 countries and covering 2 billion accumulated acres by the end of 2008 worldwide. It also predicts that the cumulative coverage of GM crops will increase to 4 billion acres by 2015 (FOCUS 2006)[3]. The GM crop promoting companies such as Monsanto, Dupont, Syngenta and Bayer Crop Science claim that consumers demand high quality nutritious food, the provision of which is possible only through GM technologies.

With the increase in GM crop production, biosafety is becoming an issue of great concern. Risks include possible gene pollution, and adverse effects on human safety and wellbeing, and on environmental health. Consumers have a right to information about the gene content of GM food crops. The Cartagena Protocol on Biosafety to the Convention on Biological Diversity (CBD) was adopted by the Conference of the Parties (CoP) to the CBD

---

[3] For additional information, also visit www.isaaa.org.

on 29 January 2000, with 187 parties and 103 signatories to date. The Parties to the Biosafety Protocol have an obligation to follow biosafety regulations, including those regarding the transboundary movement of GM products. According to Articles 7, 8, 9 and 11 of the Cartagena Protocol, recipient countries should be informed in advance of the shipment of GM crops; this is yet to be internalised and implemented (Focus 2006). To deal with the implications of GM regulation, the United Nations Environment Programme (UNEP) and the Global Environment Facility (GEF) have a mandate to support the development of national safety regulations. Similarly, the UN Codex Alimentarius has a mandate to regulate food safety, which covers GM food, and the WTO deals with trade in GM crops. The Sanitary and Phytosanitary (SPS) Agreement of the WTO is part of trade measures to deal with human, plant and animal health. The SPS clearly depicts the complexity of GM regulations and their wider application. The European Union is taking precautionary measures in relation to the commercialisation of GM crops by demanding the labelling of food with more than 0.9 per cent genetically modified components. However, the United States of America regards these precautions as a barrier to technology and trade (Focus 2006).

The increasing merger and concentration of life science companies and their interest in engaging in crops with commercial potential has led to a gradual decrease in investment in traditional crops and varietal improvement processes. This has directly eroded the diversity of local gene pools and the associated knowledge of small farmers in developing countries and created further dependency on the market to secure source seeds for next generation production. It has also seriously undermined the potential use and promotion of indigenous knowledge, practices and skills of women and indigenous people.

The increasing use of mono-cropping and consequent loss of diversity has created the risk of crop failure due to an increased incidence of insects and pests, as well as lack of proper knowledge and information from seed sellers. Such crops are also often uncompetitive due to the high cost of production, all of which affects the profit margin to producers and negatively impacts on food security. It is estimated that the top 10 seed corporations around the globe hold 49 to 51 per cent of the commercial seed market, and the top 10 agro-chemical corporations control 84 per cent of the agro-chemical market. Similarly, all GM seeds are bio-patented by multinational corporations: 13 commercial corporations own 80 per cent of the GM food market (Voice of Irish Concern for the Environment 2009). Countries with vulnerable economies are becoming dependent on imported seed and associated technologies.

The use of imported seeds, mostly for commercial farming, has led to mono- cropping; this is an increasing phenomenon even in rural Nepal. In countries like Nepal, other means of support for agricultural productivity and marketing structures are not yet well established. Consequently, the open market and free flow of imported seeds has created dependency, led to the deterioration of indigenous knowledge and required farmers to deal with competitive markets. Additionally, the use of imported seed and food items in the form of relief support after natural or human induced disasters is becoming an entry point for market-led seeds, which creates further dependency on the market. There is much speculation about the impact of the use of GM foods in developing countries as part of food aid. Concerns include the displacement of local seeds and associated knowledge through the promotion and dissemination of hybrid or genetically modified seeds either in the form of seed or processed food. The use of GM products in food aid has also been frequently questioned on ethical grounds. Risks are associated with diminishing the local knowledge and resource base, promoting monoculture, the use of imported seeds and inputs, and control over the knowledge system. In the long term this can be a threat to sustainable agriculture and food security.

Increasing knowledge concentration is not only a threat to the farming system in developing countries, but also to the sustainable food security of the local people and the sovereignty of the country of origin over bio-resources.

Power concentration

Globalisation led by the WTO regime and free trade campaign is a process of integrating the free market into global development processes. In principal, all member countries, irrespective of their level of economic development, have an equal right to share power in the global trade forum. However, lack of access to resources, weak institutional framework and human resource base, poor investment competence, and poor bargaining capacity restricts the participation of developing countries. As a result, they are constantly marginalised. Due to the different nature of the vulnerability of developing countries, particularly LDCs[4], they are entitled to receive special and differential treatment (S&DT) from developed countries and international financial institutions (IFIs) under the framework of the WTO to compensate for structural asymmetries. However, many LDCs cannot fully enjoy S&DT due to political instability and weak bargaining power, as well as lack of commitment by developed countries and IFIs. Likewise, market access by developing countries is restricted due to stringent requirements imposed by developed countries such as (i) maximum residue limit (MRL), (ii) packaging materials, and (iii) transit treaties and conditionality. The WTO has envisioned and acknowledged the vulnerability of LDCs in specific agreements, and the General Agreement on Tariffs and Trade (GATT) 1994 (the predecessor of the WTO) contains at least 16 different agreements on S&DT to enhance the trading capacity of LDCs.[5] The main thrust of these agreements is pro-LDCs in all aspects of economic growth, the development of human resource and per capita income growth. Unfortunately, so far, these agreements have not been fully implemented. The major provisions specifically in favour of LDCs are in the Marrakesh Agreement, establishing the WTO, which mentions

---

4 LDCs are group of countries identified based on three main criteria; i) gross national income per capita, ii) Human Asset Index, and iii) Economic Vulnerability Index. There are currently 49 members and Nepal assumed chair of LDCs from December 2009 for four years.

5 The details of the World Trade Agreement 1994 (establishing the WTO and including GATT Uruguay 1994) can be found at www.wto.org (accessed 5 January 2010).

the special need to respond to the vulnerability of LDCs created through market distortion and instability in the world market. Similarly, acknowledging the weak trading capacity of LDCs, it contains provisions for support to LDCs through technical and financial assistance and by enhancing trading capacities. For example, international financial institutions (IFIs) such as the World Bank (WB) and the International Monetary Fund (IMF) have provisions to provide financial support to compensate for the negative impacts caused by trade asymmetries such as, for example, the increased food import bill of LDCs.

Similarly, there are provisions for an exemption in relation to the provision of subsidies on production inputs to low input resource poor (LIRP) farmers of developing countries and LDCs, which is calculated based on Aggregated Measure Support (AMS). Similarly, GATT Part 4 on trade and development includes a provision for special and preferential privileges based on the principal of non-reciprocity and on S&DT to enhance the production and trading capacity of LDCs and LLDCs.

Another important area of debate and contention is protectionism in the agriculture sector especially in developed countries, which receives substantial support through tariff protection and by way of direct and indirect subsidies. According to the WTO, for example, the developed countries were supposed to reduce their tariffs by 36 per cent by 2000 and developing countries by the same rate by 2005, unfortunately, these commitments were not met. In this process, six multilateral institutions, the WTO, WB, UNCTAD, IMF, International Trade Centre (ITC) and United Nations Development Programme (UNDP), have created a common fund referred as the 'integrated framework', which can be mobilised for demand driven, ownership oriented and resource efficient support to vulnerable economies. However, developing countries most often receive support for policy development rather than for institutional and human resources capacity and infrastructural development. At the same time, developed countries are constantly providing farm subsidies to their farmers. However, both bilateral and multilateral development assistance in the agriculture sector has been steadily decreasing since the early nineties (FAO 2009), which can be seen in Figure 5.2.

Figure 5.2 Share of official development assistance in agriculture sector

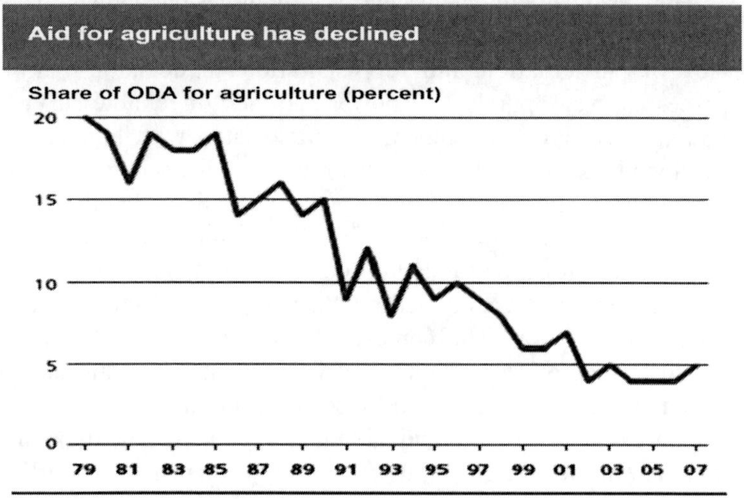

Source: Adapted from WFP and FAO (2009)

Farm subsidies in developed countries are constantly been criticised as a trade distorting factor in the global trade regime. In recent decades, the redirection of subsidies in the agriculture sector by developed countries, either in the name of bio-fuel production or to mitigate the negative impacts of climate change, has received much attention. Subsidies in developed countries play an important role in the substitution of local products and production systems in developing countries as the subsidies make such products and systems cheaper than local goods. Likewise, the volatile and unpredictable alliance of developing countries at the regional and global level does not put them in a good position to negotiate with developed countries on subsidy issues. Global and regional trade forums are constantly being used as platforms by economically powerful countries from which to exercise power, rather than to create a level playing field for all member countries. The overall trend of resource concentration linked to knowledge accumulation and power pose a threat to developing countries, specifically LDCs and can have a detrimental impact on hunger and livelihood security.

5.2.2 Hunger and livelihood insecurity

Hunger and livelihood insecurity are complex phenomena. They are the manifestation of denial of access to means of production, lack of participation and representation in decision-making processes, weak purchasing power and lack of reliable survival options. The level of vulnerability associated with hunger and livelihood insecurity differs at the individual, household, national, sub-national and international levels, as defined by the Food and Agriculture Organization (FAO). At the individual level, vulnerability might be limited to food consumption and utilisation patterns, further compounded by other important factors such as water consumption. The context becomes more complex when linked to macro issues such as availability, stability and access, which are largely determined by socio-economic conditions and the institutional, cultural and natural environment. The dynamics that determine hunger and livelihood insecurity are further linked to policy, which is governed by national governments and international commitments. Therefore, dealing with hunger and livelihood insecurity requires multiple efforts by different actors at different levels.

Likewise, the commitments made by heads and or representatives of nation states during the World Food Summit (WFS) and to the Millennium Development Goals (MDGs) have brought the issue of food security forward. These international instruments deal not only with aspects of the immediate situation of hunger, but also with long-term and interrelated issues, such as access to means of production, enhancing competitiveness and market potential, the role of developed countries and IFIs in supporting countries with weak economies, and opportunities for south- south trade, and so forth. The hunger index adopted by FAO and the MDGs deals with production factors and market dynamics, as well as the interdependence between countries at various stages of economic development (i.e., strong, newly emerging and weak economies). However, the recent trend of corporate globalisation, directly and indirectly impacts on immediate market relations leading to changes in food basket composition, an increase in malnutrition, and a risk of external shocks due to trade imbalances and emergencies; these are serious threats to developing countries.

These invisible causes of hunger and livelihood insecurity have been largely overlooked in economic development discourse, especially since the establishment of the WTO in 1995. The repercussions of failing to address systematic issues in trade governance are great and costly in the long run. Various studies have shown that the current state of hunger and livelihood insecurity is further deepened by the lack of ability of developing countries to adjust properly to the global economic and technological developments. For example, the import of cheap chickens from the European Union to the Philippines has destabilised the local production of poultry. Similarly, the import of cheap chickens from the US to Mozambique has jeopardised the local system (AAI 2005; OXFAM 2005).

The liberalisation and privatisation of means of production and processes has brought substantial change to agrarian production processes. It has resulted in the displacement of rural producers from subsistence agriculture to urban areas in search of better livelihood options, as subsistence farming is no longer providing a sufficient livelihood. The weakening of production processes and the increasing consumption of imported foods has drastically altered the food system in many developing countries. A study carried out by Jagaran Media Centre in Nepal found that only 26 per cent of people in Nepal are food self-sufficient. The study also highlighted that there are around 90 national food industries in Nepal, which account for 19.5 per cent of the total industries. This confirms that packaged foods produced locally or imported are becoming an inherent component of the food system in Nepal (Basnet & Darnal 2007). The paradigm shift in understanding hunger and livelihood insecurity has opened alternative avenues of response to the new challenges and opportunities presented by corporate globalisation. The concept and state of visible hunger has been transformed into a more invisible and complex form of hunger that is beyond the control of nation states and communities. The dynamics of hunger and livelihood insecurity are becoming more complex and increasingly controlled by market forces, and the role of the state is weakened.

Defining food security and livelihoods and opting for the best possible options at both micro and macro levels is vital. In the changing context in which food security is recognised as a right, and to respond to the increasing threat of market control over the food chain, the concept of 'food sovereignty' is gaining momentum. It is important to note that ensuring individual food security leads to national food security, but the converse is not necessarily true: individual food security is not guaranteed by national food security.

Ensuring food security is a complex task. It requires adequate and equitable allocation, ownership and utilisation of productive resources; access to safe drinking water; a balanced mix in the food basket; proper cooking and utilisation methods; and the knowledge and skills to appropriately deal with market forces. Adequate and timely irrigation, combined with the use of improved seeds, fertilizers and other technologies can enhance crop production by up to 30 per cent. However, most rural agriculture in the developing world still relies on rainfall for irrigation, which puts farmers at risk of crop failure or poor harvests. Although only one sixth of the world's farmed area is irrigated, these farms produce 40 per cent of the world's food (Rijsberman 2008). Today, water scarcity is becoming a global concern, but water privatisation is a lucrative sector for profit-oriented investment. Therefore, access to and the equitable distribution of water resources for irrigation and safe drinking water is a vital part of ensuring human rights and essential to increase agriculture production and improve food security. The recent trend of privatisation of basic services including water resources is a threat to people's right to water. For example, the privatisation of drinking water in Ghana raised the price of drinking water to 3,000 Cedis (US$ 1) for 10 buckets of water, when the per capita daily income was 7,000 Cedis. Likewise, water privatisation in Bolivia increased the cost of water by 200 per cent and in South Africa by 140 per cent. In India, 60 per cent of the water is polluted with insecticides and pesticides (Navadanya 2003; IPS 2005). This illustrates how the privatisation of water has introduced complexity into the production chain and food consumption patterns, and increased the risk of denial of access to safe drinking water and water for irrigation.

Among the poor, women in particular suffer more from the privatisation of water as high water costs force women and girls to spend more time collecting water from local sources, sometimes at a great distance. Similarly, expensive water limits the affordability of water for basic necessities. Nepal made a commitment to open 11 service sectors and 76 sub-sectors to privatisation (Bhandari et al. 2005) as part of its accession to the WTO; this has opened up the possibility of water privatisation. As Nepal is a water resource rich country, privatisation could further limit access to safe drinking water and irrigation, especially for resource poor farmers. In this context, initiatives like Water Vision-Pakistan, which prepare a long-term framework in coordination with different stakeholders, are crucial. This initiative has identified the gaps and advocated for the effective conservation of water, enhancement of water efficiency, equitable distribution of water, establishment of cffective pricing policies, good governance and the development of investment systems (Bengali 2003). Such initiatives provide a strong basis for resource specific analysis and can lead to the adoption of appropriate measures to contribute to eradicating hunger and poverty.

The agriculture sector has a multifunctional character linked with food, culture, environment and economy. This makes agriculture one of the most important sectors in relation to hunger and livelihood issues. However, the tendency to deal with hunger and livelihood issues from a sectoral perspective is one of the major obstacles to a consolidated solution to address the root causes of hunger and livelihood insecurity. Understanding and dealing with starvation, hunger and livelihood insecurity requires different and informed approaches. Starvation, in general, is a lack of enough food to eat over a particular time period within a particular context. It is important to realise that hunger can and does persist in the absence of starvation (FAO & UNDP 2008). Hunger is a deeper, systematic, and more complex phenomenon, which has been ignored by policymakers for many years. Dealing with persistent hunger, thus, requires understanding of the problem and systematic efforts by different actors.

In this context, it is important to understand the different forms of hunger presented below.

Acute or transient hunger

This form of hunger is caused by immediate circumstances such as a natural disaster (drought or flood), market disruption, or an ineffective supply chain at the local level. These circumstances can have a direct impact on physiological state and immediate access to food and production resources, which can lead to famine in certain localities at a particular time and to health problems such as influenza and diarrhoea if not addressed properly and in a timely manner.

Chronic hunger

According to FAO, people who have access to less than 1710 to 1960 kcal per day are considered to be chronically hungry. This form of hunger is generally a manifestation of the systematic denial of access to productive resources and weak purchasing power. This form of hunger can inflict permanent damage on human life due to sustained uncertainty about access to productive resources and other means of livelihood. In the long run, it can cause malnutrition and poor health, which can affect the attainment of improved livelihoods.

Hidden hunger

This form of hunger is complex and remains invisible in many instances. It is generally triggered by macro-level economic alignment and structural adjustment processes. Sometimes, the economic processes undermine the leverage and space for developing nation states to challenge the negative implications of macro- economic reforms. The influence can be seen in the production system, changes in food habits and the food basket composition, capture of the food supply chain by corporations, and the commodification and privatisation of productive resources. Corporate control ultimately creates dependency and paralyses the purchasing capacity of people. In the long run, food can become a political weapon, altering power relations and threatening national sovereignty.

In this scenario, the victims of chronic and hidden hunger are often the poor and disadvantaged people. This group of the people usually do not have an organised voice, access to information, representation in decision-making processes or political power to alter the rule of the games. The consistent ignorance of policymakers of persistent hunger and weak political commitment can lead to transient or acute hunger. The cost of recovery at that level, including rebuilding the local production system and adopting resilient measures, can be very high.

5.2.3 Right to food and livelihoods

Food is the basic necessity for human survival. Therefore, the right to food is considered to be akin to the right to life. Many international provisions have enshrined the right to food and livelihood as basic tenets of the right to life.

In 1948, the United Nations Declaration on Human Rights (UNDHR) in Article 25 adopted the 'Right to Food' for all, with special attention to widows, children and the elderly. Many other instruments, such as the Convention on Eradication of all forms of Domestic Violence Against Women (CEDAW), Convention on the Rights of the Child (CRC), International Covenant on Civil and Political Rights (ICCPR), and International Covenant on Economic, Social and Cultural Rights have also amply recognised the right to food and the right to access to means of production. These international instruments focus on the state's obligation to take into account the concerns of special categories of people such as children and women.

The concept of food security is a fundamental element of understanding hunger. FAO adopted the following definition of food security in 1996 during the World Food Summit: "Food security exists when all people, at all times, have physical and economic access to sufficient, safe, nutritious and adequate food to meet their dietary needs for an active and healthy life" (FAO 1996). FAO considers the right to food as a basic right and adopted it in an information paper on 'Safety Nets and the

Right to Food'. This paper considers hunger and livelihood security as part of a food and social safety net and highlights the importance of access to means of production; it also sets out the requirements of the safety net (FAO 2004). The 127th Session of FAO adopted the Voluntary Guideline on Right to Food in 2004. This guideline categorically defines the role of the state as to respect, fulfil and protect and to realise its citizens' right to food. The Guideline provides very pragmatic options that can support nation states to formulate necessary policy measures and programmes as required.

Global commitments envisage nation states as having the primary responsibility for ensuring food security. Similarly, nation states are also responsible for ensuring access to means of production, creating enough opportunity to enhance people's purchasing capacity, and eliminating gender, class and caste-based discrimination to fight against hunger and livelihood insecurity. In this endeavour, the role of the international community is specified as to enhance the competence of countries with weaker economies through technical and financial support.

5.2.4 Myths about hunger and livelihood insecurity

Hunger and livelihood insecurity are relative terms. Different levels of progress in economic, political and social development in the world have shifted our understanding, interpretation and way of dealing with hunger and livelihood insecurity. Free market theory based on corporate globalisation promotes the dominant role of economic growth in poverty reduction. In this context, food is perceived as a tradable commodity and means of production are being increasingly privatised. This trend has sparked concern over the control of food systems by profit-oriented private companies. Since the production system is guided by commercial interests and productive resources are increasingly being privatised and private monopolies extended, the gap has widened between resource rich and poor countries. Experiences around the world have not yet shown equitable and tangible benefits of free trade to developing countries. For example, of the total GM seed market, 80 per cent is under the control of 13 MNCs, which limits resource poor people's choices associated with new seeds, advanced knowledge, technology and information. There are many myths about globalisation, hunger and livelihood insecurity, which we will take a closer look at here.

Myth 1: Food security can be enhanced through free trade

The promoters of corporate globalisation firmly believe that economic growth accelerated through free trade can ensure food security and livelihood promotion (Jawara & Kwa 2003). Another school of thought advocates that food is the basic means of survival and that economic issues should not be given primacy over human rights. In today's world, enough food is produced. However, 24 per cent of people in Sub-Saharan Africa and 61 per cent in Asia and the Pacific were undernourished in the period from 2001 to 2003 (FAO 2008). Similarly, in Nepal, an agriculture-based economy, 40 districts out of 75 are categorised as food insecure and the trade deficit is 165 billion, 330 million. Nepal adopted a liberal economic policy in the early eighties and has been a Net Food Importing Developing Countries (NFIDC) since that time. Nepal's massive trade deficit is a clear indication that free trade is not the only, or even the best, solution for dealing with hunger and livelihood insecurity. To ensure food security for all, it is necessary to understand the dynamics of food production and availability, and the distribution mechanism.

Myth 2: Free trade facilitates economic growth and reduces poverty

Economic globalisation can bring remarkable growth at a macro level and profit for competitive multinational companies and, hence, for developed countries. However, it exacerbates inequality between and within nation (Friends of the Earth 2003). Due to weak economic power, unpredictable alliances among likeminded nation states and the institutional vulnerability of developing countries, local and small producers in developing countries are not competitive enough to reap the benefits promised by economic growth theory. Developing countries, on the other hand, are under constant pressure to fulfil the additional commitments beyond the originally agreed provisions of the WTO, which makes them more vulnerable. The increasing budget in the agriculture sector in the developed world and the dumping of their surpluses or cheap subsidised products has further widened the gap, between developed and developing countries trade potentials, rather than reducing inequality and poverty. A study carried out by Action Aid Nepal on the surge in rice imports showed that India's share of Nepal's total rice imports fluctuated between 93 to 100 per cent between 1996/97 and 2003/04 (AAN 2005). It shows the vulnerability of Nepal's rice market and the impact of the dumping of Indian rice on the local market. Hence, free trade and classical economic policy are not the most effective way for developing countries to increase economic growth and reduce poverty, or for reducing the gap between developed and developing countries. On the contrary, free trade can have a negative effect on economic growth and poverty in developing countries.

Myth 3: Free trade gives consumers access to quality and cheap products

In principal, economic liberalisation can facilitate free trade, irrespective of geographical boundaries, and can enhance people's access to a wide range of consumable goods and services. However, increasing imbalanced trade can lead to fiscal imbalances in developing countries, which can affect both short and long- term coping strategies. The privatisation and liberalisation of both agricultural and industrial sectors in developing countries has brought these industries to the verge of extinction due to global competition. It has increased the vulnerability context. Privatisation and liberalisation has reduced the pool of human resources available in developing countries by displacing unskilled and low-skilled workers who are attracted to work in other job markets, reducing developing countries' production potential. Therefore, cheap products do not necessarily ensure sustainable income and or increase people's ability to cope with external shocks created by international market dynamics. If not well consider or managed in a timely way, privatisation and liberalisation can create an external dependency and contribute to livelihood insecurity. Currently soaring global food prices are also a manifestation of the imbalance between investment priorities, resource management and the sharing of benefits. According to World Bank estimates, global food prices have risen 83 per cent over the last three years due to the increasing use of arable land to produce crops for bio-fuel, the relative inelasticity of supply, and low speculative investments, and food prices are predicted to rise by another 50 per cent by 2030 (Chatham House 2008). Nine remote districts of Nepal surveyed evidenced an increase in food prices by up to 40 per cent, from July to December 2008 compared to the same period of study in 2007 (MoAC & WFP 2008).

Myth 4: Promotion of biotechnology such as genetic engineering is the best way to overcome hunger and poverty

The promotion and transfer of technology is an important factor in global food production and the global distribution chain. However, the recent trend of genetic engineering through the transfer of transgenic genes and the granting of monopoly rights over processes and products restrict farmers' rights over genetic resources. This can create a dependency on life science companies for the use of genetic resources and production inputs. It can also erode the gene pool and have a negative impact on human health and the environment through gene pollution and the excessive use of external chemical inputs. The technologies promoted through biotechnology may not necessarily ensure easy and equitable access and are not necessarily compatible and affordable for small farmers in developing countries. Likewise, developing countries that are rich in natural resources do not have the capacity to invest in research and development of new varieties of plants, animal breeds and innovative technologies. In Nepal, 66 per cent of people are engaged in agriculture for their livelihoods, but the total budget allocated to the agriculture sector is limited and insufficient. There is a clear gap between sectoral prioritisation, resource allocation, programme implementation and expected outputs. There is also a need to invest more in the promotion of indigenous knowledge and technology-based innovation. Such investment is a more effective and sustainable solution to the problem of hunger and livelihood insecurity than reliance on imported biotechnologies promoted by commercially motivated companies.

Myth 5: Free trade regulates the global market

The promoters of globalisation believe in letting the market operate global trade. However, there are no laws or regulations requiring corporations to be responsible towards the people and societies in which they function. A free but unregulated market can undermine people's autonomy and weaken state functioning through encroachment on the production chain, and even on the policy and regulatory domains. The role of bilateral agreements in this cannot be denied. For example, the Nepal-India Trade Treaty allows duty-free trade in primary agricultural products between Nepal and India. However, to date, the benefit of the 1700 km of open border between Nepal and India has been enjoyed mostly by India. Nepal has not received the same benefits for many reasons. For example, the huge concentration of rice mills in the Terai belt on the Nepal side of the border are shrinking, and the capacity of the mills has been reduced as the import of rice to Nepal through both formal and informal channels has undercut local producers (AAN 2005). The trade potential of Nepal has been increasingly limited as the Government of Nepal, for many socio-political reasons has not been able to negotiate and take full advantage of provisions in the bilateral treaty with India, other regional trade agreements and the various global trade platforms. This alarming situation can exacerbate the gap between trading partners. Therefore, free trade should be considered as only one of many vehicles for promoting economic growth. The primary concern should be to share the benefits of trade and growth equitable based on principles of social justice.

Myth 6: Multilateral trade forums are good for economically poor countries

In principle, all the member countries of multilateral trade forums, irrespective of their share in global trade, should have equal status and an equal right to participate and table their concerns. With the expectation of receiving equal space and that their voices will be heard, many developing countries, including LDCs have been motivated to join global trade forums like the WTO. Likewise, aligning with regional trade agreements is also an increasing trend. These forums give developing countries hope of enhancing their trade competence and becoming equal trading partners. However, developing countries, especially LDCs, are increasingly being excluded from mainstream negotiation processes and their interests ignored, raising concerns over the motives of economically powerful trading partners. Similarly, negotiations in relation to bilateral trading arrangements are based on unequal power relations and often guided by political interests. Subtle pressure is exerted on politically unstable and economically vulnerable countries to align themselves with regional and multilateral trade regimes. For example, Nepal was pressurised by some of the developed country members of the WTO to adopt the Plant Variety Protection Act in line with the Union for Protection of Plant Varieties (UPOV) in its last accession specific negotiations held in Geneva in 2003. This is a clear example of WTO-plus conditionality. Likewise, increasing demands to adopt reciprocal measures has seriously hampered Nepal's autonomy. At times, Nepal has given in to such pressure simply due to in adequate preparation/homework on the issues, lack of trained human resources, weak political commitment and lack of policy space for poor countries in different trade forums. Organising developing countries on common agendas improves their internal governance, and promoting south-south trade and asserting rights to receive both technical and financial resources to improve the trade potential of developing countries is important to minimise the risks and optimise the benefits of membership of multilateral trade forums.

5.2.5 Global situation of hunger and livelihood insecurity

FAO data shows that the food available in the world is enough to provide 2,760 kcal per person for the existing population of the world. However, an estimated 854 million people worldwide are undernourished, which is quite alarming and also makes meeting the MDGs a challenge. People who consume food less than 1,710 to 1,960 kcal per day are considered to be chronically hungry. Of the total undernourished people in the world, about 800 million live in developing countries, and most are poor and small farmers (FAO 2008). Approximately one third of the hungry and micronutrient deficient people of the world live in Asia and the Pacific. Similarly, despite their huge contribution to agriculture, women are most vulnerable to hunger constituting 60 per cent of those living in hunger. According to FAO estimates, global food production will rise by 1.6 per cent by 2015. Hence, there is much speculation about how current rates of food production in the world will meet trade and fiscal imbalances. If the current rate of progress remains, it will take at least 120 years to reach the target of the first Millennium Development Goal and World Food Summit commitment: to halve hunger by 2015 (FAO 2005). This proves that production is not the only factor that determines food security at the micro and macro level and illustrates the importance of dealing with different pillars of food security such as production, availability, accessibility, affordability and utilisation patterns. To achieve the MDG target of halving hunger by 2015, we must overcome fundamental problems associated with access to and control over means of production; improve availability of food and develop effective distribution mechanisms; provide alternative employment opportunities to enable people to meet their basic requirements; and develop systematic responses to disaster induced situations. In the changing context of globalisation, food is considered a tradable commodity and is becoming inaccessible to economically and socially disadvantaged groups, especially women and children. The global agricultural trade scenario shows that 71 per cent of exports and 75 per cent of imports are governed by developed countries; in comparison, the least developed countries' agricultural exports grew from 0.4 of world trade in 1994 to 0.8 in 2004 but imports grew faster from 0.4 to 1.1 (OECD 2005). This highlights the complexity of the global food system and the increasing vulnerability of economically resource poor countries. Hence, a multi-pronged and holistic approach is needed to tackle the causes of hunger and livelihood insecurity. It is important to develop a deeper understanding of hunger and livelihood insecurity and to analyse the inter-linkages between different factors in order to adopt a progressive approach to dealing with the issues within a broader framework. The right to food, including safety net measures, is explicitly acknowledged by FAO in an information paper on Safety Nets and the Right to Food (FAO 2006).

Hunger is increasingly being understood as a political phenomenon within the larger framework of food sovereignty. Different international organisations such as Action Aid International, Green Peace, OXFAM, Third World Network, Friends of the Earth, Pesticide Action Network, Via Campesina, various Swiss NGOs and others believe that access to and control over productive resources such as land, water, credit and knowledge are prime factors that determine the food and livelihood security of small farmers, fisher folk and indigenous communities. Access to nutritious food is necessary to be able to remain productive in terms of access to education, health services and improved income. In this context, the risk associated with the free flow of GM seeds and food is high on the agenda of different farmers' organisations and likeminded networks. These organisations urge developed countries and commercial life science companies to provide scientific evidence of the safety of GM products for human kind and the environment before commercially supplying GM products. The Swiss Agency for Development and Cooperation (SDC) considers the establishment of effective regulatory mechanisms to ensure secure and sustainable technology promotion as of the utmost importance. In the Swiss referendum of 2005, voters approve a five-year moratorium on GM foods with due consideration of biotechnology-based research and GM food import (Focus 2006). The constant promotion of GM can undermine people's right to access to and control over means of production and to safe food, as well as the need for a safety net to ensure that disadvantaged communities have a secure livelihood options. Therefore, hunger must be dealt as a political issue.

The dynamics of the global food system have been dramatically altered in recent years due to the increasing promotion and consumption of bio-fuel. Soaring food prices have been understood and interpreted differently by politicians and economists. The decision to invest in bio-fuel, the changing production patterns, investment in research and development, and the links with global trade have all received increasing attention lately due to global price hikes. The promotion of alternative energy to reduce dependency on fossil fuel and also as a response to climate change to reduce carbon emissions has directly affected not only global trade, but also the food security and safety of many vulnerable communities in developing countries. Various studies have shown that climate change will alter the global production system. For example, 11 per cent of the land in Southern Africa will be unsuitable for growing crops by 2080, whereas land suitable for growing cereal in North America could increase by 40 per cent (IDS 2008). This model clearly evidences the possible increment of crops produced for bio-fuel, which could affect food security through its impact on food availability and prices, as well as making less food available for food aid worldwide.

Resource rich countries have already implemented measures to protect their agriculture sectors, as well as improve bio-fuel production targets. The cattle feed industry in the USA increasingly uses maize for ethanol production and produces cattle feed from the residue. The EU has realised the implications of the cereal shortage and adopted measures to set-aside agriculture land to produce around 10 to 15 million tons of extra grain to meet its internal requirements. China has discontinued the use of agriculture crops for bio-energy to ensure food sufficiency (Skimma 2008). At the same time, some countries have increased their investment in food aid to support the countries hardest hit by the soaring food prices. For example, the US congress approved US$ 770 million, Japan US$ 100 million, the UK US$ 59 million and Canada US$ 50 million for food aid. The support system benefits resource poor countries in terms of short-term relief, but it is equally important to understand the long-term implications of global trade negotiations and the diversion of resources in the form of subsidies, against the provisions of the WTO.

5.3 Role of trade in achieving the Millennium Development Goals

In 2000, the world leaders made a firm decision to tackle poverty and address inequality and exclusion through the Millennium Development Goals. The eight goals of the MDGs are given in Box 5.2.

Box 5.2 Eight Millennium Development Goals

Goal 1: Eradicate extreme poverty and hunger
Goal 2: Achieve universal primary education
Goal 3: Promote gender equality and empower women
Goal 4: Reduce child mortality
Goal 5: Improve maternal health
Goal 6: Combat HIV/AIDS, malaria and other diseases
Goal 7: Ensure environmental sustainability
Goal 8: Develop a global partnership for development

All the MDG goals have either a direct and or indirect role in ensuring the right of every citizen to be free from hunger and to adopt sustainable livelihood measures. The target of halving poverty and hunger by 2015 envisages trade as playing an important role from the micro to the macro level. With corporate globalisation, trade plays an unavoidable role in poverty and hunger. It has altered the dynamics of trade and 'aid for development' is gradually being shifting to 'aid for trade' in global development discourse (GCAP 2005). With the increasing realisation that hunger is a political issue, a worldwide movement is taking place to make poverty history and create a just and dignified society in which everyone can enjoy their basic rights without compromising their culture and national interests. However, the real challenge is to ensure the faithful implementation of the commitments made by nation states and IFIs to accelerate just and viable economic growth.

The disparity in benefits received from trade by different global trade partners is becoming more and more evident. The continued protection in the agriculture sector and non-cooperation by developed countries towards their commitments to support developing countries are major obstacles to fair trade. Cheap imports from developed countries have displaced people from local job markets in developing countries. On the export side, access to markets by developing countries is also limited by trade barriers such as the tariff formulation process, the ineffective implementation of tariff reduction, and by various non-tariff measures such as quality standards, which have hampered the trade potential of developing countries. Tariff escalations (charges that increase with the stages of value addition), tariff peaks (high levels of tariffs on certain sensitive products) and tariff dispersion (an increase in tariffs within the bound level when there is a high production of certain farm products) are major barriers to agriculture trade. In South Africa, the elimination of tariffs and subsidies hit maize producers and the farm workforce fell by 14 per cent (AAI 2005). Hence, developed countries are reluctant to reduce tariffs and subsidies, despite commitments to do so under the various WTO provisions.

Among global trade, the share of agricultural from developing countries was 13.3 per cent in 2004, of which LDCs contributed less than 0.5 per cent (UNCTAD 2005). Of the 4,162 products exported by LDCs to 30 major trading partners, 127 products account for 90 per cent of the export trade, showing a clear lack of product diversification. One-third of LDCs are landlocked and, therefore, have to overcome transit hurdles to access international markets. LDCs are motivated to integrate their economies with the global trade system in hope of better and quality investment, technology transfer, and of increasing their trade potential in the international market to improve trade and fiscal imbalances and reduce poverty. However, the concerns of LDCs and LLDCs are heightened as they have still not received substantial technical assistance, capacity building and trade facilitation for market access for LDC products. LDCs and LLDCs are generally characterised by underdeveloped infrastructure, a weak industrial base, high dependence on foreign assistance in national development planning and limited possibilities for economic diversification, as well as by exposure to associated environmental risks.

The potential of south-south trade has been recognised and emphasised by UNCTAD as a way of improving trade efficiency with little investment and low transaction costs. Primary commodities play an important role in south-south trade, more so than in south-north trade (UNCTAD 2005). Recognising this, and with a consistent understanding of the hunger that exists in the region, the South Asian Association for Regional Cooperation (SAARC) is working to address these issues from a regional perspective. The SAARC Plan of Action on Poverty Alleviation focuses on land administration, the provision of a safety net in the form of food assistance to vulnerable groups, and faster progress in negotiations within the South Asia Free Trade Agreement (SAFTA) as a regional effort. It is also working towards the development of a joint position before international institutions like the WTO. Likewise, SAARC has highlighted the removal of tariff and non-trade barriers and protectionism as important external policy measures. There has also been agreement among SAARC members for a regional Food Reserve containing wheat and rice stock of no less than 125,000 metric tons for use by member states in case of natural and human induced calamities, and to be replaced by recipient member states within not more than one calendar year of use (SAARC 2005a & b). Nepal committed to contribute 3600 metric tons by January 2002, and ultimately contributed 4000 metric tons. Therefore, SAARC members need to assess the production as well as trade potential of each member countries within SAARC to make provisional arrangements in responding to hunger and food insecurity.

Unfortunately, there has been constant non-cooperation by developed countries in formalising and implementing the Special & Differential Treatment (S&DT) for LDCs, including provisions for food aid. In addition, developed countries have failed to honour commitments to reduce subsidies for agriculture, which is one of major trade distorting factors. Market access for LDC products is another alarming issue. On this front, the EU had made a liberal offer to accept agricultural products from LDCs in their market within the framework of 'Everything but Arms' (EBA). Likewise, developing countries and LDCs made further proposals to receive support in protecting some of the crops with importance to food security, livelihoods and rural development in the local context. However, the counter- proposals from developed countries, including the list of sensitive products, have made the negotiations more complex and further restricted market opportunities for developing countries and LDCs in particular. Similarly, before making any formal commitment to provide technical or financial support to LDCs, developed countries have demanded that developing countries open up their domestic sectors; this is a reciprocal demand, which is against the spirit of the Marrakesh Agreement. The Sixth Ministerial Conference of the WTO in Hong Kong in December 2005 limited the LDC market to 97 per cent of tariff lines, and many speculate that the remaining three per cent may cover all potential exportable products of LDCs. Likewise, one of the major demands of LDCs under Mode 4 of the General Agreements on Trade and Services (GATS) is for the movement of unskilled and low-skilled persons to the markets of developed countries, but the proposals are not dealt seriously in any of the subsequent negotiations. This has raised doubts about the multilateral platforms and negotiation processes as developing countries, which account for at least two-thirds of the members of the WTO, have not received much benefit.

In the global trade scenario, the WTO has a meaningful role to play in facilitating global trade. As per WTO provisions, resource poor farmers in developing countries are entitled to receive agricultural subsidies. However, such subsidies have remained elusive due to non-cooperation by developed countries and IFIs in terms of providing meaningful support. The concerted efforts of developing countries and civil society made it possible to agree on the Doha Development Agenda (DDA) in the Fourth Ministerial Conference of the WTO in November 2001. But the spirit of the Doha Development Agenda was diluted by the July Package. The July Package was developed after the inconclusive closure of the Fifth Ministerial in Cancun, Mexico in 2003, which set the tone of the Sixth Ministerial in Hong Kong in 2005. The WTO Ministerial has not been able to accommodate the concerns of LDCs. Instead, developed countries have been able to continue to make empty promises about tariff reductions, without committing to any timeframe. At the Hong Kong Ministerial Conference it was agreed to apply tariff reductions and or zero tariff access to European markets for LDCs products for 97 per cent of export items. However, developing countries and civil society organisations speculate that the remaining three per cent tariff lines might cover almost all potential tradable commodities of LDCs. Similarly, the Mini-Ministerial held at Dalian in China in July 2005, which was attended by around 20 ministers from the developed world, did not rate the importance of LDCs' concerns on Mode 4 of the General Agreement on Trades and Services. There were also heavy critiques of the LDC Ministerial Declaration of Livingstone, in Zambia on 25 to 26 June 2005, at which the ministers could not concretise their strategy to enhance the trading potential of LDCs. In addition, a new form of power play has appeared through the formation of the Five Interested Parties (FIPs). The majority of developing countries and civil society organisation are not satisfied with the leadership taken by India and Brazil due to their biased focus on market access, which is mainly in the interests of India and Brazil. The process and focus has completely sidelined other issues of concern to LDCs. Similarly, several rounds of negotiations in the General Council between the Ministerial Conference deliberately excluded LDCs and developing countries. The constant exclusion of almost two-thirds of its members cannot be taken as participatory, resulting in heavy criticism of the governance of the WTO by civil society organisations. Interestingly, civil society participation was restricted in the subsequent Ministerial of the WTO.

Nepal, as a party to the MDGs, has made an effort to meet the MDG targets. The Government of Nepal (GoN) claims that the policy reforms of the mid-eighties have produced dividends. As a member of the WTO since 2004, Nepal sees significant scope for effective integration into the global economy. Towards this, Nepal requires policy reform, effective institutions, improved infrastructure and a reliable governance system. The GoN has adopted 'A Poverty Monitoring and Analysis System' (PMAS) to track the progress of the MDGs. Its sees the potential to halve the number of people living in poverty and those suffering from hunger, but admits that the existing supportive environment is weak. The GoN estimates that there is a financing gap of US$ 7.6 billion for the period 2005 to 2015 (NPC 2005a), of which 64 per cent of resources are expected to be invested in the agriculture sector to meet the MDG targets. In this context, the role of migration and the contribution of remittances to reducing hunger and poverty in Nepal are well recognised by the state. It is estimated that almost 1.5 million people are currently working abroad and remittances contribute almost 20 per cent to national gross domestic product (GDP). The proportion of households receiving remittances has increased from 23 per cent in 1995/96 to 32 percent in 2003/04. According to the Nepal Living Standard Survey (2003/04), 53.3 per cent of remittances are received from abroad, 23.3 per cent from India and the rest from within Nepal. The receipt of remittances is increasing. In 1992/93 remittances of two billion in Nepali currency were received, and this figure is expected to rise up to two trillion rupees for the fiscal year 2008/09. However, class-based migration and differences in remittance potential have increased inequality between different castes and genders. Similarly, the out-migration of men has led to the feminisation of rural agriculture, which has increased the workload of women and negatively impacted on productivity and the food security of households. The lack of investment of remittances in productive sectors and the lack of reintegration support for migrants after their return hinder the optimal utilisation of remittances to improve living conditions. It is estimated that almost 80 per cent of remittances are used to buy land and houses. Figure 5.3 shows the targets set by the GoN to meet the targets of MDG 1: to eradicate extreme poverty and hunger.

Figure 5.3 Population below poverty line

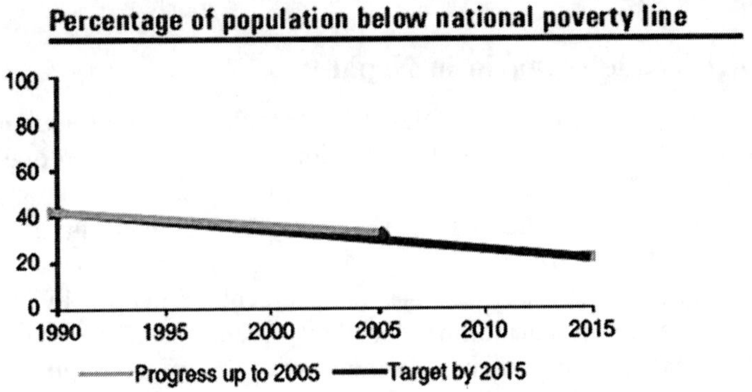

Source: NPC (2005a)

The Government of Nepal had set the target to reduce poverty and hunger from 31 per cent as at 2005 to 21 per cent by 2015. The GoN has acknowledged the dominant role of the agriculture sector in achieving this target. The agriculture sector was anticipated to grow from three to five per cent per annum in the Agriculture Perspective Plan (APP). At the same time, policy reforms were planned in both agriculture and non-agriculture sectors, although the majority of reforms had already taken place in the nineties and before. However, progress against this target has not been satisfactory due to the decade-long armed conflict, weak political commitment and implementation failures.

Dealing with hunger and livelihood security in Nepal has an intertwined relation with national targets and international commitments. It requires a minimum common understanding to realise and commit to resource sharing through trade and aid, depending on the circumstances. Mr Kofi Annan, the then Secretary General of UN, called on developed countries to fulfil their commitment to provide aid at the rate of 0.7 per cent of GNP to help developing countries to meet the MDG targets; this is yet to be met by any developed country.

5.4 National situation of trade and its impact on hunger and livelihoods

5.4.1 Trade scenario in Nepal

Since the early 1990s, Nepal has adopted a liberal economic policy. Many services and production sectors have been opened up as part of the Government's Structural Adjustment Programme (SAP). Nepal's trade has been confined largely to India as part of the bilateral treaty of 1950. According to the Nepal Living Standard Survey (CBS 2004), 66 per cent of people in Nepal are engaged in agriculture for their livelihoods, the majority of whom are subsistence farmers with fragmented and very small per capita holdings of productive land. Access to and control over productive resources is highly skewed on the basis of class, caste and gender. Being sandwiched between two giant neighbours (China and India) with large and prominent economies, Nepal has decided to align its economy with global mainstream processes. Accordingly, Nepal was accepted as a member of the WTO by the Fifth Ministerial held in Cancun, Mexico on 13 September 2003 and Nepal's membership was ratified through ordinance on 24 April 2004.

Photo: Y. Ghale, 2003

The then Director General of the WTO, Mr Supachai Panitchpakdi, handing over the accession protocol to the then Minister for Industry, Commerce and Supplies of Nepal, Mr Hari Bahadur Basnet, at the Fifth Ministerial of the WTO in Cancun, Mexico in September 2003.

In the history of the WTO, Nepal is the first LDC to accede to the WTO through the formal accession process. Nepal faced tremendous challenges in meeting the conditions set by developed member countries (Bhandari et al. 2005). The accession process was rigorous and extensive, taking 14 years to complete, during which time Nepal was unable to enjoy the provisions made for LDCs mentioned in Article XI of the GATT. The space provided by the WTO for developing countries, and especially LDCs, is insufficient and the S&DT provisions have not been consistently applied. Sincere support is needed from developed countries and effort from LDCs to ensure that the provisions for S&DT, which are supposed to be enjoyed by all LDCs, are applied.

How much Nepal can benefit from the WTO and other regional trade forums depends on how proactive it is in analysing its national potential in partnership with different stakeholders at the national level, and also how successfully it can ally itself with likeminded groups at regional and international levels to enhance its trade potential.

Agricultural trade in Nepal is largely with India. Of the total agricultural products imported by Nepal, about 80 per cent come from India. There are many reasons for the trade imbalance between Nepal and India. Nepal has been unable to effectively use tariffs to protect its domestic market due to its preferential trade agreement with India under which primary agriculture products from India face zero or little tariff barriers. Nepal has the flexibility to promote domestic agro-processing industries by applying higher tariffs to processed products (tariff escalation). However, Nepal's applied average tariff on agriculture products, which is around 10 per cent, is well below the bound rate. Likewise, Nepal has not been able to enjoy its entitlement as a member of the WTO to support for resource poor farmers to enhance their trading capacity.

Nepal has a limited export market to countries other than India, with products concentrated in carpets, textiles and agriculture. According to FAO, there have been at least three import surges of milled paddy in Nepal: 17.4 per cent in 1994,

55 per cent in 1996 and 79.8 per cent in 2000. A study by Action Aid Nepal revealed that import surges in milled rice have been substantial and surges were recorded during the period from 1991 to 2000 in Nepal. The Department of Customs recorded rice import surges in 1998/99 of 24.7 percent and in 1999/00 of 92.9 per cent (AAN 2005). The major reasons for these import surges are high production costs, lack of competitiveness of Nepalese producers and support for the agriculture sector by the Government of India. Imports as a result of south-south trade to Nepal rose from 21.2 per cent to 52.5 per cent 1990 to 2003 (UNCTAD 2005). This shows an increasing dependency on imports from other developing countries and reflects the fact that Nepal has not been able to tap opportunities presented by multilateral trade forums.

Trade and financial imbalances, global forces such as international trade regulations and emerging issues like climate change have a direct impact on consumers. At the macro level, policy regulations and the development priorities of resource poor governments and weaker economies are usually guided by the technical and financial support of IFIs. In this process, a lack of proper assessment of the micro situation and inadequate policy space for poor and small farmers, especially women, remains one of the limiting factors. With the worldwide food crisis, IFIs have published a list of 'do's and don'ts' that determines the policy measures of developing countries. Under the 'do's', IFIs have urged developing countries to scale up social safety nets, eliminate tariffs on key food items, and introduce temporary subsidies on food items vital to poor and inputs for poor farmers such as fertilizers. Likewise, on the 'don't' side are items related to export controls, price controls and general subsidies (Woods 2008). All these measures are in some way linked to production and the value chain process. These measures also direct production process and market dynamics. Such processes require adequate technical and financial resources to respond to immediate needs without undermining the sustainable use of resources and the autonomy of producers and consumers.

5.4.2 Food security and livelihoods in Nepal

In Nepal, 31 per cent of people still live below the poverty line. Poverty is compounded by multiple factors such as deprivation, denial and exclusion. The structural causes of denial, exclusion and injustice are an expression of the incompatibility of the socio-political and economic system with the aspirations and needs of the people. The five basic livelihood assets (physical, financial, human, social and political) are inter-linked and crucial to holistic empowerment. Weak links between different assets, lack of political will, weak structural processes and exclusionary policies have led to poverty and deprivation in Nepal. Hunger is the primary and most visible form of livelihood insecurity in Nepal. According to the Nepal Living Standard Survey (NLSS 1996), in 1996, 51 per cent of households had less than adequate food and 47 per cent of households had just adequate food; only two districts had more food than required. Food insecurity, leading to a large undernourished population, has resulted in low national productivity. Hence, the deteriorating status of food security and livelihoods in Nepal has larger implications for the national economy in the long run. Looking at the food production pattern in Nepal over a period of time, there is no significant improvement as shown in Figure 5.4.

Figure 5.4 Food production in Nepal for financial years 1994/95 to 2003/04

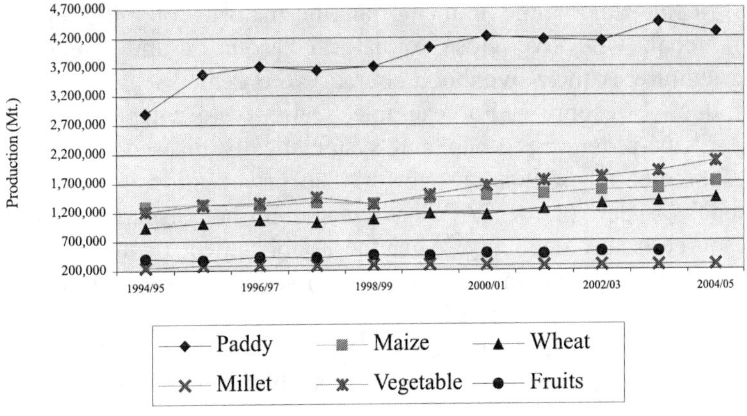

Source: WFP & FAO (2006, p 16)

The food production pattern across the whole geographic region is quite skewed, reflecting poor management of resource distribution; lack of access to information, technology and production inputs based on geographical disparities; and the weak purchasing capacity of the people. This is evidence by the existence of 72 per cent of people living in hunger and poverty in the far west hills and mountain regions of Nepal.

Nepal, as an agricultural economy, is losing its production capacity and, since the eighties, has become a net importer of food. This has had a direct impact on the national economy due to the extremely poor nutrition levels as presented in the MDG progress report of the Government of Nepal.

Table 5.1 Nutrition situation of children

Indicators	1990	1995	2000	2005	2015 (target)
Percentage of population below minimum level of dietary energy consumption	49	NA	47	NA	25
Percentage of underweight children age 6-59 months (>-2 SD)	57	47	53	NA	29
Percentage of stunted children age 6-59 months (>-2 SD)	60	54	44	NA	30

Source: NPC (2005b)

The gradual privatisation of productive resources has further increased the gap between resource rich and poor citizens in Nepal. Since time immemorial, the majority of the people in Nepal, who live close to natural resources and adopted agriculture as their livelihood source, were denied legal title to productive resources. For example, Dalits were categorised as a service-providing group and systematically disassociated by resource-based politics and power. The privatisation process in Nepal (as part of the SAP) has created further disparities and resource-based inequality. After the establishment of multiparty democracy in 1990s, non-governmental services grew and many social movements started. Landless producers also became organised to claim their rights over the means of production so that they could enjoy social justice through legal access to productive resources.

In the late nineties, the Government of Nepal introduced the concept of a 'land bank' as part of land management, supported by the World Bank. The aim of the land bank is to promote a market approach to land management (Bhusal 2006) to reduce land-based discrimination and facilitate poor people's, especially ex-bonded labourers', access to land through the provision of loans. However, the land bank has not been properly implemented due to constant protests by land rights groups. The logic of the land rights groups is that they deserve to acquire land through land redistribution as part of land reform and management, rather by taking a loan to purchase it, as they were victimised for generations through the bonded labour system. Although it is agreed that land is of prime importance in establishing social justice, economic transformation and increasing agricultural productivity, the process of land reform has been jeopardised by weak political commitment and the process of privatisation. The Government tends to commodify land as a lucrative sector for privatisation and a way of promoting Foreign Direct Investment (FDI) for other purposes such as the establishment of industries for merchandise trade.

Skewed land distribution and the system of land-based resource entitlement is a dominant factor in controlling the food production and consumption cycle in Nepal. Among the total land holding in Nepal, about 21 per cent is under cultivation, with an average holding size of 0.96 ha, and 32.1 per cent of households are landless (CBS 2002). Ensuring food security for individuals requires – if no alternative income opportunities are available – self-sufficiency at the local level, for which access to and control over means of production is necessary. It has been evidenced that households headed by wage labourers have a higher incidence of poverty (46%), followed by households headed by someone self-employed in agriculture. Among the total population of Nepal, only 10.83 per cent of women have any land entitlement, and female-headed households have a higher incidence of poverty due to their increased engagement in subsistence agriculture, without any reform in tenureship patterns. Among Dalits, 23 per cent are landless and the majority of the rest have minimal access to land; Dalits have a 15 per cent higher incidence of poverty than the national average (NPC 2005b).

Similarly, the transfer of technology plays a significant role in innovation and dissemination for development and prosperity. However, research and development has not been a priority for the Government, and so sufficient resources have not been allocated. Another important and contentious area is protectionism in the agriculture sector in developed countries through tariff protection and subsidies. The present level of domestic support for the agriculture sector in Nepal is around 1.3 per cent of Agriculture Gross Domestic Product (AGDP).

Reducing the prevalence of hunger and poverty is a daunt task for the Government of Nepal and one that requires massive agrarian reform to ensure access to and control over the means of production, substantial investment in research and development, the promotion of value addition in the production chain process and marketing, and the creation of employment opportunities. It is equally important for Nepal to align itself with the global system by tapping potential opportunities and mitigating the negative aspects of globalisation, liberalisation and privatisation.

5.4.3 Threats to Nepal from corporate globalisation

Nepal has gained both advantages and disadvantages from its membership of the WTO. On the one hand, there is potential benefit to be gained from access to outside markets. On the other hand, Nepal must be careful to protect its domestic market, and particularly its small and poor farmers. WTO membership generally deals with trade policies and procedures. However, many of the trade policies and processes deal with agriculture, biodiversity and natural resources, which have a direct impact on food security and the livelihoods of many small and poor farmers. Some of the major agreements that have direct implications for Nepal and that directly impact on food security and livelihoods are the Agreement on Agriculture (AoA), Trade Related Aspects of Intellectual Property Rights (TRIPS), and Technical Barriers on Trade and Sanitary and vhytosanitary (SPS) Measures.

Sixty six per cent of Nepalese are engaged in agriculture, the majority of which are women and people from disadvantaged groups. Therefore, trade policies, procedures and structures have a direct relationship to the food security and livelihoods of these groups. As Nepal is still a subsistence-based economy, the possibility of exposure to external shocks created by international and regional trade policies and provisions cannot be denied. Since, corporate globalisation has implications for biodiversity, farmers' rights and market access, which in turn affect food and livelihood security, the potential implications of changes in global, regional and national level trade regimes have to be looked at in detail.

Biodiversity

Biodiversity is closely associated with resources for human survival in developing countries. It has economic, environmental and social value. The prosperity of biodiversity is, to a large extent, based on the efficient use of biotechnology. In developing countries, farmers use plants as a source of food, for medicinal purposes and as cultural symbols. However, the green revolution promoted in the seventies introduced high yielding varieties requiring chemical inputs to increase production. There is evidence that the genetic resource base has been greatly affected and narrowed as a result. For example, in India, by the end of the 20th Century, 75 per cent of India's rice production came from a mere ten varieties of rice, whereas India was once home to 30,000 varieties (Downes 2003). This phenomenon has both short-term and long-term implications for food security. The short-term implications are that farmers have to buy seeds every year as hybrid seeds cannot be reused. This increases the cost of production and results in loss of knowledge and skills associated with biodiversity, creating dependency on large seed companies. Likewise, the commercialisation of agriculture and, in particular, mono-cropping, has negative implications for food security in times when crops are affected by disease or pests. Therefore, it is important to widen the biodiversity base for better food security and livelihood options.

In the long run, the narrowing of the genetic resource base can have large implications for the national economy, environment and national sovereignty. The majority of developing countries are still very rich in biodiversity and their livelihood systems are widely supported by these resources. There are plenty of opportunities for bio-prospecting and to generate employment and income from the bio-resources of developing countries. This also promotes research and technology development and dissemination. However, laboratory-based innovation and its wider application, the use (and manipulation) of the biodiversity of developing countries by multinational companies and developed countries, and the expansion of monopolies over these resources threaten the food security and livelihoods of people in developing counties. Bio-patents over life forms and monopolies over genetic resources thus prevent farmers from exercising their generations-old practices and remove their right to use, save and reuse the resources that they have conserved and promoted for centuries. Appropriate policies and procedures must be developed to ensure technology transfer and the sharing of benefits generated by the use of bio-resources with the country of origin, and resource poor countries should be assisted to conduct research and development, to enhance their productivity and trade competence.

Farmers' rights

According to the recent estimate of FAO, 1.02 billion people are suffering from hunger and majority of them are from the developing world and are primarily engaged in agriculture for their livelihoods (Ghale 2009). The majority of poor and small farmers are also net consumers. Therefore, protecting farmers' rights usually overlaps with protecting consumer rights. Globalisation and liberalisation has the potential to limit farmers' choices.

Farmers' rights were explicitly defined by the FAO International Undertaking on plant genetic resources for food and agriculture adopted in the 31st Session in November 2001, as "rights arising from the past, present, the future contributions of farmers in conserving, improving, and making available plant genetic resources, particularly those in the centres of origin/diversity" (FAO 2001). These rights are vested in the international community as trustees for present and future generations of farmers for the purpose of ensuring full benefits to farmers and supporting the continuation of their contribution, as well as the attainment of the overall purpose of the International Undertaking on plant genetic resources for food and agriculture. This provision recognises the right of farmers to save, use and exchange seeds. Other instruments like the Convention on Biological Diversity (CBD) 1992 acknowledge the sovereign right of states to utilise their resources according to their own policies for the protection of global biodiversity. The CBD also recognises the traditional knowledge of farmers and contains provisions for the equitable sharing of benefits arising from the use of indigenous knowledge, innovations and practices.

Contrary to the provisions of the CBD, the WTO's TRIPS agreement defines intellectual property rights as private rights. The TRIPS agreement restricts the right of farmers to save, use and exchange seeds, and to benefit from their role in preserving biodiversity. Although the concept of farmers' rights was introduced in the 1980's, it is still unclear as to what they actually are and how they can be reconciled with plant breeders' rights. The debatc on whether or not farmers' right to be protected within an ownership or stewardship approach is currently a hot topic of debate (SAWTEE 2007). The outcome of this debate will greatly impact on food security and the livelihoods of farmers in developing countries.

Market access

Developing countries including LDCs basically grow for their own consumption. However, they also have certain areas of potential for export. Some of the bio- resource based enterprises in developing countries would be viable to develop if regional and international markets were flexible enough to accommodate their concerns and priorities. Developing countries also need support to enhance their trading capabilities. These countries either have not been able to identify potential commodities and markets, or have not been able to invest enough resources to build their capacity to tap existing opportunities. The complexities are widening in successive meetings of the WTO, in particular, where firm commitments, especially to withdraw agriculture subsidies practised by developed countries, open market for products from developing countries and increasing development aid in agriculture and food security, are still to be achieved.

The products of developing countries are usually unable to enter the international market due to high quality standards that are beyond their capacity to meet or due to other international rules. The quality standard system and practices are becoming a trade barrier to access to international market (Ghale 2005a). The product and process specific standards for both industrial and agricultural products remain a challenge to securing market access. In the case of Nepal, a technical committee under the Nepal Council of Standards (NCS) chaired by the Minister of Industry, Commerce and Supplies (MoICS) sets standards based on internationally defined parameters and national requirements. A total of 111 companies have received quality certifications for 32 products under this system including polythene pipe, biscuits, beer and noodles. Likewise, the provisions of the Sanitary and Phytosanitary (SPS) agreement are intended to minimise the negative effects of SPS measures on international trade, considering the risks to human and animal health from food and animal or plant-borne disease, and to animals and plants from pests and diseases. The SPS is applicable to fresh fruits and vegetables, fruit juice and other fruit preparations, meat and meat products, dairy products and processed food products.

The UN Codex Alimentarius regulates food safety by setting international standards for food production. These standards act as gatekeepers to international food markets effectively blocking imports of food from most developing countries. This has resulted for two main reasons: On the one hand, developing countries are not adequately represented on Codex's committees and not actively involved in the standard setting processes of Codex. They, therefore, have to abide by standards that are predetermined by others and are often too high. On the other hand, LDCs like Nepal are usually not in a position to comply with SPS standards set by Codex. This means that products from LDCs like Nepal have limited access, if at all, to markets in developed countries. Interestingly, some recent Codex decisions reflect political compromises designed to promote international trade, not necessarily best science to protect consumers.

Nepal's export basket of food and agricultural products contains, among others, medicinal herbs, ginger, brooms, resin, cardamom, cattle fodder, biscuits, noodles, vegetable ghee, raw jute, pulses, catechu, turmeric, black tea, other types of fermented tea, sugar, spices, uncooked pasta, edible preparations of animal or vegetable fats, wheat, plants and beer. Given the country's limited technical capability to meet internationally agreed standards, Nepalese products can have very limited access to export destinations.

At the bilateral level, certain restrictions are also becoming an obstacle to regional market access. For example, India has the restricted the export of sensitive products to through only 7 of the 15 existing transit points.

5.5 Efforts to mitigate hunger and livelihood insecurity in Nepal

5.5.1 National policies and programmes

The Government of Nepal considers food security as a matter of availability (production of food), access (economic and social access to food) and utilisation (proper processing of food items into food) (NPC 2005a). Over the years, the GoN has adopted various uncoordinated strategies to address the causes of poverty and hunger in Nepal. Since the fifties and the start of periodic development planning in Nepal, almost all plans have identified poverty as the main issue in underdevelopment in Nepal. All the periodic development plans have considered agriculture as an engine of growth and poverty reduction. Implemented in 1997, the APP is considered a milestone document with its long-term plan in compliance with Nepal's WFS commitments of 1996. Likewise, the Poverty Reduction Strategy Programme (PRSP), 2002, which is also known as 10th periodic development plan of Nepal, has clearly identified four areas of intervention, as seen in Figure 5.5. There are also several sub-sector policies that deal with production, processing and trade aspects of agriculture. In 2004, the GoN came up with an Agriculture Policy 2061, with comprehensive coverage of the agriculture sector. The last Three Year Interim Plan (2007/09) also focused on agriculture-based growth to address poverty and inequality. The Government of Nepal is currently focusing on the effective implementation of public private partnerships to meet its poverty reduction targets.

Figure 5.5 Four pillars of the Poverty Reduction Strategy Programme

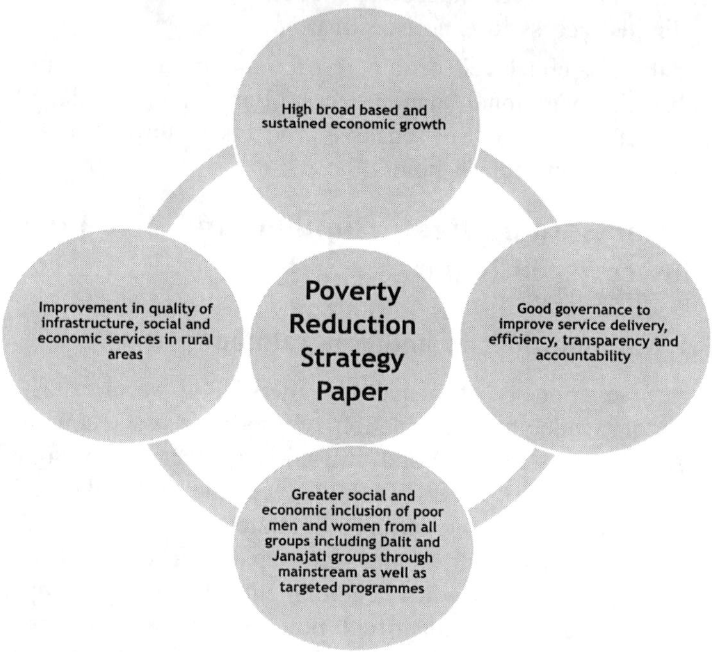

Source: NPC (2002)

However, civil society organisations like Action Aid International and OXFAM consider hunger and livelihood insecurity to be political issues created by lack of access to means of production such as land, credit, information, technology and markets, and by a lack of participation in decision-making forums. They believe that hunger can be mitigated through the promotion and adaptation of technologies to meet local needs, the creation of space for people to make informed choices and participate in decision making, and through the promotion of farmers' basic rights. Therefore, it is important to consider people's rights when implementing development approaches and to create connectivity between different sectoral interventions to bring about real change in the fight against hunger and livelihood insecurity.

5.5.2 Opportunities offered by international trade rules

The weaker state of LDCs and LLDCs has been well acknowledged by global trade platforms. Accordingly, certain mechanisms have been developed to enhance the trading capacity of these groups. In the Marrakesh Agreement (establishing the WTO), mention is made of the special need to respond to the vulnerability of LDCs created by market distortion and instability in the world market. Hence, provision is made for compensation for the negative impact of these on the food import bill of LDCs. At the same time, support measures also focus on enhancing the production capacity of LDCs through the establishment of a technical assistance framework. Under this framework, six multilateral institutions – the WB, IMF, UNCTAD, WTO, ITC and UNDP – have committed to create a common fund for technical and financial support. Likewise, the regional trade forums also acknowledged the weaker economic status of LDC member states and have made certain provisions to compensate for this. Some of these international and regional provisions are stated below:

1. Part IV of General Agreement on Tariffs and Trade (GATT) on Trade and Development provide for non-reciprocity for LDCs, and Article 3 of the South Asia Free Trade Agreement (SAFTA) also makes provision for the adoption of concrete preferential measures in favour of LDCs on a non-reciprocal basis.
2. The WTO provides for the exemption of subsidies on inputs and investment in relation to Aggregate Measures of Support (AMS) for Low Income and Resource Poor (LIRP) farmers from countries covered by the Agreement on Agriculture.

3. As per the WTO, developed countries are supposed to reduce their tariffs by 36 per cent within five years and developing countries within 10 years from 1995, with the actual calculation base year of 1986/88. These commitments have not been met substantially. Likewise, Article 7 of SAFTA requires tariff reduction by the Non-Least Developed Contracting States from existing tariff rates to 20 per cent and for LDCs to 30 per cent within 2 years from the date of the Agreement coming into force.
4. Acknowledging the weak trading capacity of LDCs, provisions have been made to support LDCs to enhance their trading capacities through technical and financial assistance with the support of IFIs and UN organisations.
5. SAARC's provision for a regional food reserve for emergencies has the potential to ensure people's access to quality food in situations of natural disaster in the region of a scale that requires a regional response.
6. The WTO provides for Special and Differential Treatment (S&DT) to enhance the trade competence of LDCs. SAFTA in Article 11 provides that all Contracting States shall provide special and more favourable treatment to LDCs commensurate with their development needs and, recognising that it is necessary to progress beyond preferential trading arrangements, SAFTA envisages moving towards higher levels of trade and economic cooperation in the region by removing barriers to the cross-border flow of goods.
7. There are no limits to 'Green Box'[6] subsidies. In addition, as Nepal is an LDC with more than 50 per cent of

[6] Green Box subsidies are one of the measures of 'domestic support' provided under Annex 2 of the Agreement on Agriculture. Fixed payments are allowed to producers for environmental programmes, so long as the payments are 'decoupled' from current production levels. Green Box measures i) must not distort trade or at most cause minimal distortion, ii) have to be government funded, and iii) must not involve any price support.

farmers holding an average of only 0.8 ha of land, most of Nepal's farmers fall into the category of Low Income and Resource Poor. Article 6.2 of Agreement on Agriculture allows for the non-inclusion of inputs and investment subsidies in the Aggregate Measures of Support if directed to Low Income and Resource Poor farmers. Those areas for support include direct payments in relation to product specific support and general support for non-product specific support, such as research, agriculture roads, agriculture extension and development, domestic food aid, irrigation, improved seeds, chemical fertilizers, and so forth.

5.5.3 Mainstreaming hunger and livelihoods: The way forward

The right to be free from hunger is enshrined in many international provisions. These instruments consider food security and livelihood security as a basic right. Similarly, every state has a responsibility to ensure that its citizens have access to means of production, and food and livelihood security. Food is not merely a tradable commodity; it is a matter of life and death. Hence, the Government of Nepal should prepare a list of sensitive products very carefully, especially when dealing with food and agricultural products for export destinations.

Meaningful public private partnerships, in which both the Government and the private sector are bound to ensure secure and healthy livelihoods for all people, especially vulnerable groups such as Dalits, women, children, the disabled and indigenous communities, are also an important way forward. In this scenario, multi- pronged options have to be considered to address hunger and livelihood insecurity in the era of globalisation, without compromising national sovereignty.

Securing food and livelihoods has to be considered a political issue requiring broad commitment at the national and international level to address. At the national level, the GoN should adopt proper policies and implementation mechanisms to ensure people's access to means of production and viable livelihood options. The schematic diagram in Figure 5.6 presents the major aspects of addressing hunger and livelihood insecurity.

Figure 5.6 Schematic diagram presenting the major aspects of addressing hunger and livelihood insecurity

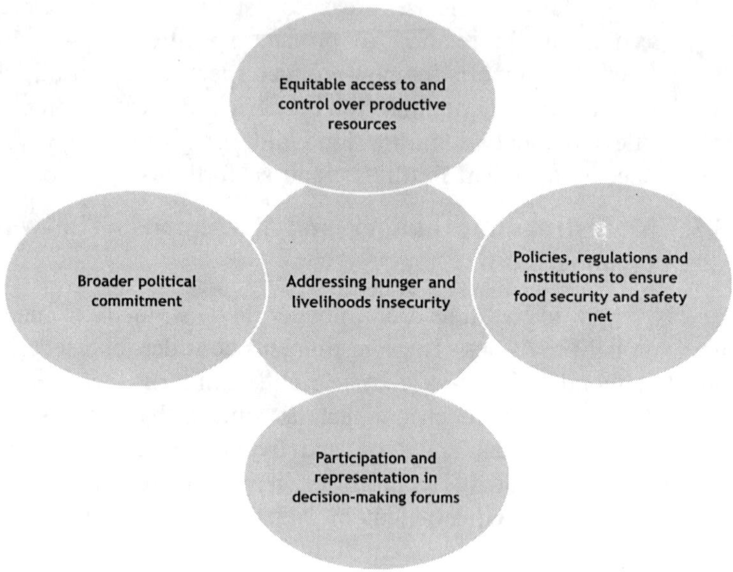

Equitable access to and control over resources

The majority of people who are hungry and vulnerable to livelihood insecurity are from economically poor and socially excluded communities such as Dalits, women, the disabled, children and indigenous minorities. They have poor access to means of production and are struggling to deal with hunger and poverty, which they have been experiencing for centuries. Among the means of production, land is the prime asset, and has both social and economic value. In Nepal, 46 per cent of total arable land is held by only 17 per cent of the population – the so-called 'elites' – and 48 per cent of the people who work the land own only 15 per cent. A very discouraging fact is that, only 8.1 per cent of women in Nepal have legal ownership of land.

Due to unequal and skewed distribution of land resources and the increasing feminisation of agriculture, agriculture productivity in Nepal is decreasing. In addition, entitlement to other support measures in Nepal, such as technology, credit and information, is land-based. There is a lack of an assured fair market on which to sell goods produced. Consequently, farmers with prior commitments to meet (e.g., to their landlord) are often forced to sell their produce at very nominal prices, which can push them towards bankruptcy.

The majority of farmers and small holders in Nepal are in need of an effective support system from the state including measures such as subsidies on irrigation, payment for power systems, the provision of seeds, and storage and export facilities for produced goods. The porous border with India and the expansion of the globalised market system are threatening small farmers.

Policy formulation needs to protect the right of farmers to produce, save and sell farm-produced seeds. The seed inflow-outflow mechanism has to be restricted to protect against loss of endangered genetic resources and to prevent gene pollution. In addition, farmers need to have better farm prices and compensation mechanisms in case of crop failure due to irregularities in the market chain or natural calamity.

Farmers and local communities have practised biodiversity conservation for centuries, which has contributed tremendously to natural resource management in Nepal. Therefore, farmers and local communities should have rights over the genetic resources that they have conserved and protected to use and reuse as they wish. As many bio-resources have trade potential, their trade value should be fully exploited. Farmers and local communities should also receive an equitable share of the benefits that arise from bio-prospecting. The basic principle of protecting local people's autonomy over production process, engagement in value chain and ensuring access to an equitable share of benefits should be upheld. Local and national governments can play a critical role in this through effective public private partnerships.

With liberalisation and privatisation, vulnerable groups will be exposed to more uncertainty and become more vulnerable.

Special protection mechanisms should be in place to protect the interests of these poor and excluded groups. There is the risk of direct encroachment on land resources and of the privatisation of water resources in the interest of profit-orientated corporations that wish to invest and privatise resources. This can negatively affect the livelihoods of people, especially vulnerable groups.

Informed participation in decision making

Information is power; it helps to develop an informed society and empowers citizens to claim their basic rights and fulfil their responsibilities. Countries with weaker economies are consistently being marginalised from the global discourse on trade and development and from participation in decision making. Investment in research and development has been weakened and priorities shifted. As a result, weaker countries lag behind in developing their trade potential and in the proper analysis of long-term implications of undermining research on crops of high importance for food security, cultural identity, environmental protection and economic prosperity. In the long run, this weakens local and national institutions, knowledge system and their bargaining capacity to tap adequate resources for relevant sector development important for food security and livelihoods. Developed countries play the game of divide and rule, to the detriment of developing countries. Global international trade forums have been predominantly occupied and influenced by the agendas and interests of developed countries. Global trade has been continuously dominated by highly industrialised countries. During the Sixth Ministerial of the WTO in Hong Kong in December 2005, it was agreed to eliminate all forms of subsidies in agriculture by developed countries by 2013. But at the subsequent high-level meeting in Geneva, no positive indications or actual plans of action were shown to ensure this reduction. Similarly, the Sixth Ministerial decided to provide duty free and quota free market access for LDCs in relation to only 97 per cent of tariff lines. The coverage by the remaining three per cent of tariff lines is still undecided. Focus on Global South suspects that this 3 per cent will cover almost 330 tariff lines and may cover almost all tradable commodities from

LDCs (Focus on the Global South 2006). At the same time, the proposal by developing countries to protect the special products of LDCs on the ground of food security and livelihood security has not fully materialised. Hence, there are enormous doubts about the ethical implementation of provisions to promote the trading capacity of LDCs and ensure that they receive benefits from integration into the global trade system.

Safety net measures

Safety net measures are vital for the immediate relief of hunger and livelihood insecurity, and can be built on through the participation of food and livelihood insecure groups as a means of empowerment. Where the equitable distribution of resources is not ensured and people's informed choices are not guaranteed, safety net measures are even more critical. Short-term relief should not be confined to immediate support measures, but should focus on the process of empowerment and lead to access to resources in the long run. In many developing countries, resource distribution is skewed based on caste, class, religion and gender. In this situation, it is pivotal to have proper safety net measures for access to food and other means of livelihood. To secure better livelihoods, resource poor farmers of LDCs like Nepal are entitled to receive subsidies for the production process. As countries like Nepal cannot generate enough revenue to support agriculture and food security sub-sectors properly, international institutions have a role to play in mitigating poverty and improving livelihoods. However, global evidence has not been encouraging on this front. Many Net Food Importing Developing Countries including Nepal are at risk of compromising timely and quality supply of food during times of emergency. The supply of GM food in food aid to some African countries has remained an international issue. Programmes like Food for Work, which was introduced in the mid-seventies; some primary school feeding programmes and food assistance programmes; and transport subsidies for transporting rice to remote areas are some of the safety measures in place in Nepal. However, the food transport subsidy has been criticised for being costly, ineffective due to the centralised distribution system, and for increasing the dependency of locals on subsidised rice, weakening the local production potential. Nonetheless, a minimal level of support, such as providing next season's crop at times of crop failure from drought or flood and by waving interest or providing loans, is essential.

There are certain provisions that have been implemented by different countries that are commendable. The Indian Supreme Court's order on the 'Right to Food' is a praiseworthy initiative that considers food as a basic human right and the duty of the state to provide. The public distribution system practised in India for people below the poverty line has facilitated poor people's access to food and other basic items like kerosene at low prices. Likewise, the 'Zero Hunger Programme' announced by Mr Lula de Silva, President of Brazil, is another step forward in the fight against poverty and hunger. The Government of Thailand has promoted various food schemes in rural areas to improve access to food and livelihood options. There have also been certain regional initiatives, such as the establishment of the Food Reserve by SAARC, which is another good example. However, hunger and livelihood insecurity cannot be dealt with by single schemes operating in isolation. Short-term support and long-term political vision are needed to deal with this important issue.

5.5.4 Measures to be taken at different levels

International level

1. Cooperate with other likeminded groups to lobby the WTO for:
   - Duty free and quota free access for LDC products
   - The phasing out of all forms of subsidies in developed countries, including export subsidies and trade distorting domestic subsidies
   - The removal of tariff escalation, tariff peaks and tariff dispersion measures
   - The provisions of S&DT envisaged for developing and least developed countries to be made obligatory
   - The dumping of any form to be discouraged

- Patents on life forms to be removed
- Predictable labour markets and access to fair jobs and benefit packages to be ensured as provisioned for LDC members in the WTO

2. International institutions to honour their commitment to provide meaningful technical and financial support.
3. Maintenance of the trading space for LDCs as envisaged in the original agreement of the WTO and in regional trading arrangements.
4. Establishment of a food-aid scheme to meet the legitimate needs of developing countries in the form of grants.
5. The removal of WTO-plus conditions in any form.
6. The international community should be responsible for mitigating the impacts of carbon emissions and potential threats posed by climate change.

National level

1. Promote public and private investment in research and development in agriculture to enhance the productivity of staple food crops and crops with export potential.
2. Build the capacities of government institutions and human resources to face the global challenges and to create a fair trade environment.
3. Provide targeted, product specific and generic support measures to Low Input Resource Poor Farmers.
4. Ensure farmers' rights over plant genetic resources to save, reuse and sell their farm produced seeds.
5. Access to genetic resources by external parties should be restricted to the level of public research and it should be subject to prior informed consent. Where prior informed consent is granted, access should be on mutually agreed terms.
6. Establish fair and equitable provisions for the sharing the benefits arising from the commercial and other utilisation of genetic resources to the local community and nation state.

7. The knowledge and skill of indigenous communities and farming communities and women in relation to plants and plant genetic resources should be protected and encouraged in line with the CBD and International Labour Organisation (ILO) Convention 169.
8. Adopt short and long-term measures to promote a sustainable production system to respond to the increasing food crisis and protect national food sovereignty.
9. Ensure a stable economy and good governance.
10. Promote justice in production relations, respect the autonomy of producers over means of production and their representation in decision-making processes, and empower poor and small producers to change the rules of the game for social justice and improved productivity.

5.6 Conclusions

In the globalised world of today there has been progress on many fronts. Developed countries, with their strong economic prosperity and financial and technology based power, are leading the world. The majority of developing countries and, in particular, LDCs are trying hard to integrate their economies into the global trading system. Although efforts have been made, the majority of people in developing countries are still unable to fulfil their basic livelihood needs. Developing countries have abundant natural resources, and the knowledge and skill associated with it, but have not been able to exploit these resources for economic gain. The resource distribution pattern in developing countries is highly skewed based on class, caste, religion and gender. Due to their poor economic status, weak institutional and human resource base, and political instability, the bargaining capacity of developing countries is weak. As a result, billions of people go to bed hungry in the developing world. Worldwide increases in food prices and the trend by developed countries to invest in bio-fuel are posing new challenges. The efforts of international institutions and support from developed countries have not been able to make a substantial difference in the lives of the many poor and hungry people in developing countries. The international provisions enshrined in the many declarations, conventions and summits have remained an illusion. Developing countries have not been able to enjoy the global market principally because developed countries, while on the one hand offering access, are at the same time restricting the import of agricultural products from developing countries through process standards. In other words, even if the product is safe, it can be denied market access on the ground that the it can't be 'proved' to be safe. In contrast, it is very difficult for Nepal to restrict the import of a product for which no international standard is available, as international agreements put the onus of proof on the importing country based on scientific evidence. Given Nepal's limited scientific capacity, the required 'proof' may be difficult if not impossible to produce. This is clearly unfair. The SPS and Technical Barriers to Trade (TBT) agreements broadly serve the interests of exporters from developed countries, particularly MNCs.

Likewise, Nepal's trade potential has not been further expanded especially in food and agriculture sectors. The surges in imports, which can take place against static or even declining export performance, are further increasing Nepal's trade deficit. As a result, imports will be difficult to sustain. More importantly, cheaper imports from abroad may kill incentives to produce at home. Farmers and other small producers will no longer be motivated to remain engaged in food and agricultural production. This would negatively affect food security, in general, and household consumption of food products, in particular. Finally, cheaper imports will contributing to changing food habits, which will affect, in many cases, the nutritional status of food. Nepal's traditional food items are rich in micronutrients. They may, however, lose out to the attractive-looking and ready-to-eat packaged food imported from elsewhere, even if they do not have the same nutritional value as home-grown products. Quality management, process control and documentation; cooperation with external partners; an enabling framework; market segmentation; collaboration with likeminded groups; and regional cooperation are some of the core areas to be developed for international trade regulation to benefit all. Some of the good initiatives like the SAARC Food Reserve can be promoted and fully operationalised for better access to food during difficult situations.

Another important issue is the regulation of GM products. One of the core elements of GMO legislation would be a requirement to positively label. In other words, the labelling of GM foods to say 'this product contains GMO' would be mandatory. The alternative to such legislation would be a negative labelling ('this product does not contain GMO'), which could be done voluntarily by suppliers. In view of the potential price premium on GM-free products (e.g., organic food), suppliers can be expected to do this voluntarily. However, a threshold limit will have to be worked out for a product to be labelled as 'GM-free'.

Therefore, in order to eradicate hunger and ensure livelihood security for disadvantaged people a dual approach is needed: those in immediate need must be supported and ways of addressing structural causes that make people vulnerable must be sought. Immediate support, such as safety net measures, need to be taken as part of the process of empowerment, which ultimately relates to access to and control over means of production. Long-term measures have to be oriented towards enhancing the production and market potential of both agriculture and non-agriculture sectors for equitable growth and good governance. Only this can ultimately lead to dignified livelihoods and social justice.

References

AAI [ActionAid International]. 2005. *Trade Invaders, The WTO and Developing Countries' Right to Protect.* London: ActionAid International.

AAN [ActionAid Nepal]. 2005. *Import Surge in Nepal: A Case Study of Rice.* Kathmandu: ActionAid Nepal.

Adhikari J, Ghimire S. 2006. *Changing Food Series* [In Nepali]. Kathmandu: Martin Chautari.

Adhikari R, Ghimire H. 2001. *Integrating LDCs into the multilateral System: Rhetoric Galore.* Kathmandu: South Asia Watch on Trade Economics and Environment.

Adhikari R, Belbase N, Ghale Y. 2000. *Seed of Monopoly: Implications of TRIPS Agreement on Nepal.* Kathmandu: ActionAid Nepal and Pro-Public.

Basnet P, Darnal S, editors. 2007. *Politics of Privilege and Reservation* [In Nepali]. Kathmandu: Jagaran Media Centre.

Bengali K, editor. 2003. *The Politics of Managing Water.* Islamabad: Sustainable Development Policy Institute (SDPI) and Oxford.

Bhandari S, Shrestha SM, Ghale Y. 2005. *Nepal's Accession to the WTO: Opportunities and Challenges.* Kathmandu: ActionAid Nepal and Law Associates Nepal.

Bhusal YR. 2006. Land Issues and the Role of Land Bank in the Context of Agriculture Perspective Plan and Poverty Reduction Strategy in Nepal. Paper presented in the workshop on *The APP: From Vision to Action.* 22-23 November, 2006. Kathmandu: National Planning Commission and World Bank.

CBS [Central Bureau of Statistics]. 2004. *Nepal Living Standard Survey 2003/04.* Kathmandu: Central Bureau of Statistics, Nepal.

CBS [Central Bureau of Statistics]. 2002. *Pocket Book of Statistics.* Kathmandu: Central Bureau of Statistics.

Chatham House. 2008. *Rising Food Prices: Divers and implications for development, Chatham house briefings paper No. 08/01.* www.chathamhouse.org.uk (Accessed on 22 August 2008).

Clive J. 2005. *Global Status of Commercialized Biotech/GM Crops: 2005, Executive Summary. Brief 34.* Webpage: http://www.isaaa.org.resources/publications (Accessed on 18 December 2005).

Downes G. 2003. *Implication of TRIPS for Food Security in the Majority World.* Dublin: Comhlamh Action Network.

ETC. 2005. *Global Seed Industry Concentration, ETC Group Communiqué.* September/ October 2005, Issue No. 90. 6 September 2005. Source: http://www.etcgroup.org/documents/comm90globalseed.pdf 6 Sep, 2005 (Accessed on 29 September 2008) .

FAO [Food and Agricultural Organization]. 1996. *Rome Declaration on World Food Security, World Food Summit.* Rome: Food and Agriculture Organization of UN.

FAO [Food and Agricultural Organization]. 1997. *FAO Undertaking on Plant Genetic Resources for Food and Agriculture.* Rome: Food and Agriculture Organization.

FAO [Food and Agricultural Organization]. 2001. International Undertaking on plant genetic resources for food and agriculture. Program held on 2-13 November 2001, Rome, Italy.

FAO [Food and Agricultural Organization]. 2004. *Right to Food Guidelines.* http:// www.fao.org/righttofood/ (Accessed on 29 September 2008).

FAO [Food and Agricultural Organization]. 2005. *The State of Food Insecurity in the World 2005. Food Security in the World 2005,*

Eradicating world hunger-key to Achieving the Millennium Development Goals. Rome: Food and Agriculture Organization of UN.

FAO [Food and Agricultural Organization], UNDP [United Nations Development Programme]. 2008. *Combating Hunger: A Seven Point Agenda.* Colombo: UNDP Regional Centre and Bangkok: FAO Regional Office for Asia and the Pacific.

FOCUS. 2006. Biotechnology and Food Security. *Info Resources*. No. 1/06. Webpage: http://www.inforesources.ch/pdf/focus06_1_e.pdf (Accessed on 12 September 2008).

Food First. 2002. *Food Sovereignty: A right for All.* Political Statement of the NGO/CSO Forum for Food Sovereignty on 14 June 2002.Webpage: www.foodfirst.org/ progs/global/food/finaldeclaration.html. (Accessed on 22 September 2008).

Friends of the Earth. 2003. *The World for Sale: An Introduction to Corporate Globalisation, Briefing.* London: Friends of the Earth. www.foe. co.uk/resource/ briefings/the_world_for_sale.pdf (Accessed on 20 December 2009).

GCAP [Global Call to Action Against Poverty]. 2005. *Global Call to Action against Poverty*. http://www.whiteband.org/about-gcap/what-is-gcap (Accessed on 20 December 2009).

Ghale Y. 2009. *World Food Summit 2009: Can the renewed commitments eliminate hunger?* http://www.nepalnews.com/main/index.php/-guestcolumn/2587-world- food-summit-2009-can-the-renewed-commitment-eliminate-hunger.html. (Accessed on 20 December 2009).

IDS [Institute of Development Studies]. 2008. *Agriculture; Research Findings for Development Policymakers and Practitioners.* www. id21.org. (Accessed on 22 September 2008).

ITCSD [International Centre for Sustainable Trade and Development]. 2006. *Bridges between Trade and Sustainable Development.* Year 10. No.1. January- February, 2006. Geneva: International Centre for Sustainable Trade and Development.

Jawara F, Kwa A. 2003. *Behind the Scenes at the WTO: The Real World of International Trade Negotiation.* London: Zed Books and Bangkok: Focus on the Global South.

MoAC [Ministry of Agriculture and Cooperatives], WFP [World Food Programme], FAO [Food and Agricultural Organization]. 2009. *2008/09 Winter Drought in Nepal Crop and Food Security Assessment: Joint Assessment Report.* Kathmandu: Ministry of Agriculture and Cooperatives, World Food Programme, Food and Agricultural Organization.

MoAC [Ministry of Agriculture and Cooperatives], WFP [World Food Programme]. 2008. *Report on Rapid Emergency Food Security Assessment; Far and Mid- West Hills and Mountains.* Kathmandu: Government of Nepal and United Nations World Food Programme.

Navadanya. 2003. *WTO and Water Privatisation: Defending Water as Public Good: Indian Movements Resist Water Privatisation as a Solution to Water Stress and Water Pollution.* Delhi: Navadanya.

NPC [National Planning Commission]. 2005a. *Millennium Development Goals Progress Report.* Kathmandu: National Planning Commission.

NPC [National Planning Commission]. 2005b. *Nepal Millennium Development Goals Report.* Kathmandu: National Planning Commission.

NPC [National Planning Commission]. 2005c. *Poverty Reduction Strategy Paper Second Progress Report.* Kathmandu: National Planning Commission.

OECD [Organizations for Economic Cooperation and Development]. 2005. *Tackling Trade in Agriculture.* OECD. Paris: Organizations for Economic Cooperation and Development.

OXFAM. 2005. *Make Extortion History: The Case for Development-Friendly WTO Accession for the World Poorest Countries.* London: OXFAM.

Rijsberman FR. 2008. Water for food: Corruption in irrigation systems. *In:* Transparency International. *Global Corruption Report 2008. The Global Coalition against Corruption. Berlin:*: Transparency International, pp 67-84.

SAARC [South Asia Association for Regional Cooperation]. 2005a. *Agreement on Establishing the SAARC Food Security Reserve.* Kathmandu: South Asia Association for Regional Cooperation Secretariat.

SAARC [South Asia Association for Regional Cooperation]. 2005b. *Declaration, Twelfth SAARC Summit.* Islamabad, 4-6 January, 2004. Kathmandu: South Asia Association for Regional Cooperation Secretariat.

SAARC [South Asia Association for Regional Cooperation]. 2004. *SAARC Plan of Action on Poverty Alleviation.* Kathmandu: South Asia Association for Regional Cooperation Secretariat.

SAWTEE [South Asia Watch on Trade Economics and Environment]. 2007. *Protecting Farmers' Rights in the Global IPR Regime: Challenges and Options for Developing Countries.* Policy brief no. 15. Kathmandu: South Asia Watch on Trade Economics and Environment.

Sikkema A. 2008. *Biotechnology/a Growing Market in Need of Direction.* Wageningen: Wageningen UR update No. 1. 2008, pp 8-11.

UNCTAD [United Nations Conference on Trade and Development]. 2005. *Trade and Development Report.* Geneva: United Nations Conference on Trade and Development.

Via Campesina. 2003. *What is food sovereignty?* International Peasant Movement. Website: www.viacampesina.org/en/index (Accessed on 23 November 2007).

Voice of Irish Concern for the Environment. 2009. *Bio-patents controlling life.* http://www.voice.buz.org/biopatenting/leaflet.html (Accessed on 26 April 2009)

WFP [World Food Programme]. 2008. *Nepal Staple Food Market Review and Outlook for 2009, Food security monitoring and analysis system, Nepal.* Kathmandu: World Food Programme.

WFP [World Food Programme], FAO [Food and Agricultural Organization]. 2009. *The State of Food Insecurity in the World: Economic Crises- Impacts and Lessons Learned.* Rome: World Food Programme Food and Agricultural Organization.

WFP [World Food Programme] and FAO [Food and Agricultural Organization]. 2006. *Food and Agriculture Markets in Nepal.* Kathmandu: World Food Programme.

Woods B. 2008. Agribusiness vs. Food Security: The Food Crisis and the IFIs. Bretton Woods update No. 61. London: Bretton Woods Project.

CHAPTER 6

A critical reflection on the sustainable livelihoods approach and its application to Nepal's community forestry

Bharat K Pokharel

Abstract

This chapter looks at the Department for International Development's Sustainable Livelihoods Approach, together with its components and framework. It also introduces four other livelihoods approaches promoted by various development agencies: the Rural Livelihood System and the livelihoods approaches used by UNDP, CARE and OXFAM. The Sustainable Livelihoods Approach is then applied to analyse community forestry in Nepal. The approach is found to be a useful tool for understanding of the elements of livelihoods. However, the approach is criticised for its inability to provide a framework for political transformation and wider social change. While the Sustainable Livelihoods Approach does acknowledge the importance of the transformation of 'policy, institutions and social processes', and of capital formation, it does not offer any explicit clues as to how such a transformation is to take place or how people can increase their capital and reduce vulnerability. The approach is silent about the factors and the means of political change to influence the policy change, such as gradual change or change through a civil or political movement. Despite its limitations, this chapter demonstrates the value of the Sustainable Livelihoods Approach as a tool for analysing development programmes such as Nepal's community forestry programme. Although the chapter portrays the Sustainable Livelihoods Approach as a widely-practised and useful approach to development, suggestions are made as to how to capitalise on its strengths and overcome its weaknesses by incorporating the human rights based approach to development. The human rights based approach to development is stronger in its focus on political and civil rights than the Sustainable Livelihoods Approach, and treats livelihood needs as human rights and 'beneficiaries' as 'rights holders' who could achieve the outcome of poverty reduction if their rights and responsibilities are recognised.

6.1 Introduction to the Sustainable Livelihoods Approach

What is the Sustainable Livelihoods Approach (SLA)? Is it just more donor jargon, or does it actually have value in practice? How can it improve the lives of the poor? What are its advantages over other approaches? How is it applied? What are the expected benefits of the approach? These are some of the questions asked by both academics and development practitioners about SLA. This chapter will attempt to answer some of these questions.

Most simply stated, a 'livelihood' is a way of making a living or obtaining the necessities of life. Chambers and Conway (1992, p 7) define livelihood as:

> *...compris[ing] the capabilities, assets (stores, resources, claims and access) and activities required for a means of living: a livelihood is sustainable and can cope with and recover from stress and shocks, maintain or enhance its capabilities and assets, and provide sustainable livelihoods opportunities for the next generation; and which contributes net benefits to other livelihoods at the local and global levels and in the long and short term.*

The Sustainable Livelihoods Approach is both a tool for analysis and a school of thought. It is a conceptual framework through which to better understand the problems embedded in the daily lives of people and, based on that understanding, it is a tool with which to design interventions. The SLA and its application have been well documented in recent years. Chambers and Conway (1992), Carney (1998), DFID (1999), Carney (1999), the IDS livelihoods website (http://www.livelihoods.org), Ellis and Biggs (2001) and Sunderlin (2005) are the main writers on the topic and give a comprehensive overview of the approach, framework, methods of application, tools and techniques, as well as practical experiences worldwide. This chapter is basically a synthesis of these writings, together with an analysis of the contribution of community forestry to people's livelihoods in Nepal using the Sustainable Livelihoods Framework (also see Pokharel 2001; Pokharel & Nurse 2004).

The SLA builds on the experiences and learning of most of the approaches of the past, such as the Integrated Rural Development Approach (IRDA) or Integrated Area Management; Sector-Wide Approach (SWAP), participatory approaches and other livelihoods approaches; it also incorporates key concepts such as sustainability (including environmental sustainability), gender equity, planning through objectives, the use of logical frameworks, policy support, institution building, and so on (DFID 1999; Carney 1998). The SLA takes a holistic view of development and highlights the need to check cross-sector, geographical and institutional links. It focuses on identifying the opportunities and constraints, multiple objectives and various factors that affect and characterise people's lives. It recognises that people are dynamic and diverse beings. Their diversity stems from differences in race, gender, age, class, beliefs, religion or value systems and prejudices, and is, therefore, not easy to model. Different people will certainly undertake different activities, adopt different strategies and pursue different objectives.

The SLA is a way of thinking about the objectives, scope and priorities of development (DFID 1999). It is a way of putting people at the centre of development, thereby increasing the effectiveness of development assistance. Adopting the SLA improves the identification, appraisal, implementation and evaluation of development programmes so that they better address the priorities of poor people, both directly and at a policy level.

This approach differs from other approaches in that it recognises the multiple dimensions of poverty as expressed and defined by the poor, in whatever way, and using whatever indicators. Under this approach, it is the poor themselves who identify the baselines.

The SLA is necessarily flexible in application, but it is based on certain core principles that cannot be compromised (Carney 1998), such as: people-centred, holistic, dynamic, building on strengths, macro-micro links and sustainability in terms of environmental, economic, social and institutional aspects of sustainable systems. Although the core principles remain the same, different development agencies have used the approach in different ways and gained operational experience in different fields and locations. Agencies such as DFID, OXFAM, CARE and UNDP have conceptualised, developed and implemented their own livelihoods approaches, which are also described briefly in this chapter, and compared with the SLA. All of these agencies are guided by the work of Chambers and Conway in the early 1990s, and most agencies adopt the Chambers and Conway definition of livelihood given above.

6.2 DFID's Sustainable Livelihoods Approach compared to other development approaches

The Sustainable Livelihoods Approach enters an already crowded conceptual and operational development landscape (DFID 1999, p 9). Although it is not within the scope of this chapter to analyse the details of all approaches to development, an understanding of the links between different development approaches is essential to avoid confusion. A brief overview of the conceptual and methodological similarities and differences and of the links between the various approaches is given in this section.

The SLA is not effective unless operationalised in a 'participatory' manner. Hence, the approach incorporates and builds upon existing participatory approaches. Similarly, the SLA and the SWAP are broadly complementary. For example, the SLA emphasises an understanding of the public structures and social processes, which are also the main elements of the

SWAP; these elements govern people's access to assets and their choice of livelihoods strategies. One of the criticisms of the SLA is that it is too similar to the failed Integrated Rural Development Approach (IRDA) of the 1970s. However, the SLA endeavours to build upon the strengths of the IRDA, while avoiding the traps that caused IRDA's downfall by not aiming to establish integrated programmes in rural areas. Table 6.1 summarises the main points of difference.

Table 6.1 Differences between the SLA and IRDA

Elements	Integrated Rural Development Approach (IRDA) (1970s)	Sustainable Livelihoods Approach (SLA) (late 1990s)
Starting point	Structures, areas	People and their existing strengths and constraints
Conceptions of poverty	Holistic, multi-dimensional	Multi-dimensional, complex, local, embraces the concepts of risks and variability
Problem analysis	Undertaken by planning unit in short period of time, viewed as conclusive	Inclusive process, iterative and ongoing
Sectoral scope	Multi-sectoral, single plan sector involvement established at outset	Multi-sectoral, many plans, small number of entry points, sectoral involvement evolves with projects
Level of operation	Local, area based	Both policy and field level, clear link
Partner organisations	National and local governments	National and local governments, NGOs, civil society organisations, private sector
Project management structure	Dedicated project management unit, external to government	Project managed by partner organisation
Coordination between sectors	Integrated execution (donor driven)	Driven by shared objectives, benefits of coordination identified by those involved
Sustainability	Not explicitly considered	Multiple dimensions considered

Source: Carney (1998, p 19); DFID (1999, p 11)

The human rights based approach (HRBA) and the SLA are complementary approaches that seek to achieve many of the same goals (for example, to empower the most vulnerable and strengthen the capacity of the poor to secure livelihoods). The primary focus of the SLA is on the linkages between public institutions and civil society, and particularly on how to increase the accountability of public institutions (duty bearers) to all citizens (rights holders). The SLA recognises the importance of these links and of enhancing accountability, although it takes as its starting point a need to understand the livelihoods of the poor within a wider political and economic context. From this starting point it then tries to identify the specific constraints that prevent the realisation of people's rights and, consequently, the improvement of their livelihoods on a sustainable basis (Carney 1998; DFID 1999). The human rights based approach to development is unique in bringing all covenants, bills and declarations on various aspects of human rights into operation. This approach, unlike others, does not start with a needs identification, but focuses on 'rights' (which rights are being affected and the specific elements of such rights). This is followed by a 'vulnerability' or 'rights holder analysis' to identify the most vulnerable groups, together with an analysis of obstacles to the realisation of rights and the existing capacities of the vulnerable groups (their strengths and weaknesses). An 'accountability' or 'duty bearer analysis' is also an important part of the HRBA, mainly to identify the roles and responsibilities of duty bearers who are responsible for the realisation of rights. Consideration of the capacity and resources to fulfil the defined obligations of duty bearers, such as state instruments at different levels, society and family, are also critical elements of the HRBA. The strength of this approach over others, including the various livelihoods approaches, is that it considers the rights that are less fulfilled than others; rights will serve as a foundation and catalysts towards the fulfilment of other rights, needs and obligations (Upreti & Timsina 2008).

Similarly, the Rural Livelihood System (RLS) (which will be described later) fills in the gaps in the SLA by considering a number of factors, forces and effects by which an individual is affected. These factors go far beyond the narrow bundle of assets and the policies, institutions and processes (PIP) identified by the SLA (Baumgartner 2006).

6.3 DFID's Sustainable Livelihoods Framework

First conceptualised in 1998, DFID's Sustainable Livelihoods Framework considers access to assets and transforming structures and processes as a starting point. It views people as operating within a context of vulnerability. Within this context, they have access to certain assets and resources or capital. Access affects, or is affected by, the prevailing social, institutional and organisational environment. This environment also influences the livelihoods strategies – ways of combining and using assets in order to meet livelihoods objectives – of individuals. The approach identifies five assets (human capital, social capital, natural capital, physical capital and financial capital) as the main livelihoods means.

The Sustainable Livelihoods Framework was developed to help understand and analyse people's livelihood situations. It also helps in assessing the effectiveness of existing development efforts in improving livelihoods. The level of understanding of the framework among top DFID personnel and among consultants is found to be high, but ownership of the framework and application of it by rural communities is yet to be seen. The main strengths of the framework are that it builds upon existing experiences and lessons learned, and offers a practical way forward in a complex environment.

To understand DFID's Sustainable Livelihoods Framework, it is necessary to have a clear analysis of the five components of the livelihoods framework and their relationship to each other. These components are:

- Vulnerability context
- Livelihood assets
- Institutions, policies and processes
- Livelihood strategies
- Livelihood outcomes

Figure 6.1 DFID's sustainable livelihoods framework

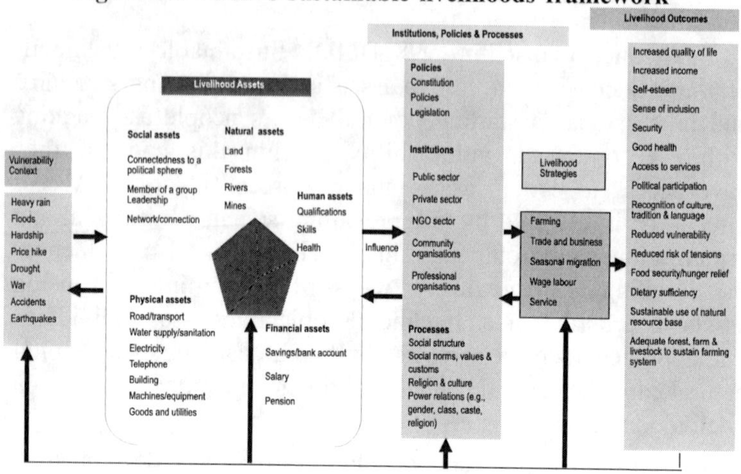

Vulnerability context

The vulnerability context frames the external environment in which people exist. This includes things like trends, shocks and seasonality, over which people have limited or no control. Table 6.2 provides the elements of the vulnerability context.

Table 6.2 Elements of vulnerability context

Trends	Shocks	Seasonality
Population trends	Human health shocks	Of prices
Resource trends (including conflict)	Natural shocks	Of production
National/international economic trends	Economic shocks	Of health
Trends in governance (Including politics)	Conflict	Of employment opportunities
Technological trends	Crop/livestock health shocks	

Source: DFID (1999)

Livelihood assets

The asset pentagon in Figure 6.2 is the core part of the Sustainable Livelihoods Framework within the vulnerability context. The SLA is based on the assumption that people require a range of assets to achieve their livelihood goals (referred to as outcomes in the framework). The five types of assets defined in the Sustainable Livelihoods Framework are given in Figure 6.2.

Figure 6.2 Five livelihood assets

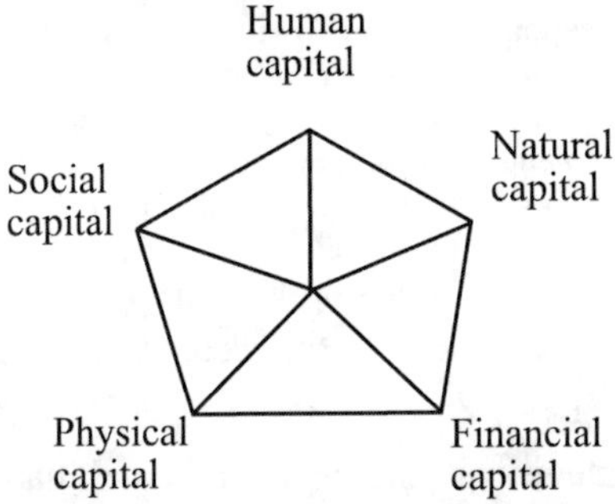

> **Box 6.1 Five livelihood assets defined**
>
> **Natural capital:** Natural resources such as land, forests, water, pastures, wildlife, biodiversity and wider environmental resources
>
> **Physical capital:** Privately owned assets such as houses, farm animals, tools, machinery, and vehicles; publicly owned economic infrastructure such as roads, transport, water, energy, communications and electricity supply; and social infrastructure such as schools and hospitals
>
> **Financial capital:** Cash income and savings, readily convertible liquid capital, supply of credit, remittances, pensions, and wages
>
> **Human capital:** Health, nutrition levels, educational standards and skills, knowledge and ability to pursue, influence and work
>
> **Social capital:** The set of social relationships on which people can draw to expand livelihoods options: e.g., kinship, friendship, patron-client relations, relationships of trust, reciprocal arrangements, membership of formal groups, membership of organisations that provide loans, grants and other forms of insurance

Source: Carney (1998)

Institutions, policies and processes

The institutions, policies and social processes within the Sustainable Livelihoods Framework shape people's livelihoods. They operate at all levels, from the household to the international level, and in all spheres, from the most private to the most public. They also have a direct impact upon whether or not people have a feeling of inclusion and rights over resources.

Table 6.3 Elements of institutions, policies and processes

Policies	Legislation	Institutions and structures	Culture	Power relations
Macro and micro level policies Special policies Redistributive policies Regulatory mechanisms	International agreements Domestic instruments/ legislation	Public, markets Private/ commercial and civil society institutions that influence access to assets Rules of the game within structures	Social norms, values, traditions and beliefs	Power relations on the basis of age, gender, caste and class

Livelihood strategies

Livelihood strategies are the range and combination of activities that people undertake and choices that they make to achieve their livelihood goals, such as productive activities, investment strategies and reproductive choices. Farming, fishing, migration, business and self-employment are some examples of livelihoods strategies.

Livelihood outcomes

Livelihood outcomes are the achievements or outputs of livelihood strategies. More income, improved food security, a feeling of inclusion, physical security and peace, a secure job, shelter, good health, and a feeling of self esteem are some examples of livelihoods outcome (see a more complete list in Figure 6.1).

6.4 Other livelihoods frameworks

6.4.1 Rural Livelihood System (RLS)

Based on intensive research in India, the Rural Livelihood System (RLS) was developed in 2004 by Baumgartner & Hoegger 2004. This approach is complementary to the SLA because DFID's Sustainable Livelihoods Framework (Figure 6.1) does not offer an explicit platform for dealing with crucial elements of decision-making, such as people's individual orientations and collective worldviews, or their experiences and emotional attachments. It is clearly important to "consider these missing aspects and to use different tools to ensure that they feed into development planning and our overall understanding of the driving factors behind livelihoods and poverty reduction" (Baumgartner & Hoegger 2004; Baumgartner 2006).

The Rural Livelihood System (RLS) is a heuristic tool and a framework for discovering the properties of a livelihood system. It emphasises the same core principles established by DFID. Its framework is represented by a nine-square Mandala with a rural house at the centre as a metaphor for livelihoods. Baumgartner and Hoegger (2004) use the analogy of a livelihoods house or Mandala, which is made up of three layers: foundation, walls and roof. According to Baumgartner and Hoegger (2004), each layer of the livelihoods Mandala represents the key elements of the RLS framework (base, space and orientation), with family at the centre (Figure 6.3).

Figure 6.3 Nine-square Mandala (RLS framework)

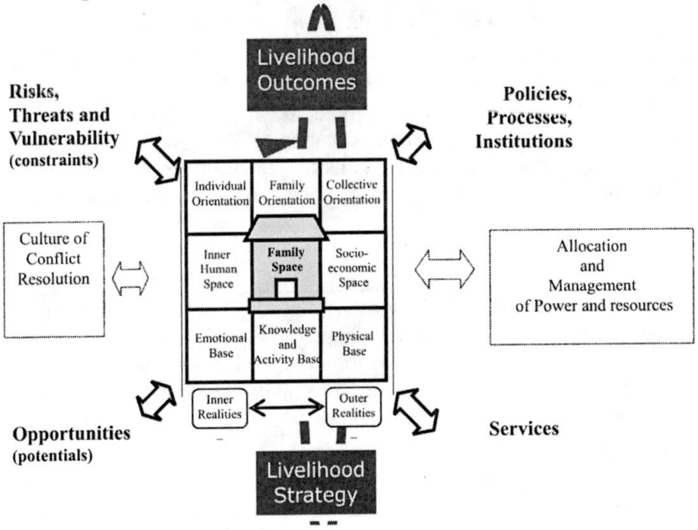

Source: Baumgartner (2006)

Foundations as livelihood base

The foundation of the house contains the three livelihood bases, namely, the emotional base of livelihoods (memories and attachments); knowledge base of livelihoods (experience, skills and technology) and the physical base of livelihoods (physical assets and natural resources).

Walls and rooms as livelihood space

The walls and rooms contain the three livelihood spaces, namely, the inner human space (integrity, identity, compassion and selfishness); family space (solidarity, gender relations) and socio-economic space (system of cooperation, community organisation).

Roof as livelihood orientation

The roof contains the three livelihood orientations, namely, individual orientation (visions, aspirations); family orientation (ancestry, caste, social status) and collective orientation (religion, tradition, worldview, education). Table 6.4 describes the RLS Mandala in more detail.

Table 6.4 RLS Mandala (a livelihoods framework)

Individual orientation Visions, hopes, aspirations, fears, self- image, respect, 'gurus', models	**Family orientation** Ancestry, caste, social status, aspirations to leadership, education, jobs, aspirations to power, wealth, social mobility	**Collective orientation** Way of life, subsistence agriculture, food security, religion, traditions, common property resources, state laws, worldviews, school, capitalistic values, urban ideals and new prosperity
Inner human space Integrity, identity, awareness, selfishness, compassion, responsibility, affection, curiosity, courage, anxiety	**Family space** Gender relations, nutrition distribution, health, family planning, distribution of workload, solidarity	**Socio-economic space** Production relations, system of cooperation, community organisations, government institutions, markets for goods, land, labour and capital, contractors, industry
Emotional base Memories, attachments, feelings, boredom	**Knowledge base** Technology, agricultural pattern, experiences, skills, traditional knowledge, labour, crafts, services, modern professions	**Physical base** Natural environment (topography, climate), natural resources, animals, habitat, accumulated wealth

Source: Baumgartner & Hoegger (2004, p 47)

Comparing DFID's SLA and RLS, the two approaches have certain similarities and certain differences.

Similarities

Both the SLA and RLS offer conceptual inspiration and a framework for development efforts aimed at more sustainable livelihoods. Both are considered tools for exploring and analysing people's livelihoods. Both are governed by a similar set of guiding principles. Although both approaches can be integrated into project cycle management and are applied in designing and implementing development support for poverty reduction, they are not bound to project-based development efforts. Both approaches are a work-in-progress and not finished products. Neither replaces other development approaches in use, but is complementary to other approaches.

Differences

DFID's SLA has a strong focus on policy, institutions and processes, within a vulnerability context, as the factors influencing capital asset formation for sustainable livelihoods. In comparison, the RLS emphasises decision-making processes and livelihoods strategy development, with a focus on emotional characteristics such as integrity, identity, compassion and selfishness. Both approaches have many strengths; if blended they have added value. Table 6.5 compares the strengths of the two approaches.

Table 6.5 SLA and RLS compared

Strengths of SLA	Strengths of RLS
Directs attention to forces and factors in the broader context of people's livelihoods, such as risks causing vulnerability, policies, services, transforming institutions	Directs attention to the centre and the process of decision-making in people's livelihoods regarding role sharing and gender and power relations
Facilitates exploration of the composition and relevance of the differentiated asset portfolio of people's livelihoods	Facilitates consideration of the role of people's threefold value orientations in the process of strategy development
Clearly focuses on the links between the asset portfolio, livelihood strategies, and the livelihood outcomes that people aim at	Extends the focus from the outer to the inner reality of livelihoods, which ranges from emotional to physical livelihood needs

Source: Baumgartner (2006)

6.4.2 UNDP's approach to promoting sustainable livelihoods

In 1995, UNDP developed a framework for formulating programming strategies, analysing strengths and assets, and assessing the coping/adaptive strategies of local people. Human, social, natural, physical, financial and sometimes political assets are analysed in this framework. For UNDP, this framework is one of five corporate mandates and an important approach for achieving sustainable human development. The main strengths of the framework are that it links micro-macro organisations, integrates poverty, environment and governance issues, and gets the most out of both communities and outsiders.

UNDP does not have a specific livelihoods framework as such; it largely uses the SLA in its programming cycle, which emphasises the assessment of coping (adaptive) strategies and the analysis of micro, macro and sectoral policies, together with the assessment of modern science and technology in the context of indigenous technologies that influence peoples livelihoods (see Figure 6.4).

Figure 6.4 UNDP's approach to promoting sustainable livelihoods

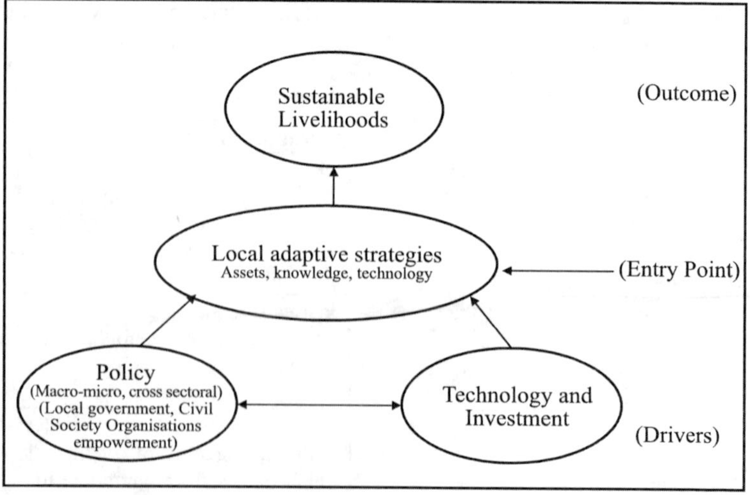

Source: Carney (1999)

6.4.3 CARE's livelihoods model

In 1994, CARE focused its efforts on improving people's capabilities, access to tangible and intangible assets, and the existence of economic opportunities. Three capital assets are identified, namely, human, social and economic. This model is used primarily as a wide programming framework. Household livelihoods security is the central focus of CARE's framework. The main strengths of the framework are that it is comprehensive yet flexible, improves sectoral coordination and increases multiplier effects. Unlike DFID's framework, CARE places less emphasis on policies, institutions and organisational factors. This is in line with CARE's focus, which is mainly on local matters such as community mobilisation, and not so much on policy (see Figure 6.5).

Figure 6.5 CARE's livelihood model

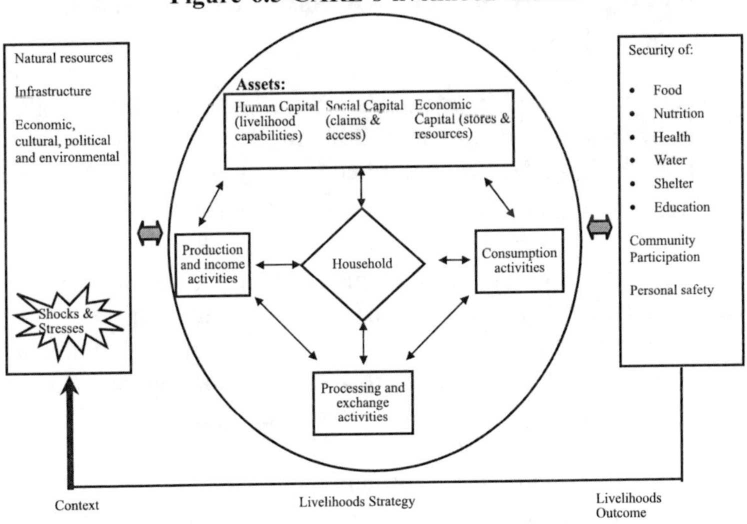

Source: Carney (1999)

6.4.4 OXFAM's livelihoods framework

OXFAM was the first agency to use the concept of sustainable livelihoods. Since 1993, OXFAM's framework has emphasised enhancing people's capabilities, working towards equity, sustainability and ensuring links between policy changes and livelihood improvement. Like DFID's framework, five assets are identified, namely, human, social, natural, physical and financial capital. For OXFAM, this framework has been an important tool for achieving poverty eradication, which is one of OXFAM's five strategic change objectives. The main strengths of the framework are that it recognises participatory analysis and enables links to social and human rights approaches.

OXFAM's livelihoods framework is similar to DFID's framework and is, therefore, not described here in more detail. The framework is basically used as a checklist in project appraisal, planning and review. Unlike DFID's framework, OXFAM uses this framework in a semi-formal way and there are no established guidelines and worksheets for applying the framework.

6.5 Strengths and weaknesses of livelihoods approaches

In the previous sections, DFID's SLA and other livelihoods approaches such as RLS and the approaches used by UNDP, CARE and OXFAM are described.

What is obvious is that these approaches have many points in common. All offer conceptual frameworks that put people at the centre, all have guiding principles that advocate for poverty reduction and livelihoods-focused methods and tools, all are complementary to other development approaches, including the HRBA. There is a need here is to look for synergies, and identify the added value of the UNDP, CARE, OXFAM and RLS approaches to DFID's SLA. For example, Haan and Zoomers (2005) provide information on the linkages among livelihood opportunities, decision making, power relations and access. Similarly, the RLS approach provides better analysis and understanding of the cultural and emotional aspects of livelihoods, and how a household's livelihood strategies are influenced by individual, family and collective orientations. In this section, the main strengths and weaknesses of the various livelihoods approaches are highlighted, with some emphasis on SLA.

Strengths

One of the major contributions of all livelihoods approaches has been the sensitisation of development actors to the need to extend development benefits to the poorest, putting people at the centre. 'Supporting and enhancing capabilities', rather than simply 'meeting needs' is the main conceptual driving force behind all the approaches described in this chapter. Making communities and households the central actors in development is the major thrust of all livelihoods approaches. These approaches demand enabling, inclusive and focused action for which multi- stakeholder participation by civil society, government and the private sector is necessary. Their emphasis on macro-micro linkage promotes bottom-up planning and policy-making processes.

All livelihoods approaches are based on holistic or system thinking, as opposed to ad hoc or piecemeal approaches. They focus on researching relations between components and subsystems. They recognise the capacities of people in terms of various forms of capital as a starting point for local development (see Chambers & Conway 1992; Carney 1998; DFID 1999; Carney (1999). Livelihoods approaches also take into account the critical elements of the human development approach of Sen (1985).

Livelihoods approaches have provided a roadmap into some pretty complex issues, and are adaptable for use in practical ways to understand livelihoods. These approaches facilitate discussion and communication between people from different disciplines, who can then talk a common 'livelihood' language.

Livelihoods approaches offer, at least in principle, a way to link poverty, at the level of the community, to actions taken by higher-level policy and decision makers, as well as to economic factors. This is a shift in approach in that it involves communities in their own needs assessment towards a process of involving communities in a holistic analysis of their own way of living, assets and coping mechanisms, and of the factors affecting their livelihood means and strategies. Livelihoods approaches also offer a way to judge poverty, relatively (not in absolute terms) against other members of the same community, while avoiding quantification.

The SLA provides development practitioners with a coherent and flexible framework for programming, while also trying to establish micro-macro linkages. The approach has some practical tools and methods, such as guidance sheets, which describe how to use the Sustainable Livelihoods Framework, what information is needed and why, and how to go about obtain and analysing such information. It provides ingredients for the analysis of social, environmental, institutional, political, and policy issues, as well as options for livelihoods opportunities.

The SLA offers communities a checklist for analysis, appraisal, planning and action. Concrete practical experiences in the implementation of the approach have now been documented, as have criteria and indicators of success and expected outcomes. These are useful in understanding SLA as a development approach. Conceptual and programmatic frameworks, which did not exist ten years ago, are also now available (also see SLLP 2000).

Weaknesses

Although the SLA has proved to be an important analytical tool for development practitioners, whether this approach has been able to solve the problems of the poor and improve their standards of living is yet to be confirmed by empirical evidence.

Among many operational issues, SLA does not provide operational tools to identify the poorest of the poor, the socially excluded and the most vulnerable households, commonly called disadvantaged households (DAH). Even after identification, the most marginalised are usually beyond the reach of development aid, because they often live in remote places and do not participate in development activities. The most marginalised are not empowered to raise their voices to demand services and have limited capacity to make use of development aid. In practice, SLA is still very much project-based rather than community-based. SLA is a conceptual framework, not a practical operational methodology (SLLP 2000).

Moreover, very few agencies have applied the SLA in sectors other than natural resources management. Under the SLA, the poor are seen as active development partners who should be involved in livelihoods analysis, rather than simply passive recipients of development. Although the approach recognises local capacities and traditional mechanisms in analysing the livelihood opportunities of the poorest, in practice, traditional practices, mechanisms and power relations are important determinants of social and economic exclusion, and of the marginalisation of the poor. Moreover, the SLA framework is complex and difficult for the poorest villagers to understand. To include them in analysis, appraisal, planning and action is, therefore, a daunting task. The SLA process demands multi-sectoral, decentralised planning. However, many development agencies tend to operate in narrowly focused sectors or disciplines. In principle, the exploration and use of locally available assets and field-level practical experience are considered to be pre-requisites for the successful application of SLA. However, theoretical ideas about SLA, concepts such as 'holistic', 'dynamic', 'environmentally friendly', 'gender sensitive' and so on, are generally put forward by Western academics. Researchers and practitioners in the 'South'[1] are barely involved in the conceptualisation and operationalisation of such concepts and approaches. Defining poverty, marginalisation and disadvantage in a diverse socio-economic context is also difficult. Poor people's involvement in this process of developing and applying SLA is still far away.

There is also scepticism about to what extent donor guided approaches, which are crafted to channel their funds, can challenge existing political systems, social structures and processes. These donor-funded programmes generally reach a particular 'class' and benefit certain power holders. If SLA is to be considered as a paradigm shift that aims at challenging the existing power structures and social relations, it could be seen as a political threat to the existing power holders for whom this kind of 'development process' is unacceptable. The key to long-term institutional sustainability lies in the successful transformation of institutions and their relationships. However,

1 The 'South' is used by NCCR North-South to refer to Africa, Asia, and Latin America, as opposed to Europe (North).

changes in power relations are difficult to bring about and can take strong civil or political movements. The SLA does not sufficiently consider power relations, entitlements or political transformation processes; the framework is silent in this regard. It tends to see the development process as neutral or apolitical. This is the weakest part of the SLA. Political transformation of local and supra-local political structures and processes are not within the scope of the SLA. Rather, the SLA, like other development approaches of the past, tends to promote 'reformist' ways and means of social and political and policy change. Although the term 'transform' is used in the framework in relation to transforming policy, institutions and processes, it is limited to 'policy' change, and does not seem to apply to 'political' change, which can ultimately lead to policy change. To increase livelihood opportunities for the most marginalised it is necessary to challenge power relations and promote redistributive systems of resource control, which is usually possible only though civil and political movements.

Some literature highlights the challenges and shortcomings of SLA, both at the theoretical and operational level (see for example SLLP 2000; FAO & DFID 2000; Haan & Zoomers 2005). It is particularly in relation to access, decision making, power relations, behaviour and structural factors that the SLA has not been able to provide adequate evidence of its contribution to altering the status quo. Similarly, at the project level, the SLA has been criticised as being used on the receiving side, basically to secure outside funding, and is not challenging the status quo of the political economy of development aid. However, the SLA does provide a conceptual framework for understanding livelihood assets in a coherent and systemic way and for understanding how they affect policies, institutions and processes, and livelihoods strategies, and vice versa. However, a weakness in the SLA lies in its focus on assets; not enough attention is paid to demand. This weakness can be overcome by a human rights based approach. The SLA can be criticised for placing too much emphasis on assets and the potential of individuals to reduce poverty themselves, thereby reducing the responsibility of authorities to respond to the demands of citizens. The HRBA, on the other hand, highlights power relations between citizens and authorities. The added value of integrating the HRBA with livelihoods approaches is the focus on both the empowerment of 'rights holders' and building the state to increase the capacity of 'duty bearers' (mainly government, non-government and private sector service providers) to respond to the demands of the rights holders/citizens (Carter 2007).

To quote Peron and Neil (2006, p 4):

> *HRBA highlights the importance of state-citizens linkages, combining a focus on developing the capacity of states to deliver on human rights commitments with citizens' awareness and capacity to claim their entitlements. Human rights are a source of legitimacy for state action, and put emphasis on the need for effective channels of accountability.*

6.6 Beyond the SLA: The human rights based approach to development

Despite its wide application around the globe, the SLA has promoted reformist views of policy processes and social change through development interventions. This approach has hardly offered anything beyond people's subsistence livelihood needs. What is becoming increasingly clear is that, to ensure improved sustainable livelihoods, people's civil and political rights need to be ensured. For this, radical structural changes are required that challenge existing power structures. In Nepal, it took a civil war to bring about institutional change and create an environment in which people's civil and political rights are now on the agenda. Such change is only possible through political processes, not just development processes. This is to say that political transformation at the political level should take place first that is then followed by social and economic transformation process at a later stage. In this sense, an alternative approach to the SLA should be sought. The newly emerged human rights based approach could be a step forward, and may build upon and improve the SLA. The HRBA aims to empower people to be involved in development and to optimise the benefits from it, using people's basic human rights as a foundation. The HRBA should be used in conjunction with the SLA and other approaches, as it fills some of the gaps that these approaches have been criticised for.

Rights based approaches to development take as their foundation the need to promote and protect the human rights that have been recognised by the global community and are protected by international legal instruments. These include economic, social and cultural, as well as civil and political rights, all of which are interdependent. Running through the rights based approach are concerns with empowerment and participation, and with the elimination of discrimination on grounds such as race, language, gender, religion, and so forth (Carney 1998; DFID 1999). Under the HRBA, human rights are considered constitutive of the goal of development, leading to a new approach to development and requiring institutional changes. HRBA considers basic human needs to be human rights, i.e., the right to life; right to live in dignity; right to education and access to information; right to a fair trial; right to participate in the political process; freedom of thought, expression and religion; right to access to water; right to access to land and its entitlements; right to access to health care; right to non-discrimination and so on (Peron & Neil 2006).

Box 6.2 What is the human rights based approach (HRBA)?

Under the HRBA, human rights are considered constitutive of the goal of development, leading to a new approach to development and requiring institutional changes. HRBA considers basic human needs to be human rights, i.e., the right to life; right to live in dignity; right to education and access to information; right to a fair trial; right to participate in the political process; freedom of thought, expression and religion; right to access to water; right to access to land and its entitlements; right to access to health care; right to non-discrimination and so on.

The United Nations' common understanding of HRBA includes the following:

"All programmes of development cooperation, policies and technical assistance should further the realisation of human rights as laid down in the Universal Declaration of Human Rights and other international human rights instruments".

Human rights standards contained in, and principles derived from, the Universal Declaration of Human Rights and other international human rights instruments guide all development cooperation and programming in all sectors and in all phases of the programming process.

Development cooperation contributes to the development of the capacities of 'duty-bearers' to meet their obligations and/or of 'rights-holders' to claim their rights.

The human rights principles identified are: universality and inalienability; indivisibility; interdependence and interrelatedness; equality and non-discrimination; participation and inclusion and accountability and rule of law.

Source: Peron & Neil (2006)

The HRBA attempts to integrate both livelihoods and human rights elements. It is now being used widely by various donors, I/NGOs and advocacy organisations. Some lesson have been learnt and documented in relation to the application of the approach (see for example: http://www.undg.org). However, a discussion of this is beyond the scope of this chapter.

6.7 Nepal's community forestry programme

6.7.1 What is community forestry?

Community forestry in Nepal involves the devolution of power from the central government authority to local communities who protect, manage and utilise forest resources. Community forestry user groups (CFUGs) are local, independent, autonomous corporate bodies governed by Nepal's Forest Act 1993, which sets their Constitution and Forest Operational Plan (see Pokharel et al. 2006 for details)

Box 6.3 Key features of CFUGs

The following are some of the key features of CFUGs in terms of their independent status, autonomy and authority that affect the formation of social, natural, financial and physical capital.

1. Social capital

- CFUGs can elect, select or change their executive committee at any time.
- CFUGs can impose penalties on members who break their rules.
- Community forest boundaries are not restricted to existing administrative or political boundaries.
- CFUGs can amend or revise their constitution at any time.
- The handover of forest to CFUGs is determined by their willingness and capacity to protect, manage and utilise the forest, and by their customary rights.

2. Natural capital

- There is no limit to the forest area that can be handed over to communities.
- CFUGs can make optimal use of their forest by growing cash crops together with forest crops.
- CFUGs can mortgage their standing forest products with financial institutions to obtain loans.

3. Financial capital

- CFUGs can utilise their funds for any purpose.
- CFUGs can freely fix prices and market their forest produce.
- CFUGs can establish enterprises and make profit.
- CFUGs can seek support from any organisation.
- CFUGs can raise funds by various forestry and non-forestry means with all income going to the group fund and with no requirement to share financial revenue with the government because the protection and management cost is borne by the groups themselves.

4. Physical capital

- CFUGs can invest in any areas, persons or development activities according to the decision of the CFUG assembly.

5. Human capital

- CFUGs can develop its human resource capacity to effectively protect, manage and utilise their forests

Source: Forest Act 1993 and Forest Regulation 1995

6.7.2 Study of community forestry and livelihoods in Swiss-supported areas

The Swiss Agency for Development and Cooperation (SDC) has been supporting Nepal to implement community forestry programmes through the Nepal-Swiss Community Forestry Project (NSCFP), which commenced in 1990. The Project is being implemented in three districts in the middle hills of Nepal: Dolakha, Ramechhap and Okhaldhunga. These districts have an estimated forest area of 238,422 hectares, of which 38 per cent (90,186 ha) has been handed over to local communities as community forests. As at July 2007, a total of 98,800 household members (87% of the population of these districts) had been organised into 919 community forestry user groups. The role of the project is to provide financial and technical support to facilitate a process in which government and non-governmental agencies and CFUGs work together to further promote community forestry for its economic, ecological and institutional sustainability.

A comprehensive survey of CFUGs, together with a monitoring and coaching exercise, was conducted by local NGOs and CFUG federation with the financial and technical support of Nepal Swiss Community Forestry Project (NSCFP) in November 2005. A total of 692 CFUGs were surveyed. Group discussions with CFUG committee members and users (at least 20 people in each group) were held. Selective CFUG committee chairs and secretaries were also interviewed. Information was compiled and stored in a database system. A desk study was carried out to analyse the ecological, economic and institutional sustainability of CFUGs at the group level. In addition, a checklist was prepared to gather information about livelihood assets, the effect of the policy environment and social processes. Household interviews and livelihoods coaching were conducted in about 500 households to help them to prepare their household livelihoods plan. Cross-section households were selected from different socio-economic groups based on wellbeing ranking categories to document the impact of community forestry at the household level.

6.7.3 Analysis of community forestry using SLA

SLA is a valuable tool for analysing the effects of development interventions on people's livelihoods. Section 6.8 analyses Nepal's community forestry programme at the group level using DFID's Sustainable Livelihoods Framework (also see Pokharel 2001) to show its contribution to capital formation, policy reform, change in governance structures and social processes, and, to some extent, to reducing the effect of the vulnerability context on the rural poor. Section 6.9 analyses the impact of Nepal's community forestry programme at the household level on livelihood strategies and outcomes using both the SLA and the RLS.

6.8 Impact of community forestry on livelihoods: A group perspective

This section analyses community forestry at the group level using the Sustainable Livelihoods Framework and based on the study conducted by NSCFP. This section focuses on livelihood assets (the five types of livelihood assets); policies and institutions, and social processes (see Figure 6.1).

6.8.1 Formation and mobilisation of livelihood assets

Natural capital

Forests handed over to a community are natural capital. In general, all over Nepal, community forestry has brought positive changes in regeneration status, canopy density, biodiversity and basal area (Branney & Yadav 1998; Jackson et al. 1998; Gautam et al. 2003; Karna et al. 2004). An analysis of the perceptions of 692 CFUG members in Dolakha, Ramechhap and Okhaldhunga districts also indicates that the condition of community forests has improved tremendously (NSCFP 2006). There are increased numbers of forestry user groups (FUGs), which are harvesting timber, fuelwood, grasses and non-timber forest products (NTFPs). The availability of forest products has also increased with a concurrent reduction in the time spent in collecting forest products (NSCFP 2006).

Despite improved forest condition, there has been a reduction in access to forest products for the poorest because of the tendency to protect and harvest trees for timber, rather than use them for small wood and multiple products. Forest tree inventory data from Ramechhap District, for example, suggests that district officials prescribe only a quarter of the actual annual harvestable increment: the prescribed volume is calculated by the Department of Forests at 1 per cent compared to a (conservatively estimated) 4 per cent mean annual increment found in matured natural forest. In addition, the CFUGs actually harvest only half of the prescribed volume (i.e., which is less than 10% of the available annual increment of the forest). In fact, the poorest households do not directly benefit at all from timber supply or sale (see

Pokharel & Nurse 2004, p 23; also see Malla 2000; Adhikari 2008; Kanel 2008; Khatri-Chetri 2008).

Despite improved forest condition, restrictive rules related to the distribution and sale of forest products (mainly timber) for domestic use deprive the poorest of access to these resources. Almost all the CFUGs stipulate in their rules on the sale and distribution of subsidised timber that subsidised timber can only be bought for household consumption. This rule benefits the rich who can afford to construct houses and make furniture out of timber; the poorest do not bother to buy the subsidised timber because they cannot sell it and they do not need timber for domestic use. A conservative mindset amongst committee members and forestry officials is responsible for these types of rules.

Social capital

It has been reported that the community forestry process has increased social cohesion, which has enhanced social capital for those who were previously powerless, isolated and excluded from mainstream social and political processes. For example, Pokharel et al. (2006) reports that the participation of women in committees has increased from 19 per cent in 1996 to 33 per cent in 2005. Similarly, the representation of Dalits (so called 'untouchables') in CFUG committees has increased from 2 per cent in 1996 to 8 per cent in 2005. In addition, the representation of women and Dalits in key positions has also increased.

Despite increased social capital, the poorest cannot afford to participate or take up leadership roles, because they cannot spare the time away from their livelihood activities. Hence, there is a high cost involved in social capital formation for the marginalised. The poorest suffer the most because, first of all, they cannot afford to participate; secondly, if they do, they hardly speak; if they do speak, they are rarely heard; and, if they are heard, decisions are rarely made in their favour (Pokharel & Nurse 2004, p 24).

Human capital

The capacity of community forestry stakeholders, government and non-government service providers, and community members has increased as a result of community forestry. They have developed skills in relation to community mobilisation, financial management and administration, and in the management of community forests, among other things. However, the poorest are often left out of capacity-building programmes run by the Government, NGOs and donors, because they are illiterate, under-valued, and perceived as having less ability to make and act on decisions (Pokharel & Nurse 2004, p 24).

Financial capital

Group funds generated from the sale of forest products, levies and outside grants are the financial capital created by community forestry. The average CFUG fund balance in each of the districts studied is almost equivalent to the Government's annual forestry development budget. Of the total 692 CFUGs studied, there are examples of 255 CFUGs (56%) establishing low interest credit schemes as well as grants to the poorest household members from the CFUG fund (NSCFP 2006).

Despite the increased financial capital and CFUG credit schemes, the bulk of money loaned to members was found to be 'captured' by those members of the groups deemed to be 'creditworthy' (i.e., able to pay the loan back on time). In many cases, the poorest are blacklisted because of delays in making repayments (Pokharel & Nurse 2004, p. 24).

Physical capital

CFUGs have carried out many community development activities on their own. Construction of village trails, small bridges, community buildings, schools and temples are examples of the physical capital created by the community forestry programme. Analysis of the data of the NSCFP (2006) indicates that 47 per cent of CFUGs have spent funds on school buildings, 36 per cent on roads and 26 per cent on drinking water (NSCFP 2006).

Policies and institutions

The Master Plan for the Forestry Sector 1989, the Forest Act of 1993, Forest Regulation of 1995, the Operational Guidelines of 1995, and the Government's Three Year Interim

Plan (2008-2011) are the forestry sector policy instruments that govern community forestry in Nepal. These instruments have legitimised community forestry user groups, which are grassroots-level institutions. According to the current legislation, CFUGs are independent, autonomous and self-governing institutions responsible for protecting, managing and using any patch of national forest with a defined forest boundary and user group members. CFUGs are formed democratically and must be registered at the District Forest Office (DFO), which hands over the forests to CFUGs with a written constitution and a forest Operational Plan (OP). These documents define the forest management objectives, action plan, and the rights, duties and responsibilities of the forest users of a particular forest. Moreover, community forestry has become an open university for policymakers and practitioners to see the evidence of the effect of policies in practice. As a result policy reforms are made based on practical experiences that take place on the ground.

6.8.3 Social processes: Gender, equity and empowerment

Nepali society is unequal in terms the social and political power held by people from different castes, classes, cultural groups, regions and religions. Discrimination is perpetuated through every day practices and contexts. Discrimination occurs at every level: within households, neighbourhoods, groups, organisations, communities and society in general. Only by changing everyday practices of discrimination can social relations of power be transformed. Community forestry is generally centred on institution building and forest management. Unfortunately, the benefits of programmes that are focused on disadvantaged groups are often captured by power elites (rich high caste males from urban areas) in the current inequitable political and social structure. The poor, low caste women from remote areas are difficult to reach through development. The current focus of community forestry on providing women and low-caste members with education, encouraging their participation in CFUG committees, as local facilitators and as local resource persons (LRP), as well as evaluating whether or not they hold positions of responsibility such as CFUG secretary or president, have helped, to some extent, to shift local power dynamics. New initiatives at the household level are also important in terms of recognising the kind of support disadvantaged groups need in order to gain access to community arenas. Further programmes can be strengthened by creating networks of support, both horizontally and vertically, in the community (NSCFP 2006).

6.8.4 Vulnerability context

The economically poorest members of CFUGs who belong to socially disadvantaged households and live in remote areas are generally more vulnerable in terms of their capacity to cope with natural disasters and health conditions. CFUGs are becoming sensitive to the need to address issues of poverty and social exclusion in relation to such vulnerable households. Information from the 692 CFUGs in the study districts indicates that up to 61 per cent of CFUGs studied have made some kind of special provision for the poor or disadvantaged groups in their operational plans and have acted as a safety net for their disadvantaged members (NSCFP 2006). Table 6.6 shows the results of the analysis of the CFUGs' information maintained in database and analysed for the purpose of the study in November 2005.

Table 6.6 Provisions made by CFUGs for poor and socially excluded household members

Areas in which positive discrimination provisions have been made	Community Forestry User Groups	
	Number	Percentage
Forest products	279	61
Group funds	255	56
Skills training	203	44
Housing materials	187	41
Scholarships	85	18
Land allocation	65	14
Employment	45	10
Share holding in local forest based enterprise	37	8

Source: NSCFP (2006)

Table 6.6 shows a significant number of CFUGs trying to move from elite-centred decision making and programme activities to poor-centred. Similarly, Pokharel et al. (2009) has found that CFUGs are becoming self-sustaining grassroots-level institutions. Pro-poor strategies are having an effect; as a result, CFUGs are able to reach poor households. Nevertheless, pro-poor practices in community forestry develop in a sequential manner, building upon a strong institutional and environmental basis. The non-inclusive operation of the institutions has a negative effect on the overarching objective of poverty reduction. Thus, any kind of exclusion, of either elites or the poor, in this process should be avoided (Schreckenberg & Luttrell 2009).

Despite this trend, Pokharel and Nurse (2004, p 24) have reported that the amount of funds allocated by CFUGs to disadvantaged households is very low compared to investment in community infrastructure. Moreover, on many occasions, the poorest have been excluded from membership of groups on account of not being 'resident' in the ward, due to the fact that they are recent migrants from other areas; they were therefore unable to be involved in protection and plantation activities from the beginning so had to bear the cost of membership. They are also sometimes excluded for not being able to participate in the voluntary labour schemes as prescribed by the CFUG committee.

6.9 Impact of community forestry on livelihoods: A household perspective

Although the SLA framework is a useful tool for analysing the impact of community forestry at the programme level, it does not consider how people's emotions and cultural values determine their livelihoods strategies. The application of the RLS can be useful for such analysis. Using the both the RLS and SLA frameworks as analytical tools and putting the household at the centre, an analysis of the impact of community forestry on livelihood strategies and outcomes at the household level is given in this section.

Gorakh Bahadur, the Chairman of Bhiteri Community Forestry User Group of Dolakha district, has a vision to make his village wealthy with improved green forest. He remembers that the forest near his village was destroyed completely when its trees were sold by the government to contractors. The revenue went entirely to the Government treasury. Villagers considered the forest to be the property of the Government, and, hence, did not protect it. Although forest guards were present in the district headquarters, it was impossible for them to prevent villagers from cutting down trees. Slowly the forest was completely destroyed and degraded. Following the emergence of community forestry, the forest was handed over to the community; Gorakh played an important role in the handover. After the handover of the forest to the community, everyone from the village contributed to planting trees. Gorakh is a respected person in the village and was elected chairperson of the group, but fears that he will be unable to fulfil the expectations of the people. He says the following:

> *Upon our demand, the District Forest Officials handed this forest over to us as a community forest. The forest is now ours. We are now protecting it as our common resources. We hold regular meetings and assemblies. Rules are made collectively in the assemblies. Labour contribution and forest product distribution are sought equally and there is no discrimination against any sex or caste. Open discussion is allowed in the meetings. Decisions are made by consensus. The committee is usually selected unanimously. All sections of people are represented in the committee including women and disadvantaged groups. The forest condition has improved: it is greener, there is more biodiversity and more forest products are available. We have started reaping the benefits. We have helped build a school and purchased furniture for the children. There are five enterprises, three for furniture making and two for Nepali paper. Many poor households are employed. We have fixed the quota for timber and Lokta (a plant used to make paper) for these enterprises. The CFUG fund is increasing. Some of the funds are deposited in the bank, some are loaned to group members and the rest is kept safely by our treasurer. The forest is strictly protected against grazing. Some of us have attended training and been on study visits and we have learnt some new things such as Alaichi (cardamom) cultivation and enterprise promotion, which we have tried out in our group. We have received support from the Nepal Swiss Community Forestry Project and other agencies to build our capacity as community leaders. We now know many things about how to run an institution. Many people have visited us to see how we are operating as a group and managing the forest. Our previous secretary, Lama Bhai is now in the District Federation of Community Forestry User Groups – he is an entrepreneur now. We have good relationships with the District*

Forest Officials, rangers and the District Federation. They are quite helpful to us. We coordinate with the local Village Development Committee (VDC) for planning. We received support from the VDC Chairperson during a boundary dispute with our neighbouring group. We are doing fine, progressing and advancing slowly and steadily. We are happy that we have been able to do this much.

Contrary to the above, Mr Mohan Kasai, one of the poorest Dalit men of Lang Lang Community Forest User Group of Nepal, describes the effect of community forestry on his livelihood in the following way:

I have just two ropani (0.1 ha) of land. I do not grow enough grain even for two months of the year from my land. I look for wage labour to survive. I have no connection to anyone like you. I do not know other things than working in Jethamukhiya's (landlord's) farm. My family has been in debt for generations and has no money or savings to buy things, do business, or to go to the city or abroad for work. No one has done anything for us so far. I do not think community forestry can do anything for us. I am also a member of the group and I have been told to come to the meetings and speak up there. I did go once or twice, but who cares about us? Who will listen to us? They (the leaders) talk of protection, fines, timber, grazing control, community building, school teachers, furniture, and so on, which sounds good to everyone, and to us also, but it does not feed us or benefit us. I am aware that some timber can be bought from the forest at a cheap rate if we build a house. I know that Bhakta Bahadur (furniture owner) got timber under this rule. But we cannot afford to buy timber. We wish we would get some dead fallen timber for free, but we are not even allowed to cut dead trees and sell them for food. If I am not allowed to sell the timber, what can I do with it? I cannot eat it. I cannot send my children to school, even if there are many teachers. People (outsiders) ask us to go to the meeting and speak out. But we do not know how to speak properly at these meetings. People laugh at us when we speak. I do not see any hope; therefore, I do not bother to go to the meetings anymore. There is no way that we can speak out. Gorakh went to Ilam on a study tour because he knows how to speak, but I do not think I will be selected for such a tour because I do not understand what people talk about, even in the assembly, and I cannot read or write. The best thing is to stay home or work as a wage labourer, as we have been doing for generations. That is how we are, and it will go on and on, I don't know for how many generations, unless we die.

This is not the end of the story. Tara Shrestha is a female member of Bichour Community Forestry User Group of Dolakha.

She is landless, works as farm wage labourer, earns NRs. 90 (US$ 1.17) per day. Her husband makes his living by portering, but his income is not enough for his four-member family. Hence, the family is in debt to the landlord. Among the 100 household members in the group, Tara has been identified by the group as one of the poor households. A few months ago, Tara was told by a facilitator that she had the same rights to the community forest as did the group's Chairperson and that she should, therefore, attend the group's general assembly meeting and raise her voice to make the group consider her situation in its decisions. In one of the group's general assembly meetings Tara surprised herself by speaking up. She said that she should be helped by the group otherwise it was a waste of time for her to come to the meetings. This forced the Forestry User Group to take some decisions in her favour. Now there is a provision in the group's working plan that Tara, together with five other poor households, will get timber and fuelwood free of charge. The group requested the project to provide her with NRs. 4500 (US$ 58) to implement a Livelihood Improvement Plan in mushroom cultivation and vermiculture (compost making). The group agreed to provide wood and small timber and community forestland for income generating opportunities. She received training related to mushroom cultivation, built a small shed from the timber that the group provided and started producing mushrooms within a year. She now sells mushrooms in the local market and makes some money for her own use, which she uses particularly for her health check-up. She was happy to know that the project has provided a scholarship to the daughter of her neighbour, who was also identified as belonging to one of the poorest households. Tara is also very happy to know that one of her neighbouring groups has allocated a part of the community forestland to five households identified as disadvantaged. She was told by a committee member that they have provided some funds to start a business producing handmade Nepali paper. Tara intends to stand for a position on the committee so that she can influence others to make decisions in favour of poor people like her. Recently, she was visited by a service provider from another Swiss- funded project called the Sustainable Soil Management

Project (SSMP). Tara made a request that the project provide her with some support for goat rearing. She now owns four goats. Recently, Tara approached a Livestock Officer to provide support for the vaccination of her goats against disease. Some user members of another district made a study visit to her home. Tara said very confidently:

> *Now I am a different woman. I am more confident and I can now put ideas forward. If I continue like this, community forestry can help me to get out of poverty.*

The analysis of the impact of Nepal's community forestry on the livelihoods of people, from a group perspective and a household perspective, indicates that the frameworks of RLS and SLA can be useful analytical tools for understanding the various elements and dimensions of livelihoods. The aim of the analysis was to use the SLA framework to analyse how community forestry has contributed to the formation and mobilisation of livelihood assets, addressing poor people's vulnerability, improving the policy and enabling environment, and make the government and non-government institutions more accountable in addressing social and environmental issues. Similarly, the RLS framework, which is complemented by the SLA framework, is used to analyse the impact of community forestry on the livelihood strategies and outcomes of three households, namely, those of Gorakh Bahadur, Mohan Kasai and Tara Shrestha. For example, personal emotions and the CFUG's collective responsibility to provide support to Tara Shrestha; a feeling of ownership of the community forest on the part of Gorakh Bahadur; and the socio- economic conditions and family base of Mohan Kasai can better be articulated by using both the SLA and RLS framework. However, neither has the ability to change existing power relations to better meet livelihood needs as human rights. The SLA, RLS and other livelihoods approaches are not the only ways of thinking, nor are they substitutes for other approaches. The most important point is that, based on practice on the ground, the SLA, RLS and other approaches need to be modified, adapted and adjusted to different local contexts and priorities. If these approaches can be used to analyse community forestry as described above, it should also be possible to use these approaches to analyse other development interventions.

6.10 Conclusion and main messages

A lot more can be written about the meaning, concepts and framework of the SLA (and other livelihoods approaches) and its linkages with other approaches. However, it is beyond the scope of this chapter to do so. In this chapter, an attempt was made to synthesise some conceptual and operational issues and observations related to livelihoods approaches, in general, and DFID's SLA, in particular. DFID's SLA was also used to analyse Nepal's community forestry programme. An alternative approach, the HRBA to development, is also suggested. In summary, the chapter contains four key messages.

First, the SLA is not a separate approach. Rather it 'adds value' to various existing approaches to development. It capitalises on the experiences and lessons learned from most of the leading concepts of the past. Although the approach is flexible and dynamic, its core principles, such as people-centred, holistic, dynamic, building on strengths, macro-micro links and sustainability are not compromised. Various livelihood frameworks have been developed by various agencies to help understand and analyse the livelihoods of the poor. In all of the livelihoods approaches, development is pursued using a humanistic, rather than a technocratic mode, which is similar to the HRBA. The livelihoods approaches are holistic in that they take a unified and integrated view of the entire social, economic, environmental and institutional system. The livelihoods approaches are reinforced, rather than replaced, by the emerging HRBA in terms of its extended focus on 'livelihood needs' as part of 'human rights'. All have common elements such as capital, policies and social processes. These are the main elements to be considered in assessing the effectiveness of existing efforts of development in achieving the aim of poverty reduction.

Second, the livelihoods approach offers communities a checklist for analysing, appraising, planning and action. This approach provides development practitioners with a coherent and flexible framework for programming, and for trying to establish micro-macro linkages. It also provides a roadmap into some pretty complex issues adaptable for use in practical ways, guidance on how to use the framework and on what information is needed and why, and how to go about getting and analysing this information.

Third, theoretical ideas and arguments on the conceptualisation of the SLA, defining and elaborating on the jargon (e.g., terms such 'holistic', 'dynamic', 'environmentally friendly', 'gender sensitive' and so on) have mostly been developed by western academics. The participation of poor people in this process is still a distant idea. Even professionals in the 'South' are not involved in this process of conceptualisation and operationalisation. For a reversal in power relations, a strong people's civil and political movement is needed, which the livelihoods approach does not recognise, or is at least silent on. This lack of emphasis on political processes and the means of changing power relations is the weakest part of the approach. Hence, the political transformation of local and supra-local political structures and processes is not within the scope of the SLA. Rather it, like other development approaches of the past, tends to promote 'reformist' ways and means of social and political change.

Fourth, many development programmes, such as Nepal's community forestry programme, can be analysed by applying the Sustainable Livelihoods Framework. However, an alternative approach should also be sought to address the issue of civil and political rights, without which people's right to access services and benefits generated by development interventions are always at risk. Therefore, the integration of HRBA, the RLS and other approaches with the SLA could be the way forward. The HRBA espouses the principle that basic human needs are human rights. The HRBA brings a new perspective to development; it looks at 'the ethics of development' by looking at causes of exclusion and sources of power. A key shift is that, under the HRBA, development cooperation is not viewed as 'charity', but as a 'right', i.e., the 'beneficiaries' become 'rights holders'. The challenges in applying the HRBA, or a combination of livelihoods approaches and rights-based approaches, both at a theoretical and practical level, are many. Caution should nevertheless be taken, as with other development approaches, to adapt the approach to the local context.

Acknowledgement: I would like to acknowledge Dr Ruedi Baumgartner, Anupama Mahat, Dr Bishnu Upreti, Bimala Rai Paudyal and Radhika Regmi for their comments, feedback and support during the process of writing this chapter. In addition, I am grateful to SDC, Intercooperation, NSCFP staff and respective community forestry user groups for allowing me to write this chapter, and for their continuous encouragement and contribution in generating the information presented in this paper.

References

Adhikari B. 2008. Is Cooperation Costly with Diverse Economic Agents? *In*: Gahate R, Narpat SJ and Mukhopadhyay P, editor. *Promise, Trust and Evolution: Managing the Commons of South Asia:* New York: Oxford University Press.

Baumgartner R. 2006. *Poverty and Livelihoods in Development Cooperation.* Unpublished working paper. Available from the author of this article.

Baumgartner R, Hoegger R. 2004. *In search of Sustainable Livelihood Systems: Managing Resources and Change*. New Delhi: Sage Publications.

Branney P, Yadav KP. 1998. *Project Report. Changes in Community Forest Condition and Management 1994-98: Analysis of Information from Forest Resources Assessment Study and Socio-Economic Study in the Koshi Hills.* Nepal-UK Community Forestry Project: Kathmandu.

Carney D. 1998. Implementing the Sustainable Livelihoods Approach. *In:* Carney D, editor. *Sustainable Rural Livelihoods: What Contribution Can We Make?* London: Department for International Development.

Carney D. 1999. *Livelihoods approaches compared: A brief comparison of the livelihoods approaches of the UK Department for International Development (DFID), CARE, Oxfam and the United Nations Development Programme (UNDP).* London: DFID [Department for International Development].

Carter J. 2007. *Meeting Minute and Office Memo. Block day on "Livelihood".* Berne: SDC [Swiss Agency for Development and Cooperation] and Intercooperation.

Chambers R, Conway G. 1992. *Sustainable Rural Livelihoods: Practical Concepts for the 21st Century.* IDS Discussion Paper 296. Brighton: Institute of Development Studies.

DFID [Department for International Development]. 1999. Sustainable Guidance Sheets. London: Department for International Development.

Ellis F, Biggs S. 2001. Evolving Themes in Rural Development 1950s-2000s. *Development and Policy Review* 19(4): 437-448.

FAO [Food and Agriculture Organisation], DFID [Department for International Development]. 2000. Forum on Operationalizing Participatory Ways of Applying Sustainable Livelihoods Approaches. *In:* A proceeding of a SLA Forum, 7-11 March, 2000 Siena: DFID, FAO, IFAD [International Fund for Agricultural Development], UNDP [United Nations Development Programme] and WFP [World Food Programme].

Gautam AP, Webb EL, Shivakoti GP, Zoebisch MA. 2003. Landuse Dynamics and Landscape Change Pattern in a Mountain Watershed in Nepal. *Agriculture Ecosystems and Environment* [Vol 99], pp 83-96.

Haan L, Zoomers A. 2005. Exploring the Frontier of Livelihoods Research. *Development and Change* 36(1):27-47.

Jackson WJ, Tamrakar RM, Hunt S, Shepherd KR. 1998. Land Use Changes in Two Middle Hills Districts of Nepal. *Mountain Research and Development* 18(3):193-112.

Kanel KR. 2008. So Far So Good: Next Steps in Community Forestry. *In*: Gahate R, Narpat SJ and Mukhopadhyay P, editors. *Promise, Trust and Evolution: Managing the Commons of South Asia.* New York: Oxford University Press.

Karna BK, Gyawali S, Karmacharya MB. 2004. Forest Condition Change: Evidence from Five Revisited Community Forests. *Proceedings of the Fourth National Workshop on Community Forestry, 4-6 August 2004,* Kathmandu, Nepal: Department of Forests and Soil Conservation.

Kollmair M, Müller-Böker U, Ejderyan O, Gamper S. 2006. *The Sustainable Livelihoods Approach.* Input Paper for the Integrated Training Course of NCCR North-South. Laos, 25 June- 2 July, 2006. Zurich: Development Study Group, University of Zurich 9WP2.

Khatri-Chetri R. 2008. Who Pays for Conservation: Evidence from Forestry in Nepal. *In*: Gahate R, Narpat SJ and Mukhopadhyay P, editor. *Promise, Trust and Evolution: Managing the Commons of South Asia.* New York: Oxford University Press.

Malla YB. 2000. Impact of Community Forestry Policy on Rural Livelihoods and Food Security in Nepal. *Unasylva 202,* Vol. 51. Retrieved via http://www.fao.org/ docrep/X7273E/x7273e07.htm on 25 December, 2009.

NSCFP [Nepal Swiss Community Forestry Project]. *2006. Consultant report. The Review, Analysis and Development of the NSCFP Monitoring System.* Kathmandu: Nepal Swiss Community Forestry Project.

Peron LH, Neil TO. 2006. *Integrating Human Rights into Development: A synthesis of donor approaches and experiences*. London: ODI [Overseas Development Institute].

Pokharel BK. 2001. *Community Forestry and Livelihoods in Nepal* http://www.livelihoods. org/post/forest1-postit.html; accessed on 2 March 2009.

Pokharel BK, Nurse M. 2004. Forests and people's livelihoods: Benefiting the poor from community forestry. *Journal of Forests and Livelihoods* 4(1):19-29.

Pokharel BK, Paudel D, Gurung BD. 2006. Forests, Community-based Governance and Livelihoods: Insights from the Nepal Swiss Community Forestry Project. *Capitalisation and Sharing of Experiences on the Interaction between Forest Policies and Land Use Patterns in Asia: Linking people with resources.* Technical papers. Vol 2: 53-60. Kathmandu: SDC.

Pokharel BK, Branney P, Nurse M, Malla Y. 2008. Community forestry: sustaining forests, livelihoods and democracy. *In:* Ojha HR, Timsina NP, Kumar C, Banjade MR, Belcher Brian, editors. *Communities, forests and governance: policy and institutional innovations from Nepal.* New Delhi: Adroit Publishers.

Pokharel BK, Carter J, Parajuli RR, Byrne S, Gurung BD. 2009. Community forestry in Nepal as a means of empowering people living in poverty: an assessment of its social, economic and environmental sustainability. Paper presented at the International workshop on community forestry held in Pokhara September 15-18, 2009. Pokhara, Nepal.

Sen A. 1985. *Commodities and Capabilities.* Amsterdam: Elsevier.

SLLP [Sustainable Livelihoods Learning Platform]. 2000. *Sustainable Livelihoods Learning Platform.* Email Conference Update, February 7th, 2000 to c.jackson@ids.ac.uk.

Sunderlin WD, Angelsen A, Belcher B, Burgers P, Nasi R, Santoso L, Wunder S. 2005. Livelihoods, Forests and Conservation in Developing Countries: An Overview. *World Development.* Amsterdam: Elsevier, 33(9):1383-1402.

Upreti BR, Timsina D. 2008. *A Brief Report for Training on Rights Based Approach and Advocacy*. Jiri, Dolakha 23-27 March, 2008.

* * * * *

CHAPTER 7

Livelihood strategies of internally displaced people in Western Nepal: Some observations

Anita Ghimire,
Bishnu Raj Upreti,
Subash Pokharel

Abstract

The livelihood strategies of internally displaced people are affected by the various factors and the new contexts that they encounter in the host communities. This topic has also been of great interest in the broader framework of migration studies. Taking the case of the Rajhena Camp in the Western Terai, Nepal, this Chapter examines the livelihood strategies of conflict-induced internally displaced persons using the Sustainable Livelihoods Framework (DFID 2002) and the Rural Livelihood System (Baumgartner 2006) as analytical tools. This Chapter attempts to understand how the circumstances endured by internally displaced persons affect their capacity to build assets or capitalise on available assets and, thus, shape their livelihood strategies. This chapter also discusses the relevance of livelihoods frameworks in studying the livelihood strategies of special categories of people.

7.1 Introduction

The aim of this chapter is to analyse the livelihood strategies of internally displaced people using livelihoods frameworks. In doing so, this Chapter also examines the analytical scope of two common livelihoods frameworks, namely, the Sustainable

Livelihoods Framework (SLF) (DFID 2002) and the Rural Livelihood System (RLS) (Baumgartner 2006).

As discussed in previous chapters, one of the main impacts of the ten-year armed conflict was the displacement of an estimated 250,000[1] people from their place of origin. Internally displaced persons (IDPs) in Nepal are facing enormous hardship and practising various approaches to make a living (Upreti 2006). Most of them are from rural areas where land and land-based livelihoods were their primary source of subsistence and income. Their life and culture, beliefs and daily activities in their place of origin were shaped by the context in which they lived. After displacement, the IDPs came to urban and semi-urban areas that they perceived to be safer. Some of the IDPs interviewed for this study reported still living in fear; they suspected that the Maoists visited the camps to keep a close eye on them and, hence, were hesitant to speak freely about their experiences.

Apart from three camps – Rajhena in Nepalgunj, Birendranagar Camp in Surkhet and Dhanusa Camp in Dhanusa – most IDPs sustain their livelihoods outside the 'camp' setting. The vast majority of IDPs have managed on their own. Some of them have settled on public lands, such as along the East West Highway, in urban slum areas, and on public lands and forest areas near road heads and towns. IDPs are cited as one of the main reasons for the rapid growth of slum areas in urban areas of Nepal especially along riverbanks (Adhikari 2006; Caritas 2005; Rai 2005; Upreti 2007). Other IDPs have melted into so-called 'informal settlements' in residential areas of cities, sharing the rent with other poor migrants. A small fraction of IDPs, in particular, political leaders and village elites who already had houses in urban areas, were able to continue their lives without any major problems.

A large number of IDPs also went to India and significant amount to the Gulf countries in search of work (Kollmair et al. 2006; Müller-Böker & Thieme 2007; Thieme 2006;

1 For discussions on the differences between the data see, Ghimire and Upreti (2008).

Thieme et al. 2005; Thieme & Müller-Böker 2004; Thieme & Wyss 2005). Others from rich and elite families migrated to Western or developed countries (Adhikari 2006).

With the signing of the Comprehensive Peace Agreement (CPA) between the UCPN(M) and the Government of Nepal in November 2006, internal displacement was expected to diminish, and so initiatives were taken to return IDPs to their place of origin. However, the Government failed to ensure the rule of law and incidences of murder, torture, abduction and so forth continued, significantly impeding the return process. The eruption of violence in certain districts in the Terai soon after the signing of CPA displaced more people, mostly the so-called 'Pahadiyas' (people of hill origin).

7.2 IDPs in Nepal

Studies on conflict-induced displacement in Nepal have mostly assessed the situation for humanitarian assistance. There have been only a few academic studies and in-depth research conducted on IDPs in Nepal.

Unlike the international practice of settling IDPs in camps that can be closely monitored, IDPs in Nepal have been largely supported by their families and social networks, and, thus, have remained beyond the reach of formal procedures for support or assistance. This is one of the reasons why there were few camps for IDPs in Nepal, compared to the total number of people displaced.

Elected local representatives and the secretaries of village and district development committees were forced to either accept the dictates of the UCPN (M) or vacate their residences and leave their villages. Hence, many people left their villages. Family members of villagers working in the army or police forces often experienced difficulties in villages controlled by the UCPN (M). There were several incidents where the UCPN (M) asked family members of the security forces for money and even forced them to pressure their sons or husbands to resign from government jobs. This situation placed members of the security forces in a vulnerable position.

Box 7.1 Suffering on both sides

During the night, groups of UCPN (M) would come and ask for food, shelter or money. If we refused, they would threaten to beat or even kill us. During the day, the security forces would come and create havoc 'atanka machauchan' in the village. They beat and harassed us, accusing us of giving shelter and food to the UCPN (M). When this started to happen regularly we were very afraid. So, we left our house to avoid such threats from the Army and the Maoists.

Source: Interview with Mr G. Shahi (name changed) from Kalikot on 27 September 2007

The situation of silent IDPs – those who are either unaware of their status or who do not want their status to be known – is unclear. During the conflict, there were problems with access to IDPs, and, now, there is still a large number of IDPs who do not want to be known as IDPs due to fear and social stigma. Hence, it is very hard to find accurate data on IDPs in Nepal. The initial official Government estimate was only 6,000 to 7,000 IDPs. The Government had counted only people displaced by the actions of the UCPN (M). Human rights activists and advocacy groups estimate the number of IDPs to be between 400,000 and 600,0002. After the CPA, an IDP unit in the Ministry of Peace and Reconstruction (MoPR) was created. It has started targeted work for IDPs, like the registration of IDPs, and is trying to maintain records and provide relief funds, among other things. As a result, the number of people registering as IDPs has steeply increased. According to the latest estimate of the MoPR, the total number of people internally displaced due to the conflict is 44,861. This number is based on the data collected by the Government taskforce for determining the conflict induced human and structural costs and includes the total number of people who have registered as IDPs with the district administration offices.

[2] The reason for such a high discrepancy between these figures is mainly due to the definition of IDP. The Government recognises IDPs as those people who have registered with a district administration office (DAO) and obtained a certificate. However, some people do not register with the DAO due to fear (as the DAO, being a government body, is a local party to the conflict) and mistrust, and others have very little incentive to register.

Simultaneously, return movements have also been counted. However, the validity of data for returnees is questionable as most of the returnees have again left the place to which they returned, which has not been monitored.

The CPA highlights that IDPs need a targeted approach to livelihood support, as they are spread across urban areas and town centres without proper support. The lives of IDPs living in settlements is compounded by the sorrow of leaving property behind, being separated from family members, grieving for loved ones killed in the conflict and so forth. Studies on the situation of displaced people in Nepal (UNHCR et al. 2006; Rai 2005; Tamang & Fedrick 2006; Dhakal 2004; Upadhaya 2006; IDD 2005; Upreti 2007; Ghimire & Upreti 2008) show that, for most IDPs, living conditions are difficult and there is little support to cope with high unemployment rates and large debts; there is also a high level of dependency on assistance from friends, relatives and the community. Some have been forced to beg for food at local hotels. Because of the distrust of IDPs among the host community, many face problems renting flats or finding jobs. Many have run up large debts to survive, having left all their property and investments behind and having used all their savings. Displaced women were reported to be working in hotels and bars and felt vulnerable to different forms of abuse. There are increasing incidences of child labour. The malnutrition rate among children was found to be very high, sometimes above the critical 15 per cent threshold set by the World Health Organization to define emergency situations (IDMC 2007). The same report found that IDPs in Nepal do not have sufficient access to clean drinking water and sanitation.

7.3 Study methodology

The methods used in this case study include observation (of IDPs' living conditions, physical facilities and livelihood bases); semi-structured interviews with 55 individual IDPs and concerned local authorities (Banke District Development Committee, Banke District Administration Office, Nepalgunj Municipality); key-informant interviews with selected individuals including representatives of the Maoist Victims Association, local social and political leaders, and IDP activists; focus group discussions with 7 groups of IDPs (5 to 10 persons per group); and interactions with informants including NGO workers, local leaders and officers, and members of community organisations working in the case study area. In addition, in-depth discussions were held with seven NGO workers, two local leaders, three community organisations and eight government officials to further explore the specific issues related to livelihoods and security[3]. Secondary sources of information were also used.

The Rajhena Camp in Banke District was selected as a case study because of its location as the main centre for IDPs coming from rural areas (mainly in the mid and far west of Nepal) to urban centres in Nepal and also to India. It is also the first of its kind (i.e., the first government run IDP camp in Nepal) and closely monitored by various NGOs. The camp is run with the collaboration of the government and international agencies and their local partners[4].

According to the respondents, the IDPs in Rajhena Camp were displaced due to the UCPN (M). The IDPs victimised by the security forces were said to be scattered because they were not ready to concentrate in an identified cluster due to fear of possible raids and action by the security forces. In addition to the IDPs in Rajhena Camp, other IDPs staying outside the camps in Nepalgunj and Kathmandu were consulted to collect information and for triangulation of the data collected in the field.

7.4 Study area

The case study site, Rajhena Camp, is located in Kiran Nala Village, Rajhena VDC, in Banke District. It is situated 20 km north-east of Nepalgunj Municipality, south of the Mahendra Highway. The nearest market is Kohalpur Market. Rajhena

---

[3] The primary data were gathered by Masters student Mr Subash Pokharel in mid-2006 and later by Anita Ghimire in 2007.

[4] In 2009, Camp Rajhena closed and at time of publishing (2010), there are now no IDP camps in Nepal.

is Nepal's first IDP camp. Hence, although the case is not representative of the national IDP situation, the study could elucidate the specific livelihood situation of the IDPs in the camp and initiate debate at a wider level.

Banke District, in general, and Nepalgunj, in particular, is known to have received a significant number of IDPs over the last 10 years, mostly from conflict-affected districts in the Mid-Western and Far West Development Regions of Nepal. However, IDPs from the Mid-Western Development Region were observed on a mass scale between 2002 and 2005 (IDMC 2006).

There are 91 houses in the camp, which are made of mud with thatched roofs. The road to other villages passes through the middle of the settlement. The camp is situated close to the security base camp, and, hence, is regarded as a safe place. There are two small grocery shops in the camp. The camp covers 6 Bighas (4.08 hectares) of land and accommodates 216 households. The land is government property, originally meant for building accommodation for female security personnel.

Children (30%) and women (33%) constitute the majority of IDPs in the camp (63%). Male members were mostly either political party workers or schoolteachers in their place of origin. Female IDPs were mainly housewives in their place of origin. The main causes of displacement were: perceived or actual security risks from the security forces and the UCPN (M), pressure from the Maoists to join them as a fulltime worker, painful family circumstance (e.g., the killing or torture of family members), and fear of being caught in crossfire.

7.5 Analytical frameworks for studying livelihoods of IDPs

Two concepts, namely, the Sustainable Livelihoods Framework (SLF), developed and widely applied by DFID in its international development cooperation projects, and the Rural Livelihood System (RLS) developed mainly to bring in other dimensions not covered by the SLF, provide the conceptual basis for examining the livelihoods of IDPs.

7.5.1 Sustainable Livelihoods Framework (SLF)

The Department for International Development of the United Kingdom's (DFID's) SLF is widely used in development practices and provides operational tools for understanding people's livelihood strategies (DFID 2002; Carney et al. 1999). It has been used by DFID almost as a condition for development cooperation in developing countries. In comparison, the RLS provides interesting heuristic tools for analysing the psychological, spiritual and emotional aspects of individuals (Baumgartner 2006) and their role in developing livelihood options and strategies. The SLF is widely used in development projects and programmes, in both rural and urban settings, in Nepal, but the RLS is less known. The SLF is relevant in terms of rural to urban migration (Thieme 2006). Its main value lies in the fact that it is able to identify the factors affecting livelihoods and show the relationships between them (see Chapter 6 for more details and Figures 6.1 and 6.2 for conceptual diagrams of DFID's SLF).

However, some scholars criticise DFID's framework for being an oversimplification of a very complex reality. The basic problem in using DFID's SLF is that it does not take into account inner realities, i.e., the emotions, feelings and memories of the individual under study. This inner reality is highly relevant in the study of the livelihoods of IDPs.

7.5.2 Rural Livelihood System (RLS)

The Rural Livelihood System (RLS) was developed by the Swiss scholars Baumgartner and Hoegger, together with their Indian research team, based on their extensive research work in India (Baumgartner 2006). It emphasises the same core principles established by the SLF, but deals explicitly with crucial elements of decision-making, such as experience, individual orientations, worldviews, emotions and attachments – dimensions that are missing in the SLF (see Chapter 6 for more details and Figure 6.3 for a diagrammatic representation of RLS's nine-square *Mandala*).

In exploring livelihoods, the RLS helps us to look at the complexity of countless forces, and factors, in addition to the lean notion of income sources, to understand how IDPs "keep their household going" (Baumgartner & Hoegger 2004). The complexity of the life experience of IDPs has, as Baumgartner and Hoegger explain, a tangible and a non-tangible symbolic aspect (Baumgartner & Hoegger 2004).

The life trajectories and experiences of IDPs are often highly emotional and even traumatic; the analytical framework of the RLS is able to grasp these dimensions. The RLS aims to understand human livelihoods by going beyond the physical dimensions and dealing with the inner human space, emotional bases and worldviews, at both the individual and collective levels. For the purpose of this study, both the SLF and RLS were adapted and combined to form a new analytical framework.

7.5.3 New analytical framework developed to study IDPs

Figure 7.1 describes a comprehensive approach to assessing the IDP issues, combining aspects of both the SLF and RLS.

The livelihoods of IDPs in their new surroundings are affected by physical and emotional factors. Similar to the 'outer realities' of the RLS (Baumgartner 2006), physical factors are those that are not part of the former life of the IDPs. They are responses by state and non-state actors in the form of policies, practices and regulations; the resources of the host community; and individual and family livelihood assets. Emotional factors are internal constraints and strengths – the psychological conditions of an individual, such as his or her fear, experience of trauma, anxiety, identity, willingness to participate, aims in life and motives. These are similar to the 'internal realities' of the RLS framework. Drawing from the RLS framework, we divide the emotional factors into the emotional base of the individual and his or her family, individual and family space, and individual and family orientation.

Both the internal and external factors interact with each other and shape the strategies and decisions of IDPs in bringing about their desired livelihood outcomes.

Displaced people, by virtue of their conditions, demand certain rights of protection and special provisions, which must primarily be addressed by the state. If the state is unable to do so due to lack of expertise or resources it can ask for external intervention. This response of protection and provision is referred to here as a 'comprehensive response'. The first response is physical resettlement. For an effective comprehensive response, the state should ensure that the environment is conducive for displaced people to either return to their place of origin, integrate with their host community, settle in another part of the country, or resettle in areas provided by different agencies. However, all of these options are voluntary. A comprehensive response includes the process of reconciliation, resettlement, rehabilitation, repatriation and reintegration, which will be explained in the coming sections.

For the outcome to be positive an integrated approach is needed. A positive outcome, in turn, affects the physical and emotional factors in favour of IDPs by giving them power to negotiate the situation for their benefit. Thus, the process becomes cyclic.

Figure 7.1 New analytical framework combining SLF and RLS

Social Field (Host Area)

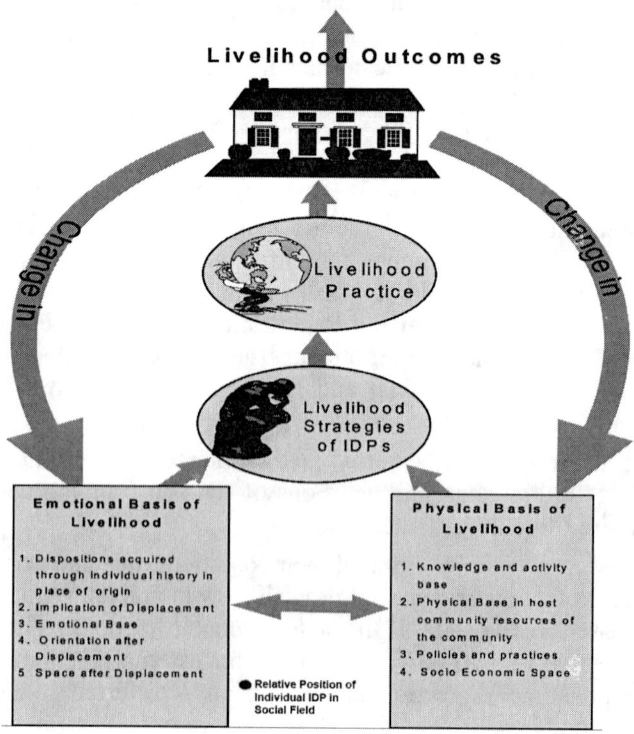

Table 7.1 Effect of policies and practices and socio-economic position on livelihood outcomes of IDPs

Policies and practices conducive to positive livelihood outcomes for IDP ↑

Good policy and practices, but weak socio-economic position makes IDPs reliant on external factors for livelihoods: • Poor economic conditions • Failure to self maintain livelihoods after assistance ends • Poor self-sustainability • Over dependence on external factors	**Optimum situation for IDPs** Strong policy and practices and strong socio-economic position creates positive livelihood outcomes for IDPs: • No IDP specific vulnerabilities • En d of status of IDPs with full exercise of rights as ordinary citizens • Justifiable compensation for all kinds of loss, such as social, human, psychological and economic loss
Most vulnerable situation for IDPs Poor policies and practices, and weak socio-economic position: • Poor economy related conditions, such as poor health and access to health services and education • Unable to exercise their rights	Poor policy and practices, but strong socio-economic position creates tension between IDPs and the state: • Good economic conditions • Self maintained livelihoods • Poor insurance and protection of rights • Poor exercise of rights

Socio-economic empowerment of IDPs →

Socio-economic empowerment and good policies and practices are both equally necessary for positive livelihoods outcomes. As shown in Table 7.1 socio-economic empowerment and policies and practices directly affect the livelihoods of IDPs. With a weak socio-economic status and 'poor' policies and practices, IDPs are in the most vulnerable position (represented by the bottom left box). Good policy and practices, but weak socio-economic status makes IDPs dependent on external factors like policies and practices for their livelihoods. However, with strong socio- economic conditions, but poor policy, the rights of IDPs are denied. This brings them into conflict with the state, as it is the state that ensures rights. The desired option for IDPs, which we have called 'positive livelihood outcomes', (Table 7.1) would be a blend of conducive policy and practices and strong socio-economic status.

7.5.4 Livelihood realities of IDPs

This section describes the factors that affect the livelihoods of the IDPs in the Rajhena Camp and how, in this context, the IDPs strategise their livelihood practices and adopt specific ways of life in the camp. The study found that the livelihoods of IDPs could only be understood by looking beyond their practices to see how these practices are formulated. The study found that the specific practices adopted by IDPs are often the result of calculated motives, driven by physical and emotional factors. These are the bases on which the person stands or determines his position in the social field when interacting with the social field. The strategies and practices are the dynamics in the space of the structure. For example, when a new person from an organisation comes to a camp settlement, from previous experience the IDPs know that they have something to offer. This experience forms the basis of knowledge that the IDPs use to strategise their practices before the new person. Their strategy may be to attract such persons to their issues. This, most IDPs perceive, can be accomplished by explaining their conditions in detail. Thus, in practice, IDPs often show representative of organisations how they have been affected by the conflict/ displacement, for example, by showing their wounds, introducing them to disabled family members or producing documents that reveal the magnitude of their loss.

Thus, practices result from calculated strategies although these strategies may produce desired or undesired outcomes. These outcomes, in turn, determine the relative position of the individual in the social field. The position we imply here is a network of social relationships, rather than a physical position in the field. By virtue of social interaction which is related to the capacity of the relative position, the person also affects the social field, i.e., the space where the individuals' livelihood practices take place. Thus, the person negotiates and renegotiates the basic physical and emotional basis of his or her livelihood.

7.6 Factors affecting strategies

In this section the factors that shape the present livelihoods of IDPs are analysed using concepts from the RLS framework. However, in contextualising the framework to explain the livelihoods of displaced people it was found that their disposition of origin and their status of being displaced heavily affected their present livelihood strategies. It then becomes necessary to know about their livelihoods before displacement.

7.6.1 Disposition of origin

Disposition of origin refers to the internalised behaviour of an IDP as a result of the structure of his or her home community. The IDPs in the camps were found to be displaced from rural areas of Nepal. These were people from villages in some of the least developed districts of Nepal. Table 7.2 presents their place of origin by district. Even within these districts, these people were living in the villages rather than in the district headquarters or urban areas.

Table 7.2 Displaced households in Rajhena Camp by district

District	Number and percentage of IDPs		Remarks
	Number	Percentage	
Mugu	73	33.8	Out of 814 internally displaced people in the camp only 36.1 per cent were literate and most of the women were illiterate.
Dailekh	63	29.2	
Jajarkot	40	18.5	
Surkhet	23	10.6	
Kalikot	9	4.2	
Jumla	4	1.9	
Humla	2	0.9	
Salyan	1	0.5	
Bajura	1	0.5	
Total	216	100	

The disposition of the IDPs before interacting with the urban environment was shaped by the rural environment. Agriculture and livestock rearing was the main occupation of all the surveyed families. The IDPs lived closely with the environment, and, in particular, with the agricultural environment, in fulfilling their basic livelihood needs. Their village communities of origin can be compared to medieval village communities: i.e., the main occupation is agriculture and there is an owner- tenant relationship in agriculture, occupational unity, and a distinct set of common traditions, habits and activities. Ninety-five per cent of those in Rajhena Camp were landlords in their villages of origin. Their thinking and practices were shaped by a strong community consciousness, the important role of neighbourhoods, activities centred around religious faith, very high social control through informal agents like norms, values, folkways and norms traditions, customs, religion and morality, and resistance to change. These informal agencies have great influences on practices, whereas formal agencies like state rules and regulation have lesser influence as most people are much less aware of the specific functions of such formal agencies.

7.6.3 Implications of being displaced

Changes in the disposition of IDPs due to the experience of displacement related to conflict also affects their livelihood capacity. Nepal has a long history of migration from rural to urban areas, mostly for economic reasons. Spatially speaking, the IDPs in the camps were also transferred from rural to urban areas. However, we presume that the conflict-induced internal displacement, which is different from the usual rural to urban migration, has different consequences than planned migration.

As Oslender (2007) states, a significant ontological change occurs through displacement. Not only have their physical selves been removed from one place to another, their being is changed. Against their will they have been categorised using a new vocabulary – as 'IDPs' – and have been bundled into a new statistic, and come under new interventions and legislation. Their identity has been changed. Most of the families in Rajhena camp had been displaced because the men in those families were active and important members of their community. They were landlords, people who had important positions in the village like VDC chairmen and teachers, or people who were politically and socially active. They had roles in all the important village decisions. They participated actively in developmental and social spheres of village life and had an ability to influence their fellow community members. For most of the IDPs, their former identity gave them a certain social status. However, in the camps, they had a new identity, which was unwanted and a source of stigma. They were bundled into a new category of 'displaced', masking their individuality.

The label 'IDP' also establishes a power relationship with the host in the socio- economic space of livelihood. When collectively labelled as IDPs, they think that they are perceived as outsiders who do not belong and are often looked upon as possible encroachers on the resources and facilities of the host population.

Beside this, there are physical implications to being displaced. Displacement is often found to have similar consequences – families are torn apart, communities dispersed, culture suppressed, normal support systems destroyed and the affected population is forced to depend on others for the basics of survival (Korn 1999). Life for migrants and IDPs, even though they are in the same urban areas, is very different. The forced nature of displacement, "the experience of displacement"[5] (Kett 2005) or the "refugee experience" (Ager 1999), makes a difference. For economic migrants, it is usually a family decision to diversify income – a common practice and a livelihood strategy connected with hopes for future success (Thieme 2006; Thieme et al. 2005; Kollmair et al. 2006; Müller-Böker & Thieme 2007; Thieme & Müller-Böker 2004; Thieme & Wyss 2005), but for the IDPs in the camp, the urban life and culture and the camp life itself is something new. Their habitual social affiliation to their community of origin is destroyed and they are forced to depend on external institutions like the government and humanitarian agencies and on the mandates of such agencies (like International Red Cross, Norwegian Refugee Council) Caritas and other local organisations (like Lumanti) for survival. It is more about overcoming immediate challenges than looking for future success.

5 "Before, during and after flight, IDPs and refugees may have experienced conflict, trauma and violence, suffered persecution, hunger, exhaustion, separation from their families and undergone many other painful experiences"(Kett 2005, p 2).

Thus, their strategies are aimed at the immediate fulfilment of basic needs, rather than a long-term sustainable future.

The specific situation of IDPs (such as having lost of property, land and documents), negatively affects the ability of IDPs to make a living in host area (The Brookings Institution – University of Bern Project 2007). Due to this, although they were generally economically well off in their place of origin, IDPs in Rajhena Camp were found to have not been able to achieve productivity after displacement. The respondents said that only a few people had managed to retrieve cash and jewellery. These assets were usually used up for health and other emergencies. Hence, the IDPs were unable to invest in income-generating activities, nor were they able to return to their villages and sell their property or retrieve cash and other valuables.

This study indicates that the present strategies of IDPs in camps depend upon their disposition acquired due to other realities, which short surveys and frameworks like DFID's SLF do not adequately explain. As Moser (1998) said, for the urban poor at the household level internal factors brought about by conflict, such as death or disability, impermanence, insecurity and lingering fear, and trauma, affect their livelihood strategy. This was also found to be true for IDPs in Rajhena Camp. All the IDP in the camp had left their place of origin due to threats and feelings of insecurity, mostly caused by the Maoists. Most of the families had witnessed the brutal legacy of the war-killings of family members, have had to look after maimed family members, have had physical and mental torture inflicted upon them or their dear ones, been separated from their families, or lost property and valuables. The conflict and displacement has caused ruptures in the continuity of life and the breakdown of social systems and safety nets. This has had a deep psychological impact. It greatly affects their ability to use present resources to achieve positive livelihood outcomes, as well as their ways of thinking and responding to daily events, and, hence, their livelihood struggle.

Some of the informants stated that, as they had left their place in a time of conflict, they did not bring important documents like citizenship certificates, property ownership certificates, etc., which determine their rights as citizens – including political rights, the right to admit their children to schools, the ability to obtain a citizenship certificate for their children, the right to buy and sell land, and the ability to obtain finance from a bank. This has crippled their ability to obtain good jobs or to obtain seed money to start a business, and much more. Now they depend on money given as assistance and on migrant remittances.

7.6.3 Physical factors that influence the livelihoods of IDPs in their host area

The physical factors that influence the livelihood strategies and practices of IDPs form the basis of livelihood. 'Physical basis' refers to the most obvious and primary external factors such as the physical environment including natural resources and other physical capital of the host community and of the displaced people, as well as policies and practices.

Assets

Rajhena Camp, as described in the previous section, is situated 20 km north-east of Nepalgunj Municipality, which is one of the most developed municipalities in the Mid-Western Development Region of Nepal. The camp is well connected by road and lies in the hinterland between Banke and the neighbouring district of Bardiya. Local transport is moderately frequent, although not scheduled. However, the local public transport from Nepalgunj Municipality stops 2 km before the camp. The land is fertile enough for cultivation, as shown by the growing of vegetables, rice and wheat. Water from the nearby river is used to water the fields near the camp. The nearest forest, which is the only source of firewood for the camp, is 10 km from the camp. Besides carrying firewood, people also use rickshaws and jeeps to transport firewood. There is no electricity or any source of lighting in the camp.

Looking at the assets of IDPs, intangible assets (World Bank 1990, Moser 1998), mostly social capital and household relations, were important to them in the camp. According to Bourdieu and Massey (cited in Arango 2000) and Thieme (2006), social capital is cumulative in nature and has a multiplier effect.

This form and nature of capital also plays a prominent role in Rajhena Camp.

Social networks formed both at the place of origin and destination have become social capital, which has facilitated opportunities for IDPs to come to the camp and gain access to services in the camp. The social capital of IDPs has reduced the cost of sustaining their livelihoods. Social capital also translates into various types of support (information, assistance in obtaining employment, facilitation of access to assistance and even provision of financial assistance, accommodation and so forth), which has facilitated migration or reduced the costs involved in migration. However, the negative effects of social networks (Thieme 2007) were also seen in the camp. For example, people who were nearest to the leaders of the IDP camp sometimes occupied two or more houses, whereas others displaced families were waiting for their turn.

The respondents explained that almost all who left the village in a hurry first went to their district headquarters where they had friends or neighbours before coming to Nepalgunj. Others who came prior to the establishment of the camp first lived in different parts of Nepalgunj. Later they acquired places in the camp. A few who had relatives, neighbours or friends in Nepalgunj, 'bonding social capital' (Thieme 2006), received information about the camp and, thus, came directly to the camp. Such networks also helped them to secure land and materials to build houses in the camp.

Housing is an important tangible asset, but there is a no formal legal title to houses in Rajhena camp. Nonetheless, when IDPs with houses moved out of the camp, there was often an unofficial trading of houses among the IDPs in the camp. Those who moved out of the camp sold their houses in whole or part to other people, sometimes members of the neighbouring community. The price is determined by negotiation between the buyer and seller and varies according to the urgency of the sale and the mutual relationship between the parties. Hence, IDPs generate social and physical capital through a continuous process of negotiation and renegotiation.

Knowledge and activity base of the individual and family

The knowledge and activity base refers to all activities that have an economic purpose, but at the same time are tied to traditions, emotions and specific forms of self-esteem. It refers to the skills and knowledge of individuals and families that are carried within the wider emotional basis of the individual and the community.

For most of the families, agriculture was the main occupation in their place of origin. All the families in the camp said that they formerly had enough land to provide food for the whole year. However, now, most of the families had no landholding in the host area.

In Nepalgunj, IDPs from Rajhena Camp were engaged in casual labour, mostly in construction, while women worked informally selling tea and food in the street ('street trading') (Siham 2005) and doing domestic and agricultural work during the harvest season. With the majority of IDPs depending on informal employment to make a living, their income is low and they have little chance of improving their economic status and access to even basic services. The analysis of livelihood options also showed that, for most (54.6%) of the people, relief assistance from different humanitarian organisations was the main source of livelihood. In Rajhena Camp, 16.2 per cent of IDPs relied on local casual labour, mostly in agriculture, and

16.2 per cent relied on loans (borrowing). Only 7.9 per cent of IDPs had regular jobs. Other livelihood options for IDPs were operating small retail shops or mobile shops ('nanglo pasal', 'gada pasal') and establishing small hotels However, none of their sources of income were permanent.

Table 7.3 Recurrent livelihood options for IDPs in Rajhena Camp (Nepalgunj)

Livelihood option	Number of households	% of IDPs
Retail shop	2	0.9
Small mobile shop	1	0.5
Small hotel	4	1.9
Local casual labour	35	16.2

Livelihood option	Number of households	% of IDPs
Regular job	17	7.9
Agriculture	4	1.9
Borrowing	35	16.2
Dependant on relief assistant	118	54.6
Total	216	100

Source: SCF-US (2005)

Note: Eighty-three families reported having two or more means of livelihood, and two IDPS were employed in government jobs.

Table 7.3 shows that relying on relief assistance was the main livelihood basis for most of the IDPs (54.6%) in Rajhena Camp, followed by local casual labour (16.2%).

Table 7.4 Proportion of IDP family members engaged in work outside Rajhena Camp

Working abroad			Working locally			
Nepal	India	Overseas	Government Job	Private job	Business	Don't know
56 (No.)	33 (No.)	10 (No.)	31 (No.)	39 (No.)	2 (No.)	27 (No.)
56.6%	33.3%	10.1%	31.3%	39.4%	2%	27.3%

Source: SCF-US (2005)

Shelter in the camp was provided by the INGO Okendon International in a phase- wise manner. However, if an individual had a good relationship (belonged to the same village or district, were related, or had another form of association) with the heads of the IDP camp, they were given shelter earlier.

Similarly, due to lack of human capital, like education and prior knowledge and experience in dealing with service providing organisations, meant that women and mostly women-headed households had to depend on men from other households for such tasks (e.g., including simple tasks such as taking children to hospital).

In unfamiliar and difficult situations, women's voices become feeble; they cannot speak up or relate their problems properly (Sammadar 2003).

Policy and practices

Structures, institutions and processes play an important role in livelihood outcomes (DFID 2002; Kollmair et al. 2006). Structures, institutions and processes in the form of material and non-material responses by government and other actors have shaped the livelihood practices of IDPs.

Sustainable solutions for IDPs involve addressing the root causes of conflict, resolution of the armed conflict (and the causes of the armed conflict) and support systems for the post-conflict situation. Resolving issues of internal displacement is inextricably linked to peace (Koser 2007), as unresolved problems of internal displacement threaten the peace-process. According to the Brookings Institution, (The Brookings Institution – University of Bern Project 2007), the peace process in general and peace agreements in particular have to address displacement- related issues, which usually involves addressing the needs and vulnerabilities of displaced people.

The United Nations developed the Guiding Principles on Internal Displacement (GPID) to address the issues of internally displaced people. These GPIDs are the major international instrument for dealing with displacement problems and are becoming an important international agenda item. The GPID defines IDPs as:

> *[P]ersons or groups of persons who have been forced to flee or to leave their homes or places of habitual residence as a result of, or in order to avoid, in particular, the effects of armed conflict, situations of generalized violence, violations of human rights or natural or human-made disasters, and who have not crossed an internationally recognized state border. (Deng 1998)*

The GPIDs were devised in 1998, but are not binding for two reasons. Firstly, there was an urgent need for a leading document to help humanitarian agencies start assisting IDPs (Cohen 2006). The GPID took two years to complete and it was considered that the ratification process would take too long. Secondly, as most governments were themselves a cause of displacement or had neglected IDPs, it was thought that they would not readily ratify such a document. However, 10 years since the GPIDs were produced, these 'unbinding principles' have not been able to fully address the issues faced by IDPs. Most often, IDPs are at the mercy of whoever wins the war between state sovereignty and international intervention. Burma's crisis, at least prior to the cyclone in 2008, is an example.

However, some argue that the GPID is only a preliminary document and that it is still the state's responsibility to devise policies to meet the requirements of the local situation. Nonetheless, countries like Nepal rely on the expertise of INGOs and external aid agencies for this.

The Brookings Institution – University of Bern Project (2007) has extensively examined the situation of IDPs and provided important insights. IDPs came to international attention after the Ethiopian famine (1984) and later during the Sudanese war (1988). Post cold war, intra state conflict was on the rise; IDPs outnumbered refugees by two to one, and their number was ever-increasing (Cohen 2006). Although this ratio is widely accepted, there is no independent body solely responsible for IDPs. IDPs are handled by a small division of the UNHCR – whose primary mandate is for refugees. There are a range of differences between refugees and IDPs in terms of needs, accessibility, realisation of impact, sovereignty v/s responsibility of state and so forth. Had 250,000 IDPs from Nepal crossed the border into China, they would have gained immediate international attention. But, as they are merely internally displaced, they have not attracted the same level of attention. Hence, it appears that it is not the seriousness of the problem that attracts prompt international or national attention, but geographical boundaries and numbers of refugees. We could similarly debate other differences between refugees and IDPs. This is what happens when there is no specific international or national body to closely monitor IDPs.

Different provisions of the CPA are directly and indirectly related to IDPs. There are several sections related to the reconciliation, reintegration and rehabilitation of IDPs and other conflict victims. Section 5.2.4 is one of the important provisions. It states:

> *Both parties agree to form a National Peace and Rehabilitation Commission to initiate the process of rehabilitation and provide*

> *relief support to the persons victimized by the conflict and normalise the difficult situation created due to the armed conflict.*

Similarly, Section 5.2.5 states:

> *Both parties agree to form a high level Truth and Reconciliation Commission on mutual understanding to conduct investigation about those who were involved in gross violation of human rights at the time of the conflict and those who committed crimes against humanity and to create the situation of reconciliation in the society.*

Section 5.2.8 states:

> *Both parties express the commitment to allow without any political prejudice the people displaced due to the armed conflict to return back voluntarily to their respective ancestral or former residence, reconstruct the infrastructure destroyed during the conflict and rehabilitate and socialize the displaced people into the society.*

Section 8 of the CPA contains provisions relating to dispute settlement and implementation mechanisms. It states:

> *Both parties agree to become responsible and accountable in an individual and collective manner and not to repeat in future the mistakes committed in the past and also to correct these mistakes on a gradual basis (Section 8.1).*
>
> *The National Peace and Rehabilitation Commission shall be set up as per the need for making the campaign for peace successful. The composition and working procedures of the Commission shall be as determined by the interim Council of Ministers (Section 8.2).*
>
> *Both parties are committed to settle all kinds of present or possible future differences or problems through mutual talks, understanding, consensus and dialogue (Section 8.3).*
>
> *Both parties express commitment that the interim Council of Ministers shall constitute and determine the working procedures of the National Peace and Rehabilitation Commission, the Truth and Reconciliation Commission, the High- level State Restructuring Recommendation Commission and other mechanisms as per the need to implement this agreement, the Interim Constitution and all the decisions, agreements and understandings reached between the Seven- Party Alliance, the Government of Nepal and the UCPN (M) (Section 8.4).*

Implementation of the various provisions of the CPA would help to solve the problems of the IDPs. However, a major challenge is to translate policies and provisions into action.

The Ministry of Peace and Reconstruction (MoPR) came into existence after signing the CPA. At present, the MoPR looks after the management of IDPs. The Government has developed an 'IDP Policy, 2006' after amending the pre-existing policy for the third time. However, due to the absence of a directive for implementing the procedure, the policy has not been fully implemented. In short, the MoPR is yet to realise the need for an integrated approach in dealing with IDPs.

The Government focus was initially on the immediate settlement of the problem mostly on the quick return of IDPs to their place of origin. The Government was unable to ensure peace and security back in the villages. The issue of return of confiscated land, the main means of livelihood of people in their place of origin, was not settled according to the provisions of the CPA. The Maoists at the local level said that they would return property after the implementation of 'scientific land reform' envisioned in the CPA. However, so far, the Government has not started the process of 'scientific land reform', and is unlikely to do so soon, as there are serious differences between the major political parties on the understanding of land reform.

The management of IDPs, irrespective of who has displaced them, is the responsibility of the state (Slim & Eguren 2004; Global IDP Project 2006; Deng 1998), so it should not matter who was the cause of the displacement. Displacement should be seen as a negative consequence of the armed conflict, with both short and long-term consequences. Consequently, the focus should be on identifying the problem and its causes and addressing them. However, over time, the Government's IDP policy has changed and the structures and procedures for implementation of the policy are not in place.

To help IDPs improve relevant livelihood skills in urban areas, the Government has at times conducted short-term training programmes. Training in candle making was given to female members of the camp. Young girls participated actively in the training, but they could not use the skills gained because they had no initial funds to start a business and had no knowledge of a market for their product. Similarly, the Government trained internally displaced girls to drive 'tempos' – the local five- wheel vehicle. After completing the training, girls were given driving licences, but no one took tempo driving up as an occupation because they couldn't hire or buy the vehicle. The Government had arranged jobs such as digging canals and roads for host communities, but, due to conflict with the host communities, who were equally in need of jobs, the jobs were terminated.

7.6.4 Emotional basis of livelihood

The emotional basis of livelihood as described by Baumgartner and Hoegger (2004; Baumgartner 2006) keeps people going when economic resources collapse. These are emotional attachments to what they consider to be their home and way of life. These are also anxieties and emotional factors inherent in every livelihood system, which influence every decision taken. They can be deep-rooted feelings, a sense of belonging or strong emotional attachments. In this study, the emotional basis of livelihoods has been divided into the following three categories: Social space within the host community, family space and individual space.

While the emotional basis of livelihoods is not a statistical reality, it was found to be of the greatest relevance to the study of the livelihoods of displaced people. Emotional realities are some of the core components of the RLS framework. The notion of emotional realities seems particularly important in the IDP study because of its value in looking at the individual's orientation, focusing on his or her own visions, hopes, aspirations, fears, self-image, integrity, identity, awareness, courage, anxiety, memories and feelings. These attachments are at the core of each individual and shape their internal orientation and livelihood strategies.

Although the vulnerability context often lies outside the IDPs control, emotional realities, being inherent in the individuals, help them to cope with shocks and risks.

Hence, an individual's emotional basis is not static and is subject to change with the context. Emotional bases are important for two reasons in IDP studies. Firstly, the experience of being displaced from their place of habitual residence due to conflict and the hardships that they have endured (killings, atrocities, torture, etc.) must be taken into account when studying IDPs livelihoods. Secondly, the experience of the new (urban) environment and having to adapt to it impacts on the capacity of IDPs to acknowledge and use their assets to produce positive livelihood outcomes.

As observed in the camp setting, the livelihood strategies of IDPs depended on individual orientations together with family and collective orientations. In many circumstances, the external or physical base becomes weak and the emotional base guides individuals to behave in a particular manner. Therefore, the notion of an emotional basis for livelihood becomes a powerful concept in the study of conflict-affected people in general and IDPs in particular.

Socio-economic space

Poor men and women in cities frequently face a set of vulnerability factors like the social context of cities, the nature of the urban economy, and urban systems of governance. This holds true for IDPs in camps who originate mostly from rural areas and are used to a different social context (like close kinship relations and ties, a close knit community and systems, e.g., division of labour according to class and caste, and so forth), economy (agriculture being the basic form) and system of governance (government members belonging to same village or neighbouring village, often from the same family or cultural group).

Displaced people, by virtue of being labelled as such, have a distinct social space that is different from that of the host community. The host community sees them as people who do not 'belong' to the place. In addition to this demarcation between IDPs and the host population, there is further demarcation within the camp. The most complete demarcation found during the study was on the basis of place or district of origin. The camps were arranged such that within each physical area, houses of people from the same district were built. There was a sense of connection between people from to the same district even if they did not know each other previously. Within the camp, daily interactions, social interactions, and trade and exchange between family groups were practised more between people from the same village or district. For example, the people form

Jajarkot (a district in the Mid- Western Development Region) regarded people from Dailekh (another district in the Mid-Western Development Region) as different. Group names were based on place of origin, for example, 'Jajarkoti' and 'Dailekhi'. There was also a distinction between groups based on class of the origin. People who knew each other in the place of origin paid respect based on their social status/class in the place of origin, rather than in the camp. The class hierarchy in the place of origin was very visible in their interactions in the camp. For example, a big landlord in the place of origin was automatically the leader of at least the people from the same district.

The working population of IDPs went to the nearest market at Kohalpur or to Nepalgunj municipality for work. Of those who migrated abroad for work, 33.33 per cent went to India. These places then become the socio-economic space within which their livelihood system develops.

The effect of socio-economic space on livelihoods will now be discussed in relation to the host community, the family, and the individual's inner space.

i. Relationship with host community

Box 7.2 Loss of identity

The same people who lived with us back in the village are now in Nepalgunj. They have built houses there. They think that they belong to Nepalgunj, but since we live in the camps, we do not. They see us as displaced 'Bistaphits' or 'Kiran Nala's'. So our identity is lost.

Source: Personal Interview with Mr R. Karki (name changed) on 20 September 2007.

The above statement raises the important issue of identity and the recognition of IDPs in the host community. IDPs are not recognised as equal in their host communities.

Forest and land are important natural resources of the host area, both to host communities and IDPs. Access to and control over these resources is of great concern to IDPs as it is in relation to the use of this space that their 'displaced' status has the most direct disadvantages. IDPs in Rajhena camp are not allowed to use the nearest forest for firewood or grass for their cattle. It is community forest and they are not regarded as members of the community. Firewood is the only source of fuel for the IDPs to cook food. The next nearest forest is 20 km from the camp. This forest is a government owned forest and they are only allowed to collect dry twigs. The IDPs complained of harassment by the forest guards. Sometimes the guards would snatch their firewood and throw it away or restrict them from entering the forest; at other times the guards verbally abused them.

There is constant conflict with the neighbouring host communities over the land settled by IDPs and the infrastructure built especially for them. Their crops are often destroyed by the people or cattle from the neighbouring host community, which has led to severe violence in certain instances. According to the respondents, they have registered 52 cases against violence by the people of the neighbouring host community. They recalled several incidents when IDPs from the camps were beaten nearly to death and dumped in the nearby river between the camp and the host community. The host community's perception is that the IDPs have been given land which was previously used by the host community, although it is government land.

Rajhena camp is located at Kiran Nala, which is around 25 km from Nepalgunj where all the government offices and international and national non-governmental organisations are concentrated. Transport services to the camp are infrequent and rates are high. Nonetheless, in order to visit government offices, organisations and the hospital, IDPs have to go to Nepalgunj. However, there is a perception that IDPs cannot pay, so no vehicle will take them. Such response by service providers frustrates IDPs and adds to their insecurity and uncertainty.

ii. Family space

Although social space is an important factor for determining strategies for action (social and economic decision-making), the family space plays an important role in determining the final strategy.

The demarcation based on gender was the most obvious demarcation of space within the family observed in the camps. Jobs were divided on the basis of gender; most of the indoor activities like cooking, cleaning and tending the house were the primary duty of the female members. The only outdoor duty undertaken by females was the collecting of firewood and fodder for the animals. The male members did most of the outdoor activities like going to the municipality and the city to visit government and other organisations, looking for help and trying to provide for basic needs.

However, within the educated younger generation, families were not very strict with gender roles. Thus, girls visited different organisations and hospitals with male members from the camp. They even represented elderly male members in organisations and at demonstrations or meetings organised for IDPs. However, among the elderly and uneducated members gender roles were still strongly defined.

Another strong differentiation of space was between generation and age. From observation of the IDPs in the camp, it was clear that the individual in the family had power within the family, not according to age or belonging to an elderly generation as in traditional cases, but according to how much responsibility they undertook within the family. There was certainly a specific respect for age, but power was distributed according to the responsibility one bears for the family. It was generally found that in a household consisting of three generations, the mother/ father, their married sons/daughters-in-law, and their unmarried sons and daughters (which was the general composition of the families in the camps), the sons and daughters-in-law were the main providers and had the major say in family decisions. The elder generations had their space and respect, but rarely had the final say in decisions, although their concerns (old age, health status) were taken into consideration in decisions.

iii. human space of individuals

According to Baumgartner and Hoegger (2004), neither the broadly accepted rules of socio-economic space, nor those of the family, alone determine how strategy is devised and actions are taken. Such actions depend on very personal considerations and the qualities of individual people, irrespective of their social and family position. Although the mainstream opinions of the society and family exert their influence upon individuals, the ultimate actions that they take depend upon personal decisions and how much these individuals allow their family/society to influence them. These decisions are in turn affected by their personal individual qualities, like integrity, awareness, maturity, capacity to accept change, capacity to integrate, courage, endurance and so forth.

Differences in individual space can be traced to individual dispositions acquired as a result of their positions in their home villages. Most of the elderly males living in the camp were very active in their villages of origin. They held significant political and social positions (e.g., they were VDC chairmen, important political cadre, influential members of important social organisations like the forest users group). All of those in the camp were displaced because they did not comply with the Maoists and for their position of influence over the local population. Because of this previous disposition resulting from their previous social status, these IDPs had a stronger individual capacity to resist the influence of society and family. They had knowledge of their status as IDPs, legal procedures, and services provided by the Government and of initiatives, projects and incoming resources targeted to IDPs, as well as access to these resources. Those who had knowledge and were accustomed to dealing with government and other organisations were able to access benefits. These people (mostly male members of the camp) were approached for help and also had their say in the distribution of resources[6]. They were also more aware of the political processes of the country, like different negotiations and policies regarding IDPs and conflict victims, making them more capable in negotiating and less influenced by the larger social forces of the society in making livelihood decisions.

The women in the camp were more guided by the decisions of the male members or by the collective orientation of the camp community. The collective orientation of the host community is also structured by the decisions made by the majority of male

6 This is highly applicable outside the camps. Political elites shape the policy and distribution of compensation highly in their own favour.

members. One strong manifestation of this was the fact that all of the women in the camp wanted to stay in the urban area because they thought that urban life offered more educational opportunities for their children and better healthcare. The same was true of the young people. However, most of the men in the camp had a strong determination to return back. When the issue was discussed within groups of both men and women, women supported the men with gestures of agreement. When the issue was discussed only among women (the same women who had participated in the mixed group earlier), the women said that they wanted to stay in the urban area. This has two implications for women's inner human space, both of which relate to being influenced by other forces. Firstly, the IDP group is fighting with the Government for their sustainable return to their place of origin. This is the most specific and manifested collective orientation of the group in the camp. However, the women within the group had a different opinion, which they could only express discreetly. In the absence of a discreet environment they tended to be influenced by the collective demands of the group (which can be read as the will of the senior male population).

The second implication is that, within the family, women's decisions are influenced by the decisions of the male household head. So even when women participate in the family decision-making process, their decisions are influenced by the ideas of the male members, due to their relatively weak inner human capacity to resist influence.

Similarly, the influence of male power relations within the broader camp was also seen in the socio-political status of the women. In the camp there was an IDP committee. Women representatives who fulfil quota for women on the committee were generally household members or relatives of male committee leaders. These women were readily accepted by the other women in the camp because they are dependent on the male leaders of committee in dealing with various administrative issues. So, displaced women without access to power and networks suffered more than those women who had male family members active in the camps and thus better access.

The young people, however, displayed a greater capacity to resist outside forces (e.g., in relation to the issue of return, forces such as influence by the head of the family and the collective orientation) in their individual decision making. This can be attributed to individual qualities such as awareness, education, capacity to accept change, identification with the urban population, capacity to integrate and integrity.

The dynamics of the influence of individual human spaces has a significant effect on the livelihood dynamics of IDPs as a group, and, through a ripple effect, affects all the intervening players and the whole intervention scenario. This will be discussed further in the section on results and discussion.

The above-mentioned factors, which influence livelihood strategies, are in turn influenced by the mental process that shape and guide individuals. Such mental guidance, according to the RLS framework, comes from their orientation.

Orientation

Orientations are the mental processes that shape and guide the practices of individuals. This concept is most adequately depicted in the nine-square RLS Mandala by the roof – something that one looks up to. So, orientations are mental process, like visions and aspiration that guide our practices. However, as individuals live and interact within societies, their practices are also fostered or restricted by the collective orientation of a collective natured superstructure.

i. Collective orientation

At the wider group level, the collective orientation of the IDPs in Rajhena camp as a specific group is their group aspiration for a better life, shared sense of loss and hope of regaining what can be regained. Their common motivations include to improve their current livelihood situation in an urban setting, as well as to get to the end of the plight of displacement. This leads to a vision of demanding their rights and the expectation of protection and the fulfilment of basic needs by the Government and other players in this field. This is, however, guided by and complies with the general collective orientation, which is based on traditions, religion, values and worldviews. This broader orientation defines what counts as loss and what counts as compensation, what to fight for and the rules of the fight, as well as broader rules for social interaction. All these forms of specific and general orientation provide the drive for collective action, such as forming a group and fighting for their rights.

However, in the midst of the collective sense of loss and the collective vision of fighting for their rights in the hope of ending their plight of displacement, families within the camp differed in the magnitude of their involvement in collective action. For example, in the family of one of the leaders all of the family members were involved in group activities either through physical action or mental support; whereas in other families, although they live in the same camp and share the same collective sense of loss, the members participated less in group actions, preferring to work or look for work. This is shaped by the family's orientation – a common family aspiration for wealth, power, social status, and so forth.

ii. Family orientation

In the camp, family orientations differ. As stated above, although there is a common vision to better their lives, the paths they choose are different. For some families, based on knowledge and activity base and family space, the motivation is to use the urban environment for the betterment of their life, for example, by positively using the physical base and socio-economic space of the host environment, complying with the wider orientations of the host community and trying to integrate into the host community. For others, the motivation is to achieve betterment by fighting for their rights, rather than using the opportunity provided by the urban environment. Some of the families maintain a dual role, dividing the roles among family members: some of the members go for demonstrations when asked to do so, while others work. However, in the midst of the polarization and duality, the difference in family orientations is evidenced by the fact that, even in the same camp, in a similar environment, some families initiate demonstrations and lead the group, whereas some simply comply with such collective action to maintain their social relationship with the group.

The family's history and status in the place of origin was frequently referred to by all interviewed families when they remembered their previous life. All of the families were proud of their socio-economic status in their place of origin. The influence of their status of origin was seen in how people were treated in the camp. Thus, the previous socio-economic status was maintained in the camp. Most families preferred traditional gendered roles within the family to keep their status – so the role of women was more restricted in families with a high socio-economic status in the place of origin. For example, the female family members of big landlords (in the place of origin) did not work in others' fields for money.

The decisions of the household regarding their future and, hence, their daily activities were also shaped by their perceptions of the future. For some, returning to their place of origin offered a more secure future and, therefore, their strategies were centred upon making this happen. For example, elder male members of such families frequently went to the Informal Sector Service Centre (INSEC) office, which is responsible for returning IDPs.

However, there are others who do not intend to return and would not like to do so. These are mainly people who, until 2007 had left the camps to settle in the host community (however, most of them took the money that the Government gave to returnees). In general, those who had invested in Nepalgunj or had nothing in their place of origin did not wish to return.

no matter how attached an individual is to their family or community, everyone ultimately makes their own final decision. There is always a situation where the individual may not comply with the general orientation of the family or community. These ultimate decisions are very personal decisions guided by individual orientations according to personal hopes, visions, and aspirations and influenced by role models, self-image and so forth.

iii. Individual orientation

In in-depth interviews, most of the IDPs revealed fear, depression, frustration and suicidal tendencies. These IDPs were full of pessimism, hopelessness, helplessness and uncertainty for the future both in their speech and facial expressions. They often compared life in the camps with life back in the village. Many respondents still measure time of displacement according to the festival that was approaching when they left the village, and by the fruits and crops that would have been found in their fields at this time of year. They still get together and discuss how a particular festival might have been celebrated back in their villages. They are curious and ask people who travel back and forth about what happened during certain festivals.

In the camp, the people with strong individual orientations were mostly the male leaders and the educated young people. For the elder leaders, their vision and aspiration was to re-establish their lost socio-economic and political status in their place of origin. They identified themselves with the Maoists Victim Association-led movement which is centred in Kathmandu. They were interested in the mainstream politics of the centre and discussed the scope for return in the context of the ongoing situation. They wished to return to their villages of origin.

Most of the elderly IDPs stated that they did not feel at home in the new environment. They kept remembering their life back in village and found it hard to adjust to the new semi-urban life where norms and worldviews are different than what they were used to. They had never heard of or seen a camp before – let alone experienced camp life. Many were living away from their ancestral home for the first time, and at an old age. They had a hard time adjusting to the new, remote and semi-urban life of the city and life in the camp. Life for them is just a means of subsistence until the time comes to return. Thus, their capacity to use resources for positive livelihood outcomes is severely restricted. This is further complicated by the fact that they were not engaged in constructive and collective (group work) activities in the camp, nor did they have any active interaction with the host population.

The interviews also showed that those who didn't have much property back home were reluctant to return as they said that, while the income for them is the same, in the urban areas their children have better opportunities. This indicates that coming to urban areas has had some positive outcomes, although the status and circumstances of being displaced are still assessed as traumatic.

Contrary to the above discourse, from an age perspective, it was found that in the same situation younger groups of people are more optimistic. The youth want to stay in Nepalgunj because they feel that Nepalgunj has more opportunities than their village to obtain academic and professional qualifications and employment. For young people, the way of life was closer to what they aspired to. They easily accepted the broader ways of the same culture. For them, the outcome is positive or at least has a hope of being so. As they see a positive future in Nepalgunj, to the extent that their resources allow, they are engaged in academic and job-oriented skill learning processes that they think will be useful in the future.

The factor of fear for IDP's in relation to livelihoods is due to the perceived or expected temporariness of their existence in the camp. According to the concept of human security (Leaning & Arie 2001), if people do not have hope for the future they tend to use resources rather than invest. The people in the camps were people who had worked actively in their villages for better livelihoods. However, as they perceive the camp as impermanent and believe that one day they will eventually return home, they do not use resources available inside the camp (land, trees) properly. Although some people have lived in the camp for more than four years, they still they do not plant even seasonal vegetables around their house, a common practice back home. Most of the elderly and women who were used to doing such work said that they didn't plant anything on the land (small plot of vegetable garden) because they were told that they would soon be returned back to their place of origin.

Box 7.3 Uncertainties about their return

They (people managing the camp) always told us that our turn to go back would come next month or after two months. So we just waited doing nothing rather than tending these lands. But it has almost been one and half years and there is no sign of them taking us back.

Source: Personal interview with Mrs Tika Maya Rokaya (name changed) on 25 September 2007

7.7 Strategies and practices

In line with global trends (IDMC 2007), one of the main strategies adopted by IDPs was to go to urban areas, but their motive being to escape the conflict rather than to diversify income like most economic migrants (IDMC 2007). Regarding the livelihoods of IDPs in urban areas, most of the literature is unanimous in saying that the livelihoods of IDPs are precarious (Upreti 2006; Tamang & Fedrick 2006 Duijn 2003; Adhikari 2006; Caritas 2005; IDMC 2006). If we take informal sectors as defined by Ray (2003) as a loose amalgam of (usually small-scale) organisations that escape the cover of many of the regulations and do not receive access to privileged facilities, then most IDPs, both outside and inside camps in Nepalgunj and other urban areas in Nepal, are absorbed by such sectors.

Human security frameworks (Leaning & Arie 2001) assume that people tend to make investments for positive outcomes in the future only when the future is visible and holds promise. The impermanence of life in camps has shaped IDPs' strategies for livelihoods such that they focus on meeting immediate needs rather than on positive outcomes for the future. For example, using children for household work is a common strategy in camps. Children accompanying women to labour forces or working in the household is another important strategy in response to vulnerability for urban poor. However, this increases vulnerability in the long term, rather than keeping households out of poverty (Moser 1998). Children played an important role in doing household chores like cooking, bringing firewood and looking after young ones in the camp. When households depend upon their children's labour as an asset to maintain current consumption, rather than investing in their children's future human capital, they risk future income and earning capacity (Moser 1998).

Most IDPs move from the camp and settle in the neighbouring community as soon as they can afford to do so. This a way for them to overcome the stigma associated with being 'displaced' and also to gain access to important resources like community forests. As a result, a migrant community has formed in Nepalgunj. However, some of them still continue to make their presence felt in the camp to gain facilities and benefits such as assistance provided by governmental and non-governmental organisations to IDPs in the camp. This is done either by staying in the camp when such organisations come, or are likely to come, like in the morning or during the day.

To cope with their new situation, IDPs have to change the way that they make their living (Siham 2005). Most women surveyed were actively engaged in the agriculture sector in their place of origin. Thus, they were economically productive. Most of them described themselves as well off in their place of origin and not used to working in others' fields to earn money; they shun such practices as not respectable for women from respected households. In the camp, where they have no land of their own, initially they did not work as labourers in others' fields. However, as their stay became prolonged, a significant number of women started to work in the fields in the neighbouring community, changing their general habit. Some also started moving out of the house to keep small shops in the nearby market – a job they had never done before. However, these women, mostly of women-headed households, have not ventured very far from their camp for jobs. This may be because mobility is still to a large extent gendered and limited for women in rural Nepal (Thieme 2006).

Some women also migrated to India, however, this was only with their husbands.

The lack of lighting in the camp makes it difficult for IDPs to work during the evening and early morning. The people in the camp depend upon either kerosene lights or candles, but prefer to finish their work (which in the evening is dinner and washing and cleaning after dinner) early so they don't have to use kerosene or candles.

The IDPs who had taken on a large amount of debt were hoping to sell their land to repay their loans once they returned to their village after the peace accord. But the few IDPs whose land was returned were not allowed to sell their land and still had to pay tax to the Maoists on their crops. The IDPs who returned were unable to stay in their village, despite the Government's assistance. They now regularly visit organisations that advocate for their rights and attend the camp when the organisations come to the camp. The people who had been migrating to Nepalgunj as economic migrants and those who moved out of the camp were working actively to enhance their status economically and otherwise, whereas the IDPs in camps were mostly dependent upon the intervening organizations for their basic needs and were working towards making the government aware of their issues.

7.8 Results and discussion

The growing phenomenon of displacement has numerous implications. The most visible – similar to that shown by studies elsewhere (Goudner 2005; UNDP 1997) is the rise in squatter settlements. In Kathmandu, the population has increased from 1.5 million at the start of the conflict to about 2.8 million in 2007) (for details Upreti 2007). We only can assume that a high proportion of IDPs have settled in Kathmandu.

On the macro-level, besides inducing an increase in international migration at an alarming rate (Thieme 2006; Thieme et al. 2005; Kollmair et al. 2006; Müller-Böker & Thieme 2007; Thieme & Müller-Böker 2004; Thieme & Wyss 2005), displacement has posed a serious challenge for local government to effectively manage this group, which is partly created by the Government as one of the parties to the armed conflict.

Although the reasons for coming to an urban area are different for migrants and IDPs, one of the similar consequences, as predicted by migration theory is increased competition in the unskilled labour market, which was previously occupied mainly by people of rural origin who came to cities for economic reasons. However, due to the conflict and the associated slowdown of the labour market's absorption capacity, these masses were already having a hard time maintaining their livelihood in urban areas. IDPs, like other poor urban migrants, live in economic conditions shaped by the existence of almost-saturated labour markets that do not provide many employment opportunities (Schutte 2005). Competition and consequent mistrust and conflict between IDPs and the host population, especially between IDPs (and migrants) living in separate settlements such as slums and camps and their neighbouring residential community, are on the rise. This mistrust has resulted in the erosion of social relations and Nepal's rich culture of hospitality.

The presence of displaced people in the host community has been accepted as an expression of the country's internal conflict, although the displaced are not accepted and still face discrimination (Oslender 2007). For the host population, IDPs are people in distress and in need. The fact of being an IDP has eclipsed their individual personalities, skills and knowledge. Their broader inner human space (Baumgartner 2006), in terms of their capacity and skills, and their socio economic space and interactions with communities are constricted in the new environment of the camps.

Women-headed households found it hard to obtain benefits and services from the government because of their lack of knowledge and ability. The support they received depended mainly on the proximity of their relationships with male camp leaders. Women back in the villages were mostly uneducated and limited to managing their households and farms. When they came to the camps they neither had the required knowledge and experience, nor could they access these organisations. So, although the state has a policy intending to facilitate women, in practice it is not of much effect. This is because the implementation procedures are structurally patriarchal (male officers in the field, official procedures not suitable for women, etc.) and not women friendly. What and how they received their rightful share depends upon the male camp members who help them. This is how patriarchy is reinforced in humanitarian assistance, although policies are framed to be power-neutral (Upreti & Ghimire 2008).

The Government and its approach towards IDPs keeps changing, leading to more uncertainty. The Government's priority is to maintain and strengthen power sharing. Hence, not enough attention has been given to IDPs, which also creates confusion. Furthermore, the project duration of agencies involved in camp management, their frequently changing mandates, procedures and staff, as well as their assessment of the situation, has created further uncertainties among IDPs in the camp.

The first IDP policy was designed to create negative publicity for the UCPN (M), rather than to solve the problems of the IDPs. This first policy defined IDPs as only those who were affected by the UCPN (M), excluding those affected by the state security forces. Duijin rightly observed: *[I]t clearly excludes the following several important categories of IDP, including: families of security forces forced to flee by the Maoist; ex-Maoists; those fleeing, conscription; people who are too frightened to register or see no benefit in doing so* (Duijn 2003, p 6).

Furthermore, both governmental and non-governmental agencies have predefined mandates, budgets and timeframes, which are far less than required to properly respond to IDP needs. Most children in the camps were sponsored for education, but when the term of the project expired in 2005, almost all girls had to quit their education. A project responsible for medicine was also phased-out and leaving lots of medicine behind, which was distributed to some people with some instructions for use. This is a glaring example of how projects funded by aid agencies are inadequate to address IDP issues. Similarly, the provision of electricity was neither a mandate of any agency, nor regarded as a basic need. So, although there is electricity in all the nearby communities, and electric wires pass right above the huts of IDPs, there is no electricity in the camp. Children were sponsored for education, but were not able to study at night because they could not afford to light their houses.

Another main problem is the lack of interest in long-term solutions. Agriculture was the main source of livelihood for displaced people in their place of origin. Nepalgunj is a semi-urban area with lots of cultivable land. If, instead of giving 5 to 6 kg of rice per day, agencies had encouraged farming, given seed money for the initial investment and training on urban methods of agriculture, the IDPs would not have become so dependent and non-productive. Engaged in productive occupations, they would have been better able to cope with their grief and loss, which would also help once they return to their place of origin. Some agencies did supported IDPs to sustain their livelihoods. However, services provided to IDPs were inadequate and occasional in nature.

Thereturn process was initiated without the reconstruction of damaged infrastructure; this infrastructure had contributed significantly to the daily livelihoods of people. A large number of youths, who had gained skills and found better livelihood opportunities in the urban area, preferred to stay in Nepalgunj. The Government, looking for an immediate solution, failed to understand or consult these youths, rather hoping that giving assistance to return would make the IDPs return to their place of origin. The consequence was that a lot of people took the assistance, and from many districts (even though an IDP is entitled to take assistance for return from only one district), but didn't go back.

Nepal represents a unique case for the GPID and raises questions about the definition of IDP. Around 2 million (Aditya et al. 2006) people are estimated to have crossed the Indo-Nepal border to go to India due to the conflict. Because of the treaty between India and Nepal, the border is porous and Nepalese in India do not enjoy refugee status according to the definition in the GPID. Hence, the refugee provisions do not apply, nor are they considered IDPs. Consequently, these people are in a unique situation. The concerns of those who have gone to India due to the conflict are neither addressed by the refugee law nor the IDP policy. Furthermore, even if they were considered refugees, India has not signed the refugee convention.

Displacement is a social phenomenon that requires preventive strategies. Social and economic development is the only way of avoiding the permanent dependence of IDPs on humanitarian assistance. Hence, a comprehensive approach is needed to properly address IDPs issues.

Experiences in post-conflict countries show that dealing with the issues of IDPs requires huge resources, which governments alone cannot provide; therefore, donor assistance is needed (Brun 2003; Aditya et al. 2006; the Brookings Institution– University of Bern Project 2007). There is a need for an independent body both nationally and internationally with sufficient resources to identify and quickly respond to this emergency in an effective and co-ordinated manner.

A functional early warning system in the context of conflict does not exist in Nepal. Minor threats, fear, conflict and disputes could be resolved at the local level by negotiating with the concerned parties. There should be a mechanism that constitutes conflict experts, legal advisors, human rights organisations, credible individuals and human rights activists to negotiate with local people and warring parties to stop conflict from escalating. Peace Brigade International is the example of such a mechanism aimed at serving people in the conflict zone in rural Colombia (Slim & Eguren 2004).

Human and social conditions, shaped by widespread illiteracy and child labour, as seen in Rajhena camp, also have long-term negative effects on health and education, and result in fewer income-earners per dependents (Schütte 2005).

Women's economic contribution to the household varies depending on their opportunities and on their constraints (e.g., education level and their need to balance employment with household responsibilities) (Moser 1998). Similarly, asymmetries in rights and obligations on the basis of gender within households also translate into differences (Moser 1998) and influence women's abilities.

The urban poor, including IDPs in urban areas, live in political conditions arising from an evolving and largely uncoordinated policy environment, poor governance and widespread insecurity (Schütte 2005). The situation for IDPs in camps is similar. As the Government is witnessing a rise in the number of urban poor, local authorities like municipalities, district hospitals and district administration offices are finding it hard to cope with the added burden with the already scarce resources. This has placed pressure on existing basic infrastructure, such as roads, water supply, sanitation, waste management and housing, increasing the exploitation of the scarce natural resources of the host areas (Upreti 2007). The problem is aggravated by poor preparation in terms of strategies, resources and policies in response to such an immediate crisis. In times to come, this will have its own negative consequences for the Government.

In such a situation, tangible assets (WB 1990; Moser 1998) like labour and human capital become important, in the absence of other productive assets like housing. Although housing is an important productive asset, which IDPs are provided with, as Moser (1998) points out in relation to other urban poor, for IDPs, housing insecurity (lacking of formal legal title) creates vulnerability and a disincentive to upgrade their homes and use them productively. Like other urban poor, IDPs live in particular environmental conditions such as cramped neighbourhoods without basic infrastructure and with inadequate housing, high population density, and significant health risks, all of which create added vulnerabilities (Schütte 2005).

Although there may be certain arguments against the urban informal sector, it can also open up a lot of opportunities for the unskilled unemployed and for budding entrepreneurs (Goudner 2005). Coming to urban areas has also created positive outcomes for a few IDPs. Firstly, in situations of protracted displacement of eight to ten years people have learnt skills (like driving vehicles) for better earning opportunities in urban areas. Secondly, the fieldwork found that a lot of young people no longer worked in farms in their villages. Previously, they had no other significant income opportunities. They said that the urban areas offer them more opportunities than they had in their villages, enabling them to pursue both education and employment at the same time. These, however, are only some of the immediate effects of displacement – the long term consequences remain.

7.9 Comprehensive response

Positive livelihood outcomes for IDPs imply their increased wellbeing, both in material and non-material aspects. The recommendations outlined in this section reshape IDPs' inner realities, which again influence their capacity to recognise and use assets, thus contributing to positive livelihood outcomes in the future when they will no longer be IDPs.

This section provides recommendations for a comprehensive or integrated approach to addressing the issues faced by IDPs.

This approach covers general and specific provisions that offer long-term and permanent solutions to IDPs.

General provisions:

1. State takes responsibility for the IDPs and sincerely follows the Guiding Principles of Internal Displacement
2. Integration of IDP issues in peace agreements and provisions
3. Responsible institutional setting and regulatory provisions
4. Allocation of sufficient human and financial resources
5. International human rights and humanitarian provisions are followed when responding to IDPs concerns

Specific provisions (options):

1. Return of IDPs to place of origin and reintegration
2. Local integration in place of displacement
3. Resettlement in IDP's place of choice inside the country
4. Resettlement in the resettlement areas provided by different agencies

For the wellbeing of IDPs, regardless of which of the above options they choose, five integrated and complementary components are needed, namely, reconciliation, rehabilitation, resettlement, reintegration and repatriation (for details see Upreti & Ghimire 2008). The IDPs must be allowed to voluntary choose between options.

7.10 Conclusions

To date, IDPs have been treated as a homogenous entity and a blanket approach has been applied to dealing their issues. However, IDPs are not homogenous groups, therefore, a single approach cannot deal with the livelihood issues of all IDPs. The worldviews of different categories of IDPs, age, power relations, and socio-economic status in place of origin significantly affect the current livelihood strategies and overall status of IDPs.

The livelihoods of IDPs in Nepal are very insecure. IDPs' problems are multidimensional in nature and demand comprehensive policies and measures to address them. Political, social, psychological and economic issues are attached to displacement. Therefore, a comprehensive approach is needed to address humanitarian components, security needs and special legal requirements, as well as the short and longer-term needs of IDPs.

When considering IDPs, rehabilitation and return are important, but are not the entire solution. IDPs' past experiences will very much shape their attitudes towards integration, return and rehabilitation. This study found that the circumstances that IDPs have endured also affect their capacity to build assets or capitalise on available assets at the place of origin; their experiences also affect their livelihood strategies. Because the SLF fails to consider the psychological or human aspects of livelihoods, which play an important part in shaping the livelihoods of IDPs, a combination of the RLS and SLF was developed as an analytical tool to study the livelihoods of IDPs. However, these frameworks are just for conceptual analysis, and do not constitute complete theories. The authors agree with Thieme's (2008) argument that using these frameworks together with existing social theories results in a more complete analysis of livelihoods.

This study confirms that the SLF is a suitable tool for explaining the assets situation of IDPs staying in camps. Its strengths lie in the physical aspects of assets. However, the accumulation or expansion of assets by an individual largely depends upon the internal aspects of individuals such as personality, willingness to develop networks and generate capital, and psychological satisfaction or dissatisfaction, which are not able to be explained by the SLF.

References

Adhikari S. 2006. *Internally Displaced Persons: An Assessment of Social Situation and Development Planning Implications* [MA Thesis]. Kathmandu: South Asian Institute of Technology, Purbanchal University.

Aditya A, Upreti BR, Adhikari PK, editors. 2006. *Countries in Conflict and Processingof Peace: Lessons for Nepal.* Kathmandu: Friends for Peace.

Ager A. 1999. Perspectives on the refugee experience. *In:* Ager A, editor. *Refugees: Perspectives on the Experience of Forced Migration.* London: Pinter.

Arango J. 2000. *Explaining Migration: A Critical Review.* Oxford: Blackwell Publishers.

Baumgartner R. 2006. *Poverty and Livelihoods in Development Cooperation* (first draft). Zurich: NADEL-ETH [Postgraduate Course on Developing Countries Swiss Federal Institute of Technology Zurich].

Baumgartner R, Hoegger R, editors. 2004. *In Search of Sustainable Livelihood Systems: Managing Resources and Change.* New Delhi: Sage.

Brun C. 2003. *Permanent Impermanence: Dilemmas of Long term Displacement in Sri Lanka, Conference on Researching Internal Displacement: State of the Art, Trondheim, 7-8 February 2003.* Trondheim, Norway.

Caritas. 2005. *Caravan of Conflict: A Study of the Dynamics of Conflict-Induced Displacement in Nepal.* Lalitpur: Caritas.

Cohen R. 2006. *Developing an international System for Internally Displaced Persons*. International Study Perspectives. 2006 (7), 87- 101. London: Blackwell Publishers.

Deng FM. 1998. *Guiding Principles on Internal Displacement.* Washington: United Nation Office for the Co-ordination of Humanitarian Affairs.

DFID [Department for International Development]. 2002. *Sustainable Livelihoods Guidance Sheets*. London: Department for International Development.

Dhakal DR. 2004. *Plight of Internally Displaced Persons (IDPs) in Nepal: A Call for An Urgent Intervention by The HMG/Nepal, United Nations, and International Community.* Kathmandu: Community Study and Welfare Centre.

Carney D, Drinkwater M, Rusinow T, Neefjes K, Wnmali S, Singh N. 1999. *Livelihoods approaches compared. A brief comparison of the livelihoods approaches of the UK, CARE, OXFAM and the UNDP.* London: Department for International Development.

Duijin LV. 2003. *Nepal IDP Research Initiative Findings*. Kathmandu: Netherlands Development Organization (SNV).

Ghimire A, Upreti BR. 2008. *Conflict induced displacement: An emerging phenomenon of internal migration in Nepal. In:* Pyakuryal KP, Upreti BR, Sharma SR, editors. *Nepal: Transition to Transformation.* Kathmandu: Kathmandu University and NCCR North South. pp.101-140.

Global IDP Project. 2006. *Internal Displacement: Global Overview of Trends and Developments*. Geneva: Norwegian Refugee Council.

Goudner N. 2005. *Rural Urban Migration in Fiji: Causes and Consequences.* Suva: University of South pacific.

IDD [Internal Displacement Division]. 2005. *Report on Inter Agency Internal Displacement Division Mission to Nepal. 11-22 April. 2005.* Internet: www. reliefweb.int/idp/docs/reports/2005/IDDRepNepal11-22April05.pdf. Accessed on 5 May 2007.

IDMC [Internal Displacement Monitoring Centre]. 2007. *Internal Displacement: Global Overview of Trends and Developments in 2006.* Grensen: Norwegian Refugee Council.

IDMC [Internal Displacement Monitoring Centre]. 2006. *Internal Displacement: Global Overview of Trends and Developments in 2005.* Grensen: Norwegian Refugee Council.

Kett M. 2005. Vulnerable group of displaced population. *Med corps, 2004.* 150:256-263.

Kollmair M, Manandhar S, Subedi BP, Thieme S. 2006. New Figures for old stories: Migration and remittances in Nepal. *Migration Letters 3(2):151-160.*

Korn D. 1999. *Exodus within Borders: An Introduction to Crisis of Internal Displacement.* Washington DC: Brookings Institution Press.

Koser K. 2007. *Internal Displacement in Afghanistan.* Washington: Brookings.

Leaning J, Arie S. 2001. *Human Security Report 2000.* New Orleans: United States Agency for International Development.

Moser C. 1998. The asset vulnerability framework: Reassessing urban poverty reduction strategies. *World Development* 26(1):1-19.

Müller-Böker U, Thieme S. 2007. Livelihood strategies in a marginal area of Nepal (Far West Nepal) with emphasis on labour migration to India. *In*: Jones G, Leimgruber W, Nel E, (eds). *Issues in Geographical Marginality: Paper presented during the Meetings of the Commission on Evolving Issues of Geographical Marginality in the Early 21st Century World, 2001-2004.* Grahamstown: Rhodes University.

Oslender U. 2007. Violence in development: The logic of forced displacement on Colombia's Pacific coast. *Development in Practice* 17(6):752-764.

Rai DR. 2005. *A Pilot Survey on Internally Displaced Persons in Kathmandu and Birendranagar.* Kathmandu: South Asia Forum for Human Rights.

Ray D. 2003. *Development Economics.* New Delhi: Oxford University Press.

RUPP [Rural Urban Partnership Programme]. 2006. Assessment of migration status in different Municipalities: Kathmandu. Rural Urban Partnership Programme.

Sammadar R. 2003. *Refugees and the State: Practices of Asylum and Care in India, 1947- 2000.* New Delhi: Sage.

SCF-US [Save the Children Foundation – United States]. 2005 *Major Findings of initial assessment at Rajhena IDP camp, 200.;* Assessment conducted by Save the Children-US UN Volunteer support with NRCS, NGO Coordination committee Banke, DLGS Banke and DOCFA Banke.

Schutte S. 2005. Emerging trends in urban livelihoods. Afghanistan Research and Evaluation Unit.

Siham MS. 2005. *Improving Urban Livelihoods*. Sudan: Practical Action.

Slim H, Eguren LE. 2004. *Humanitarian Protection: A Guidance Booklet.* London: Overseas Development Institute.

Tamang A, Fedrick JF. 2006. *Asylum of Exploitation: Internally Displaced Children in the Worst form of Child labour Due to the Armed Conflict in Nepal*, Kathmandu: Save the Children, Centre for Research on Environment Health and Population Activities and Terre des Homes.

Terres des Homes Nepal. 2005. *A Survey report of IDP children in Banke district (2005): Nutritional Status of Conflict Children Victims of the Armed Conflict in Nepal.* Kathmandu: Terres des Homes Nepal.

The Brookings Institution – University of Bern Project. 2007. *When Does Internal Displacement end- A framework for Durable Solutions.* Washington: Georgetown University.

Thieme S. 2006. Social Networks and Migration: Far West Nepalese Labour Migrants in Delhi. *Culture, Society, Environment - South Asian and South East Asian Studies, Vol. 7.* Münster: LIT Verlag.

Thieme S, Müller-Böker U. 2004. Financial self-help associations among far west Nepalese labor migrants in Delhi, India. *Asian and Pacific Migration Journal* 13(3):339-361.

Thieme S, Wyss S. 2005. Migration patterns and remittance transfer: A case study of Sainik Basti in Western Nepal. *International Migration* 43(5): 59-98. (WP2).

Thieme S, Bhattrai R, Gurung G, Kollmair M, Manandhar S, Müller-Böker U. 2005. Addressing Nepalese Migrant Workers' Needs. *Mountain Research and Development,* 25(2):109-114.

UNHCR [United Nations High Commission on Refugees], UNICEF [United Nations Children Fund], UNOCHA [United Nations Office for Coordination of Humanitarian Affairs], OHCHR [Office of the High Commissioner of

the Human Rights] and NRC [Norwegian Refugee Council]. *Final Report Joint Inter Agency Mission to Mid-Western Region. 9-16 December 2005.* Kathmandu: United Nations High Commission on Refugees.

UNDP [United Nations Development Programme]. 1997. *Sustaining Livelihoods: Promoting Informal Sector Growth in Pacific Island Countries*. October, Suva: United Nations Development Programme.

Upadhaya U. 2006. *Insurgency Affected people of Nepal: Rehabilitation.* Kathmandu: Kaushila Foundation for Peace and Innovative Initiatives and Institute for Integrated development Studies.

Upreti BR. 2006. *Armed Conflict and Peace Process in Nepal: The Maoist Insurgency, Past Negotiations and Opportunities for Conflict Transformation*. New Delhi: Adroit Publishers.

Upreti BR. 2007. A study on effects of Maoist insurgency on environmental sanitation and health of internally displaced persons of urban areas of Kathmandu city of Nepal. A paper submitted to the *Internal Conference on Health and Environmental Research Challenges in Urban Poor Settlement going to be organised by Swiss Centre for Scientific Research.* Cote de Ivorie, 3-5 September 2007.

Upreti BR. 2008. Peace process in Nepal. *Swiss Peace Policy, Publication of the Swiss Federal Department of Foreign Affairs* 2008(1):4-13.

Upreti BR, Ghimire A. 2008. The policy response to internally displaced persons: Reconciliation, rehabilitation, resettlement and reintegration, repatriation. A paper presented at the national seminar on *IDP National Policy, 2007: Implementation for Rehabilitation, Resettlement and Reintegration to Internally Displaced Persons in Nepal.* 30 July 2008. Kathmandu: National Human Rights Commission.

Upreti BR, Karna VK. 2007. Reconciliation and Social and Political Reintegration in Nepal. A Background Paper prepared for National Human Development Report 2008 going to be published by UNDP in collaboration with the National Planning Commission. Kathmandu: United Nations Development Programme and National Planning Commission.

World Bank. 1990. *World Development Report 1990: Poverty.* New York: Oxford University Press.

CHAPTER 8

Addressing livelihood insecurity and the need for further research

Bishnu Raj Upreti

Abstract

The livelihoods of people in conflict-ridden countries like Nepal are threatened by various conventional and non-conventional factors. The decade long conflict and the ongoing peace process have altered the livelihood options in Nepal, creating new options while constraining others. This Chapter highlights the need for a proper understanding of livelihoods in Nepal in the current transitional context to develop a response strategy to address livelihood insecurity and to capitalise on the opportunities brought about by the political changes in the country. It also suggests some areas for further research and analysis.

8.1 Introduction

Livelihood insecurity has been identified as one of the structural causes of the armed conflict and continuing instability in Nepal (Upreti 2006; Hutt 2004). The decade long armed conflict was the result of economic insecurity, social discrimination and political marginalisation in the mid and far western hills of Nepal, and quickly spread across the whole country (Kumar 2006; Karki & Seddon 2003). Researchers, analysts and policymakers have now realised that peace and stability is not possible without addressing livelihood insecurity (Upreti 2009). In the following section some of the potential ways of addressing livelihood insecurity are presented.

8.2 Addressing livelihood insecurity

Livelihood insecurity is connected to many factors ranging from bad policies, poor implementation of policies and programmes, bad governance, climate related stresses, market distortions and price hikes, the weak purchasing power of people, and lack of employment opportunities, among other things. Livelihood security is primarily dependent on people having access to food that is affordable and available (see Chapter 4 for detailed discussion and Box 5.1 in Chapter 5 for the seven principles of food sovereignty) and the existence of diversified livelihood options (Adhikari & Ghimire 2006; Adhikari & Bohle 1999; Seddon & Adhikari 2003; Upreti 2009; WFP & FAO 2006; SAARC 2005; Adhikari et al. 2000; Strasser 2009). Livelihood security is also affected by environmental security, skill training and vocational education, and the policy and institutional environment.

8.2.1 Food security

Food security is one of the fundamental bases of livelihood security (see Chapters 4 and 5). The Interim Constitution of Nepal acknowledges access to food as a basic human right, making the state responsible for upholding this right. Food security depends upon the availability of food, people's ability to access food and their ability to purchase it (Adhikari & Ghimire 2006). The state in collaboration with the people are responsible for ensuring food security, which requires appropriate policies, responsive institutions, appropriate operational procedures, and the commitment of the state and the private sector (Adhikari & Bohle 1999; Seddon & Adhikari 2003). Availability is becoming one of the major factors affecting food security in the remote rural areas and hills of Nepal, as transportation is extremely poor (WFP & FAO 2006). The South Asian Association for Regional Cooperation (SAARC) has also realised that food insecurity is an issue in its eight member countries including Nepal (SAARC 2005). One of the causes of food insecurity is the conditions imposed by international aid agencies on the granting of assistance (Adhikari et al. 2000). In Nepal, such conditions include the abolition of government subsidised food depots from remote food deficit areas.

8.2.2 Livelihood diversification

The livelihood base in Nepal is very narrow: most of the people in rural areas depend upon subsistence agriculture, daily wage labour and seasonal migration. In urban areas, poor people engage in daily wage labour for their livelihoods. Hence, diversifying livelihood options by providing alternative income options is essential to overcome livelihood insecurity. Tourism, ecotourism and rural tourism have great potential in Nepal for diversifying livelihood options. Other areas with potential for livelihood diversification include water-based development (e.g., hydropower, rafting, rural electrification and electricity-based small cottage industries); non- timber forest products, especially medicinal plants; and rural non-farm enterprises, cottage industries and small scale industries (e.g., wood carving, knitting and weaving, tailoring, vegetable farming, fruit cultivation, jam making, and poultry and pig farming). These activities can provide broader livelihood options to rural women and marginalised people, if the state is willing to support them through accessible finance, a conducive policy environment and market expansion (Upreti 2009).

8.2.3 Environmental security and environmental justice

Livelihood security is linked to environmental security. Environmental security, for the purpose of this chapter, is defined as freedom from social instability due to environmental degradation and the maintenance of the physical surroundings of society for its needs, without diminishing the natural stock. In other words, it is a state of human-environment dynamics in which the balance of the environment is maintained, environmental damage caused by human activity is restored, and resource scarcities and environmental degradation that may cause conflict are ameliorated. Hence, environmental security is the proactive minimisation of anthropogenic threats to the functional integrity of the biosphere and, thus, to its interdependent human component. Environmental security aims to achieve economic and social development without depleting natural resources (Upreti forthcoming). Hence, environmental security is a precondition for livelihood security.

Similarly, environmental justice is ensuring justice to people suffering from environmental inequity. The concept of environmental justice requires that the burden from the use of environmental services by certain groups should not be unfairly borne by those who do not receive the benefit (such as people living around garbage dumping sites or communities displaced by mines). The equitable redistribution of burden and benefit and securing ecologically sustainable livelihoods are essential for livelihood security.

8.2.4 Skill training and vocational education

The diversification of livelihood options requires vocational training and the development of the skills of rural people. The generation of alternative income options for rural people and migrant workers requires specific skills and vocational training. A state policy focusing on industrialisation will also create employment for those with skills. The Government, policymakers, international organisations and farmers' associations have to work together in this area to strengthen livelihood security.

Skill training and vocational education for youth is essential, not only for livelihood security, but also for peace and stability. Massive youth unemployment in Nepal provided the UCPN (M) with a reservoir of combatants during the armed conflict.

8.2.5 The policy and institutional environment

Underdevelopment and extreme poverty are major livelihood problems in Nepal. The overall economic conditions are characterised by extremely low per capita income – more than half the population is living below the absolute poverty line with an average economic growth rate of two per cent during the last five decades. Hence, the Government's priority should be to break the vicious cycle of poverty and underdevelopment and remove the structural bottleneck in the Nepalese economy through rapid economic growth along with the equitable distribution of the benefits of such growth.

Stagnation of the agriculture sector is identified as another key problem in improving the livelihoods of the poor and marginalised sections of society, because it is the major factor in underdevelopment and poverty. Although the agriculture sector provides employment to almost 68 per cent of Nepalese people, its contribution to Gross Domestic Product is only 32 per cent. Rapid economic growth and poverty alleviation in Nepal is only achievable through an increase in productivity in the agriculture sector and the creation of alternative employment opportunities to absorb the excess manpower currently relying on the agriculture sector. The overall transformation of the agriculture sector is possible only by breaking the century-long feudal production relations where the farmers cultivating the lands do not own the land and those who own the land do not cultivate it. A High Level Land Reform Commission (HLRC) was constituted by the Government to recommend how Nepal should implement land reform to address equity and social justice, while at the same time enhancing the productivity of agriculture to contribute to broader economic growth. However, this Commission has not been able to complete its work due to the current political deadlock. Land reform has been a political rallying cry for more than five decades. Now scholars and researchers working on land issues are arguing that land reform is not just for economic growth, but is also essential for strengthening democracy, promoting justice and socio-cultural rights, sustaining the ecology and environment, and generally making society prosperous.

Nepal has a huge labour force, which is not fully utilised, and there is widespread unemployment and under-unemployment. Hence, Nepal's youth are compelled to seek risky, low-paid unskilled or semi-skilled employment in foreign countries. Educated youth are also attracted to working abroad, increasing the brain drain of educated and trained human resource. While remittances have contributed to the country's economy, their sustainability and regularity is uncertain, and they are not without personal and social costs. Creating employment opportunities within the country for youth and marginalised people should be the priority. This can be done only through massive sectoral development (such as hydropower, road- networks, irrigation and communication, as well as tourism and off-farm activities). Such sectoral development will also address the problem of widespread under- unemployment and disguised unemployment in the agriculture and rural sector. The Government's Three Year Interim Plan has captured some of these concerns. However, the political commitment to translate these policies into action is in question, and the Government lacks the financial resources to do so.

The Three Year Interim Plan has identified inequality and discrimination, economic dependency, the quality of services such as health and education, corruption and weak governance as some of the other sources of livelihood insecurity and conflict. Pervasive socio-cultural and economic discrimination and inequality on the basis of class, caste, region and gender also are a serious problem in the country. Political forces have concluded that these problems cannot be solved by a centralised and unitary political system. It is hoped that the proposed federal system will provide a broader basis for addressing these concerns by properly addressing the concerns of the various oppressed castes/groups including Madheshis, various regional groups, women, Dalits, indigenous and ethnic groups, and other marginalised groups. Unfortunately, Nepal is still in a transitional phase and in the process of drafting a new constitution; hence, it is not possible to address all of these concerns at present. However, if the new constitution is drafted with these issues in mind it could provide a broader framework for tackling these issues.

The inadequate and disproportionate development of physical infrastructure is one of the factors impeding the overall development of the country and fuelling inequality in society. Basic infrastructure, such as hydropower, road networks, electricity, drinking water, irrigation facilities and communication services, has not yet reached the majority who live in rural areas. The absence of a nationwide road network, low road access in remote districts, and the lack of expansion of agricultural roads are also hindering the economic transformation of Nepal. While the Three Year Interim Plan and the annual budget and plan for the year 2008/09 made some provision for infrastructure development, implementation is a major challenge in the current political situation.

The quality of the public education system and educational discrimination is of great concern and impacts directly on livelihoods. Large numbers of the population are still illiterate despite the huge investment by the Government. The quality of public schools, attended by the majority of children, continues to deteriorate. The divide between the well off and the poor is reflected in the country's education system: those who can afford to prefer enrolling their children in private schools because of the poor quality of the education in public schools. Consequently, there is a huge difference between the performance of public schools and private schools, which determines the level of opportunities open to graduates. The unregulated fees charged by private schools have increased class discrimination, prohibiting children from disadvantaged families from competing. The only way to end such discrimination rests with the Government's ability to provide quality and skill- oriented education in public schools. 'Education for all' and other various education policies are there to address these concerns, but have been largely unsuccessful so far.

The above discussion presents the various challenges and problems facing Nepal at present. A few of the main reasons for these problems and challenges are the high level of corruption and extremely weak service delivery of the public system. Political mistrust, competition and opportunistic behaviour among the major political parties, a lack of sufficient resources, and the ineffective and inefficient use of available financial and human resource are the major causes behind these issues. In relation to resources, several potential sources exist. The international community has indicated that it is willing to support the Government of Nepal if the governing system is transparent, functional and non-corrupt. The domestic private sector is willing to invest if there is a conducive environment for investment. The potential for foreign direct investment in hydropower and other sectors is also high if the Government is able to provide a secure investment environment. More importantly, the Nepalese people are supportive and willing to contribute to national development.

8.2.6 State restructuring for livelihood security

Nepal changed from a centralised, monarchical, feudalistic, and socio-culturally, politically and economically exclusionary state, to a federal democratic republic with the declaration of a republic on 29 May 2008 by the newly elected Constituent Assembly. Hence, the state structures (judiciary, bureaucracy, security) and the policies, rules and programmes of the old regimes are no longer adequate to deal with the changing context. It is essential to restructure them to meet public expectations and to ensure the livelihood security of the Nepalese people. State restructuring is a complex, risky and lengthy process that requires a huge amount of resources, time and commitment at the political level. Furthermore, it has to be done in a comprehensive and integrated manner.

Important governing structures of the state, such as the security apparatus, bureaucracy, judiciary and legal apparatus, are not responsive to the people; they are systematically structured to strengthen feudal and centralised governing practices. Hence, the very first step is to restructure them to bring them into the 21st Century and make them more responsive to the people. Some important governing structures to be reformed are:

Security sector

Nepal is currently in a transition from war to peace; it is, therefore, the right time to undertaken a holistic restructuring of the security sector, including the restructuring of the Ministry of Defence, Nepal Army, Armed Police Force, Civilian Police, National Investigation Department and Intelligence Service, Ministry of Home Affairs, and other security related agencies. The armed conflict has had a very detrimental effect on society. This period saw the militarisation of society, which consequently created insecurity. Nepal needs to address the sources of conventional insecurity like crime and violence, as well as non-conventional sources of insecurity such as food insecurity, livelihood insecurity and environmental insecurity.

Bureaucracy

The existing state bureaucracy is facing challenges in relation to competency in the changing context. The entire bureaucracy is politicised and unprofessional. Many of the staff in government offices and government managed public sector offices are inclined towards particular political parties or recruited to fulfil the vested interests of political parties instead of improving organisational performance and efficiency. The current oversized bureaucracy needs to be reduced and restructured to provide effective services to the people. The restructuring of the bureaucracy will also provide opportunities for livelihood diversification as the existing bureaucratic orientation is controlling in nature and not conducive to decentralised, people- centric development. Once the existing bureaucracy is restructured to facilitate the promotion of local ownership in development, it will enhance the performance of the development sector, expand employment opportunities and widen livelihood options.

Table 8.1 Major tasks to perform in the changing political context for livelihood security and to address the root causes of conflict

S.N.	Issue/sector	Reason/objective	Actors
1	Restructure of economic sector	To address poverty, inequality, discrimination and livelihood insecurity	Parliament, National Planning Commission (NPC), Ministry of Finance (MoF), Federation of Nepalese Chambers of Commerce and Industry (FNCCI), Confederation of Nepalese Industries (CNI), Nepal Rastra Bank, bankers associations, concerned ministries
2	Restructure of judicial sector	To ensure access to justice for the poor and marginalised and to address impunity	Parliament, Supreme Court, Nepal Bar Association, Attorney General, Judicial Council
3	Restructure of governing units	To ensure the meaningful participation of people in decision making	Parliament, Office of Prime Minister and Council of Ministers

S.N.	Issue/sector	Reason/objective	Actors
4	Refine electoral system	To increase the representation of non-represented people	Parliament, Election Commission
5	Redefine foreign policy	To improve international relations towards changing domestic and global contexts	Parliament, Ministry of Foreign Affairs (MoFA)
6	Reform political parties	To make parties accountable to the people, strengthen internal democracy and promote good governance	Political parties, Parliament,
7	Reform religious sector	To move from an orthodox to a liberal system of government (religion secularism) and avoid religious extremism and biases	Concerned ministries, Parliament, religious networks
8	Reform social sector	To provide better health, education and other social services To provide social security to people and safety net measures for vulnerable people To address the problems of the conflict victims, internally displaced people, and the families of people killed and wounded during the conflict To promote reconciliation and provide a conducive environment for better livelihood options	Parliament, concerned ministries
9	Strengthen human rights apparatus	To promote and ensure the rule of law	Parliament, National Human Rights Commission (NHRC), security providers, concerned ministries

S.N.	Issue/sector	Reason/objective	Actors
10	Implement transformative land reform	To promote social justice based and productivity oriented land reform for economic development	Parliament, Land Reform Commission, Ministry of Land Reform and Management (MoLRM), Prime Ministers' Office, NPC, MoF
11	Redefine access and utilisation of natural resources	To promote and protect indigenous knowledge and practices, and to conserve and protect biodiversity	Parliament, concerned ministries, associations related to natural resources, private companies
12	Restructure security sector	To provide national security and human security To control criminals and disreputable people, arms traders and human traffickers	Parliament, Ministry of Defence (MoD), Ministry of Home Affairs (MoHA), Nepal Army, Armed Police and Civilian Police, Central Investigation Department

8.3 Further research needs

Chapters 1 to 7 have discussed the many important dynamics of livelihood insecurity associated with conflict and tension. One of the important conclusions is that too much generalisation and the oversimplification of the realities of a socially complex and politically unstable society do not provide in-depth insights about the diversity of people, their livelihood strategies, coping mechanisms and plurality. This book has presented the livelihoods of the people of a conflict-ridden country as a very complex, interrelated and interconnected phenomena. The issues that have emerged from the discussion in the different chapters and some other issues directly related to the content of this book are presented in this section as areas for further research, analysis and debate to strengthen the various dimensions of livelihoods in a country in transition from war to peace.

8.3.1 Strengthening analytical frameworks for the study of livelihoods

The discussion in Chapters 6 and 7 clearly demonstrates that the different analytical frameworks and tools developed so far to study the livelihoods of people are strong in some aspects, weak in others and even silent in some important dimensions, such as negotiating power and resources. The strengths of the Sustainable Livelihoods Framework (SLF) lies in the understanding of the various types of capital that contribute to the livelihoods of people, but needs further elaboration to deal with the psychological and inter-personal dimensions of the individual actors and their livelihoods. The Rural Livelihood System (RLS) is strongly conceptually orientated to inner realities, covering emotional, spiritual, and psychosocial dimensions, and even attempts to combine the important elements of the SLF. Its focus on rural systems and individuals and, hence, its wider conceptualisation and operationalisation, is a major step forward. Other livelihood approaches developed by different non-governmental organisations are mainly development oriented and are weak conceptually. Important work has been started in the conceptualisation, operationalisation and strengthening of analytical frameworks for the study of livelihoods, but further efforts are needed to refine and expand these frameworks.

From the above discussion it is clear that livelihood realities are related to policies, governing systems and institutions. However, a livelihood analysis alone is not sufficient to examine the institutional context. Analytical frameworks related to governance and policy analysis have to be introduced here. Conceptually, governance is a set of values, policies, technologies and institutions through which societies manage their political, economic, social and environmental resources in a transparent, accountable and sustainable manner. The 'good governance' concept, promoted by many development agencies, aims to provide adequate space for each and every citizen to exercise his or her rights and accomplish his or her duties. Traditionally, governance was perceived to be the activities of the government; now it is understood as a process that should involve all the stakeholders in a society. Hence, good governance is the framework for the rules, institutions, values and policies by which a society manages economic, political, and social processes and ways of exercising power in the management of resources (Upreti 2009). Hence, governance in the context of livelihoods is a critical process that helps achieve sustainable economic growth, social development and environmental quality for people. The quality of governance directly affects the livelihoods of the people. Poor governance causes poor delivery of services and promotes conflict, mistrust, and corruption and, consequently, the marginalisation of the poor and powerless in society. In contrast, good governance promotes mutually supportive, transparent process and equitable and democratic practices wherein people enjoy a secure livelihood. However, in order to achieve good governance, an understanding of the livelihood realities of the people is crucial.

8.3.2 Spatial dimensions of livelihood strategies

Multi-locality livelihood strategies are becoming a regular phenomenon (Thieme 2006) with globalisation and in the changing global and local context. Internal and international migration is becoming a powerful livelihood strategy. To keep up with people's multi-locality (rural to urban, villages to cities, villages to big cities and capital to international) livelihood strategies, the framework for livelihood studies also needs to be broadened. Similarly, changes in society and in state policies brought about by the spatial dimensions of livelihood strategies need further research and analysis to understand their complexity. However, a lot of conceptual and empirical progress has been made on the spatial dimensions of livelihood strategies (cp Müller-Böker 1991, 1999).

8.3.3 Participation of displaced people in socio-political spheres

Chapter 7 demonstrates that the lack of participation of displaced people in policy decisions and socio-political spheres affects their access to services and influences the processes and outcomes of these policies. Hence, in-depth analysis of the relationship between people's participation in policy making and the livelihood outcomes of specific groups of people is needed. A blanket approach cannot address the livelihood needs of IDPs and other groups (women, children, disabled, conflict victims, elderly people, etc.).

Displacement in Nepal is largely understood to mean conflict induced displacement. However, large numbers of people (far more than induced by the conflict) are displaced each year due to natural disasters and calamities (e.g., more than half a million people were displaced by floods in the far western Terai in September 2008 and the same number again in the eastern Terai in August 2008); their livelihood strategies and coping mechanisms are not receiving enough attention in studies and analysis.

8.3.4 Property versus possession debate in livelihood studies

One of the important issues emerging in the livelihood debate is property versus possession. From the livelihood perspective, property ownership, particularly of land, may not be important if people possess land as tenants and can generate a living from it. In a society with feudalistic production relations and a subsistence agrarian economy, land ownership is viewed as important to sustaining livelihoods. Hence, an in-depth analysis of property versus possession vis-à-vis livelihood strategies is needed to conceptually contribute to the livelihood debate.

8.3.5 The relationship between power and livelihoods

Power plays an important role in negotiating the livelihood strategies of individuals and groups. Level of awareness, social status, knowledge and skills, social networks, access to centres of power and access to resources shape the livelihoods of people. However, the relationship between power and livelihoods needs further research and analysis to establish a definitive relationship between livelihood strategies and power in a society.

Both external (international) and internal (domestic) actors engage in creating livelihood opportunities, setting the policy framework and creating institutional arrangements. Their relationships, ability to manoeuvre each other and the power balance between them affect the creation of livelihood options for local people. This relationship also needs further analysis.

8.3.6 Policy formulation and implementation

In a power-skewed society, the people to be affected or benefited by a particular policy are often excluded from the policy formulation process. Policies are negotiated or renegotiated mainly at the centre by political leaders and policymakers/bureaucrats. Such negotiated policies affect rural, marginalised, poor and powerless people the most. Agrarian policies and their implementation determine the livelihoods of people. However, an understanding of the determinants of policy production, dissemination and revision in the context of a developing country like Nepal (particularly in the changing political context) is important to positively contribute to the livelihood debate.

8.3.7 Vulnerability and resilience

Vulnerability to social, economic and political threats and stress create livelihood insecurity. Furthermore, the physical weaknesses of individuals and natural calamities create additional vulnerability. However, local people have developed coping strategies (social, economic, political) and resilience mechanisms. It is important to study the coping strategies and resilience mechanisms that help people to overcome or minimise vulnerability.

8.3.8 Land, food security and climate change

Livelihood issues are directly connected to some of the new issues and challenges facing Nepal, such as climate change and related non-conventional insecurity issues such as arsenic contamination, acid rain, prolonged drought or unusual precipitation, and glacier lake outburst floods. Such issues are contributing to land use change and negatively impacting on the food security situation, which is creating livelihood insecurity. A thorough analysis of the relationship between climate change, land use issues and livelihood insecurity is, therefore, necessary to better understand the issues and formulate appropriate responses.

It is increasingly being realised that indigenous knowledge is important in the livelihood strategies of people in the context of climate change and climate change adaptation strategies. Some pioneering work has been done in Nepal by one of the editors of this book (Müller-Böker 1991, 1999). However, very few people are presently engaged in this field. This is another area that needs research and analysis to further develop our understanding.

8.3.9 Emerging policy and institutional frameworks in post-conflict countries

Global experiences in war-torn and conflict-ridden counties (UNEP 2006; Aditya et al. 2006; Colletta et al. 1996; Schmidt 1997; OECD 2001; Nyheim et al. 2001; Murdoch & Sandler 2002; Fitzpatrick 2002; DFID 2002; Adedeji 2005; Upreti 2006) have demonstrated that policy frameworks used during times of war or earlier policies and strategies do not work in post-conflict situations. Policy frameworks often have to be generated from peace agreements and are driven by the new needs and opportunities brought about by the changing political context. New institutional arrangements, new regulatory provisions and new operational procedures are needed to tackle the changing circumstances. Hence, it is necessary to examine the emerging policy and institutional frameworks in Nepal to better understand the livelihood options and opportunities for people. Research on natural resources governance focusing on rural land policy, irrigation policy, and access to and use of natural resources by marginalised sections of society is essential to understand the livelihood options of rural people.

8.4 Conclusions

Addressing livelihood insecurities in a troubled, insecure and transitional political environment is a new challenge for policymakers, planners, politicians and researchers in Nepal. However, haste in devising policies, strategies and operational arrangements without a proper understandings of the relationships between elements of the changing context and livelihoods (including livelihood constraints, opportunities and possible threats) could lead to further complications and the consequent failure of response strategies. Hence, the thorough research and analysis of livelihoods in Nepal in the new context is needed. New policies and institutional frameworks are needed in the post-conflict situation; hence, existing fundamental sectors such as the security sector, judiciary, and bureaucracy must be restructured to appropriately respond to the demands of the changed political context. Addressing livelihood insecurities and expanding livelihood options for poor and marginalised people requires coherence between research and policy; they must complement each other to enhance the outcomes. A holistic understanding of livelihood issues and operational strategies requires a combination of the livelihood perspective and governance framework.

References

Adedeji E. 2005. The Challenges and Opportunities of Security Sector Reform in Post- Conflict Liberia. Geneva Centre for the Democratic Control of Armed Force. Occasional paper No. 9.

Adhikari R, Belbase N, Ghale Y. 2000. *Seed of Monopoly: Implications of TRIPs Agreement on Nepal.* Kathmandu: ActionAid Nepal and Pro-Public.

Adhikari J, Bohle HG. 1999. *Food Crisis in Nepal. How Mountain Farmers Cope.* New Delhi: Adroit Publications.

Adhikari J, Ghimire S. 2006. *Changing Food Chain* [In Nepali]. Kathmandu: Martin Chautari.

Aditya A, Upreti BR, Adhikari PK. 2006. *Countries in Conflict and Processing of Peace:Lessons for Nepal.* Kathmandu: Friends for Peace.

Colletta N, Koster M, Wiederhofer I. 1996. *Direction in Development: The Transition from War to Peace in Sub-Saharan Africa.* Washington: The World Bank.

DFID [Department for International Development]. 2002. *Post Conflict ReconstructionTask Framework.* London: Department for International Development.

Fitzpatrick D. 2002. Land policy in post-conflict circumstances: Some Lessons from East-Timor. Working Paper No. 58. 'New Issue in Refugee Research Series. New York: United Nations High Commission on the Refugees.

Hutt M. 2004. *Himalayan 'People's War': Nepal's Maoist Rebellion.* London: Hurst and Company.

Karki A, Seddon D. 2003. *People's War in Nepal: Leftist Perspective.* New Delhi: Adroit Publishers.

Kumar D. 2006. Proximate causes of conflict in Nepal. *In:* Simkhada SR, Oliva F, editors. *The Maoist Insurgency in Nepal (Monograph),* pp 67-122.

Müller-Böker U. 1991. Knowledge and Evaluation of the Environment in Traditional Societies of Nepal. *Mountain Research and Development* 11(2):101-114.

Müller-Böker U. 1999. *The Chitwan Tharus in Southern Nepal: An Ethnoecological Approach.* Nepal Research Centre Publications No. 21. Kathmandu: Stuttgart.

Murdoch J, Sandler T. 2002. Economic growth, civil wars, and spatial spillovers. *Journal of Conflict Resolution* 46:91–110.

Nyheim D, Leonhardt M, Gaigals C. 2001. *Development in Conflict: A Seven Step Tool for Planners.* London: Forum for Early Warning and Early Response (FEWER), International Alert and Saferworld.

OECD [Organization for Economic Co-operation and Development]. 2001. *The DAC Guidelines: Helping Prevent Violent Conflict.* Paris: Organization for Economic Co-operation and Development.

SAARC [South Asia Association for Regional Cooperation]. 2005. *Agreement on Establishing the SAARC Food Security Reserve.* Kathmandu: South Asia Association for Regional Cooperation Secretariat.

Schmidt H. 1997. Healing the Wounds of War: Memories of Violence and the Making of History in Zimbabwe's Most Recent Past. *Journal of Southern African Studies* 1 21(2):301-10.

Seddon D, Adhikari J. 2003. *Conflict and Food Security in Nepal. A Preliminary Analysis.* Kathmandu: Rural Reconstruction Nepal.

UNEP [United Nations Environmental Programme]. 2006. *Environmental Considerations of Human Displacement in Liberia: A Guide for Decision Makers and Practitioners.* Geneva: United Nations Environmental Programme.

Upreti BR. 2006. *Armed Conflict and Peace Process in Nepal: The Maoist Insurgency, Past Negotiation and Opportunities for Conflict Transformation.* New Delhi: Adroit Publishers.

Upreti BR. 2009. *Nepal from War to Peace: Legacies of the Past and Hopes for the Future.* New Delhi: Adroit Publishers.

Upreti BR. Forthcoming. Environmental security and development. *In:* Matthew R, Floyd R, editors. *Environmental Security: Frameworks for Analysis.* London: Cambridge University Press.

WFP [World Food Programme] and FAO [Food and Agricultural Organization]. 2006. *Food and Agriculture Markets in Nepal.* Kathmandu: World Food Programme.

About the authors

Anita Bhattarai-Ghimire is a PhD student at the Human and Natural Resources Studies Centre, Kathmandu University. She holds a Masters in Sociology and is doing her doctoral research on conflict induced internally displaced people (IDP) in Nepal. Her areas of interests are human migration and human rights. She has been published on topics such as migration and internal displacement issues in various books and journals. She has participated in various national and international conferences and workshops.

Bharat K Pokharel has a Doctorate in Community Forestry Governance (1997) from the University of East Anglia, United Kingdom, and over 22 years of experience in community forestry in Nepal, working for both the Government of Nepal forest service, and DFID and SDC funded projects. Dr Pokharel is active in the promotion of community forestry in the region and is on the board of trustees of the Regional Community Forestry Training Centre (RECOFTC), which is based in Bangkok. His main interest is in natural resource governance and the linkage with forest livelihoods. Dr Pokharel is currently the Project Director of the SDC funded Nepal Swiss Community Forestry Project and the Country Representative of the Swiss Foundation for Development and International Cooperation (Intercooperation) in Nepal.

Bishnu Raj Upreti holds a PhD in conflict management (2001) from Wageningen University, the Netherlands. He is actively engaged in conflict transformation and peace related research in South Asia. During his 28-year professional career, he has been engaged in teaching and research at the University of London and Surrey in the United Kingdom and at Kathmandu University, Nepal. He has worked for the Government of Nepal and in different international organisations in the capacity of professional staff, resource person and consultant. He has 18 books to his credit on conflict related issues and many articles published in different national and international journals, magazines and edited books. His latest book is Nepal from War to Peace: Legacies of the past and hopes for the future (Adroit Publishers, New Delhi 2009). He has been widely quoted in the national and international media about Nepal's armed conflict. He has served as a resource person for several international organisations. He is currently Regional Coordinator, South Asia Coordination Office of the Swiss National Centre of Competence in Research (NCCR) North-South, based in Kathmandu and is teaching at the Human and Natural Resources Studies Centre, Kathmandu University.

Jagannath Adhikari received his PhD from the Australian National University, Canberra, Australia in 1996. He works mainly as an independent researcher and consultant. His main areas of interest are agricultural change, rural development, labour migration, natural resources management and food security. Some of the books he has authored/co-authored include The Beginnings of Agrarian Change: A Case Study in Central Nepal (1996), Food Crisis in Nepal (1999), Pokhara: Biography of a Town, Changing Livelihoods: Essays in Nepal's Development Since 1990 (2008), New Lahures: Foreign Labor Migration and Remittance Economy of Nepal (2001). He is editor of about half a dozen books on various subjects such as poverty, environmental justice and conflict. He has also extensively published journal articles and contributed chapters in books.

Netra Prasad Timsina holds a PhD in the Political Economy of Forest Resources. His development and research experience encompasses diverse aspects of natural resource management spanning the last 20 years. He held the position of Coordinator at ForestAction from 2003 to 2005, and continues to work at ForestAction as a researcher in natural resource governance with a focus on people's rights, justice and knowledge systems drawing largely on the framework of the political economy of natural resources. In addition, he has been engaged in national and international networking and alliance building, particularly in defending the livelihood rights of marginalised people. He has co-edited books including Knowledge System and Natural Resources: Management, Policy and Institutions in Nepal (Foundation Books, 2008) and Communities, Forests and Governance: Policy and Institutional Innovations from Nepal (Adroit Publishers, 2008). His papers have been published widely in national and international journals. He is currently Vice President of the NGO Federation of Nepal (an umbrella organisation of more than 4500 NGOs in Nepal).

Subash Pokharel obtained his Masters degree from South Asian Institute of Technology (SIAT), Purbanchal University, in 2006 and is currently working in the development sector. His research interests include displacement, development and regional planning. He is active in different social activities and writing on the issues of displacement.

Ulrike Müller-Böker is Professor of Human Geography and currently Director of the Department of Geography at the Zurich University (Switzerland). She is head of the NCCR North-South programme component 'Livelihood options and globalisation' and is in charge of the research in South-Asia. Within the broad field of human geography her research concentrates on development-related issues. Fields of competence include: the analysis of the institutional dimensions of livelihood strategies; the impact of globalisation processes; local resource-use conflicts; labour migration patterns; nature conservation; and development and participation processes focusing on South Asia, Central Asia and Switzerland. Since 1977, she has been working regularly in Nepal (Kathmandu valley, Gorkha district, Chitwan district, and in east Nepal and far west Nepal).

Yamuna Ghale obtained a Masters in Ecological Agriculture from Wageningen Agricultural University in 1998. Her areas of engagement are international trade, livelihoods and food security, gender and social inclusion, and natural resource management. She is currently the Senior Programme Officer at the Swiss Agency for Development and Cooperation (SDC), Nepal. Her professional experience includes positions with SNV-Nepal as an Agronomist, ICIMOD (International Centre for Integrated Mountain Development) as an Agronomist and Gender Specialist, and ActionAid International Nepal as a Team Leader (Livelihoods and Economic Rights). Her work has been published in various books, edited volumes, international journals, magazines and newspapers. She is affiliated with many national and international networks working on the right to food, trade and natural resource management.

* * * * *